THAT ETERNAL SUMMER

THAT ETERNAL SUMMER

Unknown Stories
from the Battle of Britain

RALPH BARKER

COLLINS
8 Grafton Street, London W1
1990

William Collins Sons & Co. Ltd
London · Glasgow · Sydney · Auckland
Toronto · Johannesburg

BRITISH LIBRARY CATALOGUING IN PUBLICATION DATA

Barker, Ralph (1917–)
That eternal summer: unknown stories from the Battle of Britain.
1. World War   2. Battle of Britain
I. Title
940.5421

ISBN 0 00 215585 0

First published 1990
by William Collins Sons & Co. Ltd, London

Copyright © Ralph Barker, 1990

Photoset in Linotron Meridien and Bembo by
Rowland Phototypesetting Ltd, Bury St Edmunds, Suffolk
Printed and bound in Great Britain by
William Collins Sons & Co. Ltd, Glasgow

'Eternal summer gilds them yet.'
Lord Byron, *Don Juan*

'It must be the finest English summer for years.'
Flying Officer George Barclay, pilot,
249 Squadron, 6th September, 1940

ACKNOWLEDGEMENTS

For the basic material in this book I am principally indebted to the central character or characters in each story, where they survived, and to colleagues, relatives and friends where they did not. Supporting material has come from documents and files made available at the Public Record Office at Kew, whose help and Crown Copyright is gratefully acknowledged, and from countless other sources, published and unpublished. None of the chapters could have been researched in detail without generous help.

Special mention must be made of those expert compilations *Battle Over Britain*, edited by Francis K. Mason (Alban Book Services, 1969), and *The Battle of Britain Then and Now*, edited by Winston G. Ramsey (After the Battle Magazine, 1980). I must also thank my friend and fellow author Chaz Bowyer for help with selecting photographs and in many other ways.

Many of the stories originally appeared at various times and in an abbreviated form in the *Sunday Express*.

Other main sources are listed below.

Chapter 1   Brigadier C. Aubrey Dixon, OBE (since deceased) and Mrs Kay Dixon, who lent me all her late husband's documents and files. Departmental Records, Ministry of Defence. *London Gazette*.

Chapter 2   Group Captain H. S. Darley, DSO, RAF (Retd). Group Captain Sir Hugh Dundas, DSO, DFC, RAF (Retd). Mrs Marjorie Darley (since deceased). Frank H. Ziegler, *The Story of 609 Squadron* (Macdonald, 1971). David Crook, *Spitfire Pilot* (Faber and Faber, 1942). Norman Franks, *Wings of Freedom* (Kimber, 1980). PRO File AIR 27/2102.

Chapter 3   Wing Commander R. A. B. Learoyd, VC, RAF (Retd). Group Captain J. D. D. Collier, DSO, DFC, RAF (Retd). Anthony O. Bridgman, DFC. R. G. Low. PRO Files AIR 2/5686 and 6102; AIR 14/816, 2666 and 3363; AIR 24/220; AIR 25/109A; AIR 27/480 and 686; AIR 30/157; AIR 35/156.

Chapter 4   Survivors: Squadron Leader R. M. M. 'Tim' Baden, RAFVR; J. F. H. Bristow; Wing Commander R. A. G. Ellen, MBE, RAF (Retd); W.

Greenwood; W. J. Q. Magrath, MM; J. E. Oates. Detective Inspector Ole Rønnest of the Danish Police. Edmund L. B. Lart (brother of the late Edward Collis de Virac Lart). Air Historical Branch, Ministry of Defence (RAF). Alan Cooper. Max Hastings. Wing Commander F. F. Lambert, DSO, DFC, RCAF (Retd). PRO Files WO 208/3323 and 3369; AIR 2/6102; AIR 14/746, 3361–8, 3414; AIR 25/22; AIR 27/681; AIR 30/157.

Chapter 5 Mrs Muriel Nicolson. BBC Recording dated 2nd December 1940. Wing Commander T. F. Neil, DFC, AFC, AE, RAF (Retd), *Gun Button to Fire* (Kimber, 1987). Dr (formerly Squadron Leader) Roland Winfield, DFC, AFC, BA, ChB, *The Sky Belongs to Them* (Kimber, 1976). PRO Files AIR 2/5686; AIR 27/498.

Chapter 6 Una 'Bunny' Ford, née Lawrence, and letters and documents which she kindly lent. Group Captain F. R. Carey, CBE, DFC, AFC, DFM, RAF (Retd). Air Vice-Marshal C. G. Lott, CB, CBE, DSO, DFC, RAF (Retd) (since deceased). Salesian College, Farnborough, Hants. Dennis and Betty Woods-Scawen. Leonard Green, Brenzett Aeronautical Museum. Doreen Green. Colin Brown. Aldershot News. Farnborough Week-End News. AR8b (RAF), Ministry of Defence. PRO Files AIR 1/1186 and 1220; AIR 2/4095 and 9456; AIR 16/956-7 and 960; AIR 27/44 and 703; AIR 29/619 and 630; AIR 30/150 and 157; AIR 50/10, 19 and 36.

Chapter 7 Air Commander J. B. Coward, AFC, RAF (Retd). Mrs Cynthia Coward. Wing Commander W. A. Smith, DFC, AFC, RAF (Retd). Mrs Joan Coward. Reuben Litchfield. PRO File AIR 27/252.

Chapter 8 Mrs Janet Hannah, widow of John Hannah. Surviving crew members Douglas A. E. Hayhurst, DFM, and George 'Buffy' James. BBC broadcasts by Pilot Officer C. A. Connor and Sergeant John Hannah, October 1940. Michael Tomlinson. R. S. Curtis. R. G. Low, formerly L. A. C. Low, 'A' Flight, No. 83 Squadron. PRO Files AIR 2/5686; AIR 27/686.

Chapter 9 Jane Somerville, née Egan, sister of Eddy Egan, and Alastair Somerville. Inquisition taken on 25th February 1977 in HM Coroner's Court, Croydon by Dr Mary P. McHugh; notes of evidence taken (kindly supplied by Dr McHugh). Anthony Graves, co-leader of the John Tickner Excavation Group (London Air Museum). Peter D. Cornwell. Eye-witnesses John Adams, J. Curwen and Doreen F. Smith. Fellow members of No. 501 Squadron, including Air Vice-Marshal H. A. V. Hogan, CB, DFC, RAF (Retd), Wing Commander P. C. P. Farnes, DFM, RAF (Retd), P. R. Hairs, MBE, Squadron Leader J. H. 'Ginger' Lacey, DFM, RAF (Retd) (since deceased), Squadron Leader P. F. Morfill, DFM, RAF (Retd), T. G. Pickering, C. J. Saward, G. H. E. Welford. David Watkins, Hon. Sec. No. 501 Squadron Association. Various departments of the Ministry of Defence. R. J. 'Dick' Luckhurst. Chilham Castle Museum. Joy A. Turner. PRO Files AIR 27/1949, 2059, 2093 and 2123; AIR 50/162.

Chapter 10   R. T. Holmes, interview and correspondence. Peter D. Cornwell, article in *The Battle of Britain Then and Now* entitled; 'September 15 – The Traditional Climax to the Battle and Its Most Famous Casualty'. Alfred Price. PRO File AIR 27/1964.

Chapter 11   Wing Commander K. G. Mackenzie, DFC, AFC, RAF (Retd), interview and correspondence. His autobiography, *Hurricane Combat* (Kimber, 1987). Don Everson, *The Reluctant Messerschmitt* (Portcullis Press, 1978). David Watkins, Hon. Sec. No. 501 Squadron Association. PRO File AIR 27/1949.

Chapter 12   Air Marshal Sir Harold Maguire, DSO, OBE, RAF (Retd), interview and correspondence. Battle of Britain Memorial Flight, Flying Displays, Appendix D: Extracts from the Pre-Display Brief – 1983 Season. Dale Donovan, Command Public Relations Officer, HQ Strike Command. Air Ministry Bulletin 40058 of 11th August 1959 (Air Ministry Information Division). Bruce Robertson. Oxo Sports and Social Club. Streatham Hollingtonians Cricket Club. PRO File AIR 20/9719.

Copyright and/or source of photographs is acknowledged individually on page xiii.

CONTENTS

OF ILLUSTRATIONS

ERRATUM

The publishers regret that the illustrations fall between pages 82-83, 98-99, 162-63 and 178-79, not as specified in the list of illustrations.

xiii

MAP

The Man from Woolwich Arsenal

THANKS TO Sidney Camm and R. J. Mitchell we had the Hurricane and the Spitfire. Thanks to Rolls-Royce we had the engines. Thanks to Henry Tizard and R. A. Watson Watt, backed up by the prescience and persistence of 'Stuffy' Dowding, we had radar warning. From the Colt Company of America (built under licence in the UK) we had the Browning machine-gun. And thanks to the Royal Air Force, the Royal Auxiliary Air Force, and the Volunteer Reserve, we had the pilots. But in 1939 the crucial element needed to effect the destruction of German aircraft was missing. The bullets.

For all the speed and manoeuvrability of both the Hurricane and the Spitfire, for all the advance intelligence of enemy aircraft approaching the coast, the vigilance of the Observer Corps inland, the skilful vectoring of the fighter controllers, the complex system of communications, and the courage and flair of the pilots, the moment of truth in air combat lasted no more than a fraction of a second and depended in the last instance on marksmanship and the destructive properties of a handful of bullets – perhaps of a single bullet. And against self-sealing petrol tanks the ordinary .303 bullet, whether ball, armour-piercing, or the existing type of incendiary, was powerless.

Now, fifty years after the Battle of Britain, it is time to add a new name to the roll of back-room boys and 'boffins' who helped to win it. Incredibly, the name is that of an infantry officer holding what seemed a dead-end job in the Design Department of the Royal Arsenal at Woolwich in London.

Captain C. Aubrey Dixon, of the Bedfordshire and Hertfordshire Regiment, one-time head-boy at Bedford School and a former Sandhurst cadet, was the third officer to be offered this appointment, the first two having turned it down as offering no scope and no future. But Dixon, a small arms expert, accepted it – on 17th May 1937, at the age of thirty-six – with enthusiasm. It made him responsible for the design of all ammunition for all three Services up to a calibre of one inch, so the potential seemed vast. But he soon discovered that this all-embracing responsibility meant very little in practice. No money was allocated to design work, and even with special authorization he was allowed to spend no more than £5 on any one project.

The more Dixon studied the problems of air-to-air fighting between the types of aircraft then coming into service (as opposed to the types used in World War I and between the wars) the more convinced he became that the existing Air Staff requirement for ammunition was years out of date. What was needed, he believed, was an explosive incendiary bullet, one that would incorporate a nose which would pierce the target's outer surface before exploding. Dixon tried many times to interest the production department at Woolwich in such a project, but his efforts failed, partly because his proposals demanded new methods and techniques of manufacture for which Government factories were not equipped.

All the incendiary and explosive ammunition previously designed had suffered from practical defects; much of it, indeed, had been intended to do no more than set fire to airships and gas-filled balloons. Dixon could find no trace of serious research into the ignition of aviation fuel in modern heavier-than-air craft. He was not alone, however, in sensing the requirement and starting research. In December 1938 two Swiss inventors, Paul René de Wilde and Anton Casimir Kaufman, gave a demonstration in Geneva in front of British Service attachés of a new and revolutionary bullet designed for just this purpose. Reports on the demonstration were so enthusiastic that the Air Ministry asked the two inventors to repeat it at Woolwich.

The first Dixon heard of it was when he was asked to be

present with others at these trials, which were to take place on 11th January 1939.

To meet estimated Air Ministry specifications the Swiss bullet was to be fired at a sheet of duralumin, 0.028 of an inch thick, at 200 yards range, with a half-filled two-gallon petrol tin placed six inches in rear of the burster plate. Dixon doubted if a bullet meeting this specification would be effective in air combat, but he was junior to most of the officers present and he kept his doubts to himself.

The trial was not an unqualified success: out of nine rounds fired, only three ignited the petrol. But no one at the demonstration had seen petrol ignited in this way before, and the sight of a large hole being blown in the duralumin sheet followed by an explosion of petrol behind it caused considerable excitement. A ratio of one success in three might have been modest enough to condemn most projects, but Dixon, who had made similar progress with his own design, reflected cynically that this invention had one outstanding merit: it was foreign.

Dixon would not have thought of proffering his own design in its present state; but now he had to listen to a barrage of enthusiastic comment. 'This is the answer!' 'This is what we've been waiting for!' 'Superb!' 'We must have this at all costs!' Meanwhile he continued to keep a low profile – so successfully that his name did not even appear amongst those listed in the subsequent report as present. His principal aim at the demonstration was to acquire a sample of the bullet that was being tested – but Kaufman divined his intention and sat on the box.

The Swiss inventors were invited to attend a conference at the Office of the Ordnance Committee a week later, where the RAF's first serving member of this Committee, Group Captain C. Hilton Keith, would be in the chair. Dixon was convinced he could do just as well or better with his own bullet and save the country thousands, and he spent the week filling and firing a number of bullets in feverish haste, eager to produce results at least equal to those obtained by de Wilde and Kaufman and to demonstrate them to the Ordnance Committee. His experiments were so promising that he began to pass his bullets round, furtively, because he was acting without instructions, but urgently, to the men who were proposing to buy the Swiss design.

When Group Captain Keith arrived for the conference, Dixon took him to one side. If anyone would listen it would be 'Happy' Keith; the two men had struck up a friendship. 'Look sir,' said Dixon, 'could you possibly postpone this conference, even if only for a short time, until the results of some trials I've been having this morning come through? I'm certain I can give you as good an answer as de Wilde.' At that moment a messenger arrived with a chit from the factory manager who had been carrying out Dixon's private trials; they had given results at least equal to the de Wilde demonstration. Dixon showed the chit to Keith but it was too late. 'I'm sorry, Dixon, but yesterday at the Air Ministry we virtually bought the de Wilde design and the Swiss have been offered a substantial sum to disclose the details. Further large sums will be payable if the bullet goes into production. Even if you could sway the conference, the decision could only be reversed at a very high price.'[1]

How could the unofficial experiments of a captain in the infantry be compared with the mature work of established inventors? In spite of Dixon's protests the conference endorsed the decision taken at the Air Ministry, and the secrets of the de Wilde bullet were duly bought and disclosed. So revolutionary was the concept that it was accepted almost without comment. Only the Research Department remained sceptical. 'It is impossible to ignite neat petrol with an incendiary bullet,' they pronounced. 'The whole project is a waste of time.'

Dixon didn't think so. But he had to put his private experiments aside, for the time being anyway. It would now be his job to make the Swiss bullet work.

The original de Wilde demonstration had been given with 7.6 Swiss ammunition. The next move was to make up 500 rounds of .303 calibre for further tests. Woolwich were to make and fill the bullets, and Kaufman was to remain in England to monitor the trials. De Wilde returned to Switzerland.

1. The agreement provided for an initial payment of £3,600, a further £1,400 on commencement of production, and £1 per thousand rounds produced up to a total of £35,000.

Kaufman told Dixon that he was a clerk employed in the League of Nations offices in Geneva, ostensibly working for peace. But like many Swiss he had a flair for mechanics, and his true trade was watchmaker. He had conceived the notion of an incendiary bullet two years earlier, but having no knowledge of explosives he had approached de Wilde. The latter, a Belgian who had taken refuge in England as a boy during World War I, owned an explosives and ammunition factory in Switzerland. De Wilde had provided the facilities and the expertise, the ammunition, the fillings and the firing range, and sponsored the tests.

Kaufman laid out his samples in Dixon's office, cut into sections with fully dimensioned drawings, and proceeded to explain the proposed methods of manufacture. Dixon soon hit on a fundamental weakness. The de Wilde design relied for efficient functioning on methods of construction and dimensioning that allowed for no tolerance whatsoever in manufacture. The design was exposed as a good hand-made job but impracticable for mass production. Even the five hundred trial rounds would take weeks to make.

Dixon pointed out to Kaufman the absurdity of trying to produce hand-made bullets in quantity, while Kaufman insisted that everything must be exactly copied or the bullet wouldn't work. Eventually Dixon worked out a modification which was consistent with a possible method of manufacture and Kaufman had to agree.

Dixon rushed a sketch down to the factory and had some empty envelopes – a selection of cupro-nickel, steel, and gilding metal – made up ready for the fillings to be inserted. This was just the sort of job he had failed to get the factory to take on for his own experiments, but now the attitude had changed. Here was a foreign design with a foreign name enjoying the direct support of the Air Ministry, and they got on with the job.

Ironically, the empty bullet, with the modification suggested by Dixon, was now almost identical with another prototype he had himself prepared for experimental production several months earlier.

The next task was to fill the bullet. Dixon was allocated an experimental filling shop at the factory, and when he went along there with Kaufman he was given a charge-hand named Bill Kay. Kay was a man typical of his kind, forthright and outspoken, resentful of being pushed around by outsiders, but a thorough professional at his job, and a firm friend to anyone he took to. Kaufman's method of filling the bullets appalled him.

Everything still had to be done by hand at this stage, and Kaufman insisted on doing it himself. Each of the nine increments in the filling process had to be weighed exactly – and some of the measurements were as small as 0.2 or 0.3 of a grain. Kaufman would measure out the particles of powder and drop them into the empty cartridge case, insert the filling punch behind it, put the point of the bullet against the edge of the test bench, and press against the punch with his stomach. All this was repeated for each ingredient, Kaufman judging the right filling pressure, which differed for each one. Unless he had a uniquely sensitive midriff, thought Dixon, Kaufman's methods were hardly likely to achieve the degree of accuracy which he himself claimed was necessary to the proper functioning of the bullet.

In any case the whole process violated the safety regulations laid down, and Bill Kay's face was a study.

The first ten cartridge cases were made up into bullets and sent to the range for firing. The result was two premature explosions, each bursting the gun-barrel.

For the next six weeks Dixon tried everything to overcome the prematures, and at length, under pressure from Kaufman, he agreed that the design could be tested in another demonstration. Air Ministry representatives were invited, de Wilde came over from Switzerland, and expectations were high. There were no prematures this time, but it was evident that the modified bullet was less sensitive than the original 7.6 calibre Swiss model; even more frequently than before, it failed to ignite the petrol. De Wilde was furious and blamed Dixon, accusing him of deliberately tampering with the design with the aim of impairing performance; he had learned from Kaufman of Dixon's prior experiments and saw him not as an ally but as a rival. The Air Ministry, too, looked askance at Dixon and demanded a report.

Eventually Dixon's explanation that the de Wilde bullet could not be copied for mass production and that after modification its sensitivity was bound to suffer was grudgingly accepted, and de Wilde and Kaufman returned to Switzerland. But with no alternative in sight the Air Ministry placed a firm order for one hundred thousand rounds, and a list of acceptance trials was issued. Sufficient rounds were ready in time for the first trials to begin on schedule at Woolwich on 23rd June 1939. The result was complete and utter failure. Every time a burst of any duration was fired, even from a new barrel, a 'premature' resulted and the barrel was 'bulged'.

Technically the problem had now become one for the research department. But they had already indicated their view that the design was unworkable and that further experiments were a waste of time. As for Dixon, no one had any faith in him, not even the brigadier in charge of the design department. Dixon was the fly in the ointment, an infantry officer who had altered the original design and reduced its sensitivity. The de Wilde bullet was quietly left to rot.

Yet for Dixon there remained that Air Ministry order for one hundred thousand rounds. No cancellation had been promulgated, no directive issued to stop work. This meant that there was real money to spend, money which he intended to appropriate for further experiments with his own design, passing them off for the moment under the trade-name of de Wilde. The order was on the file and work could go ahead. It might not be strictly orthodox, but for Dixon the end justified the means.

As for the Ordnance Committee and the Air Ministry, the former, having recommended the de Wilde design to the latter, believed that provisioning was going ahead, while the Directorate of Equipment at the Air Ministry believed for their part that Woolwich were finding out why the de Wilde bullet had failed. This left a vacuum in which Dixon, for a time at least, could operate.

Totally absorbed in the task, he worked for the next three

months day and night, keeping a notebook at his bedside when he did try to rest so as to jot down his thoughts if and when he awoke during the night. Throughout July and August 1939, driven by his conviction that war was imminent and RAF ammunition inadequate, he threw his health and career into jeopardy. The risk he was taking in misapplying public funds was worrying enough; the burden was enhanced by the need for speed and secrecy.

Working as he was on a project that demanded that others be drawn into the conspiracy, and catching up with his official work in the night hours when the factory was closed, he was bound to be found out sooner or later. He had to be able to produce something of real significance in his own defence when that moment came. Only success with his bullet would justify him.

In his race against time he was starting again, almost from scratch. Not only did he have to invent the bullet, he had to recalculate a realistic Air Staff requirement – and this for a man who knew very little about aircraft design and performance, had no practical experience of air combat, and had never flown in a Service aircraft in his life. But he soon realized he was only probing more closely into a subject that had always fascinated him. His elder brother Gerald had been a pilot in the Royal Flying Corps in World War I and had been idolized by the younger boy. 'Just wait until you're eighteen,' Gerald would say, 'then you can become my observer and the Dixon brothers will shoot all the Huns out of the sky.' The war had ended before this fancy could be tested, but it was not so far-fetched as might appear at first glance. The younger boy, although turned down when he applied to join the RAF, had always been an exceptional shot, and while in the Army in the inter-war years he became a crack marksman, representing his country in competitions. Now, at thirty-eight, with an appointment at Woolwich, he was unlikely to have any chance of employing that skill in action; but the vicarious satisfaction of arming Britain's fighter defences against the Luftwaffe would be ample compensation, if only he could bring it off.

He dug out all the information he could find about British

and German aircraft from diagrams and data published in aviation books and magazines, and he found he could remember almost all he had ever read in his youth about air combat. His studies confirmed his belief that his bullet must fulfil at least one essential requirement: it must ignite instantaneously on hitting the aircraft's surface, with incendiary properties so controlled and retarded that it would burn long enough to penetrate through to the fuel tank.

Often Dixon would leave his office in mid-morning and go along to the small arms ammunition production shop with a rough pencil design and ask the foreman, one of his many accomplices, to get something made up. Together they would rummage about for whatever tools they needed for the job and then look around for a vacant machine. With the connivance of one or two of the old hands in the shop they would run off in the next two hours perhaps fifteen or twenty empty cartridges, enough for a trial. Slipping these into his pocket, Dixon would make for the filling factory, where Bill Kay would put a hand-press at his disposal and Dixon would fill his illicit bullets. Finally, leaving it until late afternoon, he would jump on the motor-bike on which it was his habit to cover all distances that could not be readily accomplished on foot and hurry away to the ranges, where the range foreman, Dickie Maughan, was another of the conspirators.

Maughan's answer to Dixon's frequent requests for secret firings was always the same: 'You'll get me shot, sir, you'll get me shot.' But he always obliged. In the gathering dusk of the deserted ranges the two men would erect a target and Dixon would try out his bootleg bullets. Mostly it was the same story: a small improvement, keeping his hopes alive but necessitating further work on the drawing board and more prototypes and trials. Every detail of the bullet and its ingredients was tested and many alternatives tried and discarded during these trials, and Dixon also made numerous furnace tests to see what kinds of bullet and filling would withstand the heat generated by a 300-round burst.

One evening, after yet another abortive test-firing, it was eight o'clock before he got back to his office, and his in-tray still lay uncleared. He had hardly settled down to it when he heard footsteps outside and the door opened. It was the Chief Superintendent of Design, Brigadier A. E. Macrae. Fortunately he had put away all the papers concerning his experiments, and the files piled high on his desk all referred to routine matters. The Brigadier sniffed.

'Working late, Dixon? What's the problem?'

'Just catching up on a few things, sir.'

The Brigadier glanced round the office, turned an inquiring eye on Dixon for a moment, and then left. He had heard something of Dixon's nocturnal habits. Now he had first-hand evidence.

Macrae's visit had been stimulated by a letter from the Ordnance Board requesting that Dixon be provided with an assistant. Macrae was an expert in big gun design, and small arms ammunition was not his speciality, but he knew of nothing that would explain Dixon's sudden spasm of overwork and need for reinforcement, and his suspicions were aroused. Next morning Dixon was summoned to his presence.

'I've had a complaint from the superintendent in charge of the ranges,' began the Brigadier. 'It seems that trials have been carried out without proper notification, and your name was mentioned.'

This was something Dixon could not deny, and he took refuge in silence.

'In future,' continued the Brigadier, 'I must ask you to give notice in writing when you want to use the ranges, with details of any trials you wish to make.'

'Yes, sir.'

'Quite frankly, Dixon, I don't understand what you're up to. You've been here two years and you know the procedures. What purpose you think is served by ignoring them I fail to see.'

Again Dixon held his peace, and a note of exasperation crept into the Brigadier's voice. 'Anyway Dixon, it's got to stop. Whatever it is, it's got to stop.'

'Very well, sir.'

But of course, it couldn't. It was quite impossible to explain to Macrae, or to anyone else in authority, that he was in the process of evolving a bullet which might be just in time to equip Fighter Command in the coming war. But he was doing something that was against all his training and background, and it was with something approaching panic in his heart that his experiments went on.

To his long list of accomplices he now added the elderly, grey-haired, benign figure of J. S. Dick, a chemist in charge of the pyrotechnic section of the research department. Dick's pedantic manner and nervous giggle recalled the popular notion of a 'boffin', as did his unbridled enthusiasm, and he helped Dixon in his quest for a chemical which would ignite aircraft fuel and yet escape the inherent defects of the de Wilde fillings and all the other fillings tried thus far.

At last, on 8th August, Dixon achieved a successful firing with an envelope and filling which withstood sustained fire from a barrel worn to Army limits. It was only now, quite by chance, that he learned of the much stricter limits demanded for barrels mounted in RAF aircraft. This was a major setback, forcing him to re-think the requirement all over again.

Haunted by fears of detection and the prospect of failure, he began to lose his upright military bearing and become haggard and cadaverous. When the war started on 3rd September he was no nearer a breakthrough, and all the weeks of over-work, the risks he was taking with his career, and the burdens of deception, brought him almost to the point of admitting defeat. On 27th September he turned in desperation to Dick for just one more suggestion that might be worth experiment.

'I'm sorry,' said Dick. 'I've dug out just about everything I can think of. It doesn't look as though the answer to your problem exists. I'm afraid there's nothing more I can suggest.'

Dixon paced restlessly up and down the laboratory, still unwilling to come to terms with the final admission of failure. Lying on the floor under one of the benches was a battered old tin, shabby and dust-laden, which he imagined had contained one of the chemicals that had failed him. All his anxieties and frustrations went into the satisfying kick which he aimed at the empty tin.

He was surprised at the tin's resistance. It wasn't empty after all. It cavorted briefly, fell on its side, and rolled away, trailing a thin stream of silvery grey powder. Dixon bent down to pick it up. 'Sorry,' he said, 'I've spilt one of your tins.' He recovered the tin and examined it. 'What is it?'

'That? It's a pyrotechnic composition that I made up for some experiments a long time ago, must be nearly fifteen years. Come to think of it, it was never used. No one had the nerve to try it out.' He chuckled. 'Too sensitive, they said.'

'Can I have it?'

'For your bullet?'

'Yes.'

'You can try it. But I doubt if you'll get a safety certificate for it.'

Dixon scooped up the spilt powder and clamped on the lid. 'I'm going to try it.' Mixed with his other chosen ingredients, it might do the trick.

Seeing the futility of protest, Dick shouted a warning as Dixon left. 'Be careful how you handle it!'

Next day Dixon called at the filling shop and asked Bill Kay for an empty booth. 'On my own.'

The significance of this was not lost on Kay. More than once he had witnessed, during some critical experiment, the sudden flash and explosion from a premature detonation, scorching the hands and faces of employees. 'As bad as that?' asked Kay.

'Well – I've been warned.'

'Booth 3A is empty – and pretty isolated.'

The booth was about six feet square. Straight ahead of Dixon was the filling bench, with scales, filling punch, plastic beakers for measuring, and scoops, all made of and finished in copper and bronze – non-conducting metals. Dixon took the tin of pyrotechnic powder out of his bag, together with a handful of empty bullets, and started work. Clamping the cartridge into position on the bench, he weighed exact measures of selected powders and poured them almost grain by grain into the case. Then he set the filling punch to the desired pressure and levered it home.

Now and again he stopped work briefly to inhale deeply and settle his diaphragm. Flowing from the scoop at the tips of his fingers was a fine grey sand a proportion of which had been dubbed too sensitive for an earlier experiment. It might be just right for his bullet. On the other hand, chemical changes might have taken place in the meantime which might reduce or even increase its sensitivity. He had been right to insist on working alone.

He picked up another bullet and chose marginally different increments this time, marking each bullet with the quantities used. The fact that he had filled one or two bullets without incident gave no guarantee of future immunity. Each time, as he pressed down the punch, there was danger.

Other than the occasional deep inhalation and exhalation, his nervous system seemed unaffected. The fear he felt was instinctive, but his brain achieved an icy clarity as he filled three bullets, then four, then five, marking each one with a steady hand. When he got to ten he was tempted to leave it at that, but he had set out to fill twenty, and in the loneliness of the booth he went through the filling process ten times more.

When he emerged from the booth Bill Kay hardly recognized him. It was as though the chemical changes that might have occurred in the mixture had been transferred to his complexion, which was ashen. A moment later the colour came flooding back and he was standing his full height again, bright-eyed with relief. 'Thanks, Bill,' he said. 'Now to fire them off.'

It was late evening before the range was clear and Dixon could safely approach Dickie Maughan. For the 78th time, according to Dixon's notes, they put up the usual target – a 2-gallon tin of petrol with a dural screen six inches in front – and retired to the watchers' hut ten yards away. Back at the butts a hundred yards distant, one of Maughan's men was loading a Browning on a fixed mounting preparatory to retiring ten yards and firing single shots by remote control.

Dixon and Maughan crowded together at the armoured glass window as they had done so many times before. Directly the shot was fired they knew that at least it was successful at the firing end. They could always detect a premature. But disillusion followed. The new mixture, although an improvement, failed in its primary task of igniting the petrol.

They trudged back in silence to the research department, where they knew Dick was awaiting them. He suggested inserting a steel anvil in the nose of the bullet with a steel ball embedded in the mixture behind it – a standard method – so that, on the bullet striking its target, the inertia of the steel ball would cause it to fire the composition against the anvil. Dixon immediately adopted this suggestion, and in addition he designed and developed overnight a specially weakened nose which would collapse on hitting the target, so causing the filling to ignite.

All other characteristics of the bullet – the method of filling, the content and weight of components (there were only three, against Kaufman's nine), and the pressing loads – were determined by Dixon, and next evening he was back at the range. This time, as well as the bullet firing successfully, the petrol exploded.

But that was one bullet. It might have been a lucky strike. They beat out the flames and placed another petrol tin in position.

By the time they had fired six bullets it was nearly dark. All six had ignited the petrol. They had proof enough.

Next morning Dixon rang up the Air Ministry and asked to be put through to the department responsible for the order of one hundred thousand trial rounds of the de Wilde bullet. 'I think', he said, 'that you'd better come down.'

Further trials confirmed all Dixon claimed to have achieved and his bullet went into production at Woolwich. But he still found his activities shrouded in secrecy. Believing that the purchase of the de Wilde bullet and approximate details of its performance would be known to German Intelligence, the Air Ministry persisted in the use of the de Wilde trade-name for Dixon's new bullet. Superficial features of the foreign bullet were retained, so that capture would not necessarily mean discovery. De Wilde and Kaufman were given the agreed second payment, as though in accordance with their contract, when the bullet went into production; thus it was hoped that any suspicion that the RAF had something far in advance of the de Wilde bullet would be kept from the enemy.

The bullet was just in time to undergo its first operational test in the air battles over Dunkirk. Max Aitken, Douglas Bader, Al Deere, Victor Beamish, Colin Gray, Sailor Malan, and many others, testified to its magical properties and to the scramble there was amongst pilots to get their share of the bullet when, in the early days, it was in such short supply that only one gun out of eight could be loaded with it.[1] A hit on an enemy plane by a Dixon bullet was immediately visible as a tiny burst of flame, making it invaluable for aiming purposes, and the incendiary qualities were dubbed again and again 'spectacular'. 'No aircraft that was built in the last war could stand up against it,' wrote Max Aitken, and R. M. 'Dickie' Milne wrote: 'It was a killer in comparison with other ammunition.'

To minimize the risk of the enemy capturing unused samples of the bullet and discovering its secrets, Prime Minister Churchill in July 1940 ordered that its use be restricted to Fighter Command. Although the bullet became available in increasing quantities during that summer, the restriction remained in force until late January 1941. Then Air Chief Marshal Sir Charles Portal, the RAF's Chief of Air Staff, suggested to Churchill that considerations of secrecy had lost some of their force and asked for the restriction to be lifted.

Not until then did it emerge that Churchill had had an additional reason for imposing the restriction: he feared that the Nazis would shoot any pilot taken prisoner if incendiary ammunition was found in his plane. 'May they not [the Nazis] make a great public outcry in order to prepare the ground for the use of gas or other illegalities? How far can it be said that this ammunition is illegal?'

Portal explained that incendiary and explosive ammunition had been in general use by all the combatants in World War I, that the Germans were certainly using a type of incendiary ammunition themselves, and that they could not easily alter their production plans to accommodate what they would learn from the de Wilde model, nor could our use of it serve as a valid

---

1. A typical loading of the other seven was: armour-piercing in two, the old-type incendiary in another two (which gave a smoke-tracer effect), and ball in the other three.

---

excuse for the use of gas or other illegal weapons. With this Churchill was satisfied, and the restriction was lifted.

As part of reverse Lend-Lease, Dixon – with the approval of Lord Beaverbrook, Minister of Aircraft Production – flew to Washington and sold his invention to the Americans for one dollar, and over three thousand million rounds were manufactured in the States, spreading the influence of the Dixon bullet into all theatres of the air war. 'Those pilots who are in daily conflict with the enemy,' said General H. H. Arnold, Chief of Staff of the American Air Forces, 'swear by the effectiveness of the incendiary ammunition and would as soon go up without their machine-guns as without this type of ammunition.' Specifications for the bullet also went to Canada and South Africa.

'Stuffy' Dowding, in his official despatch dated 20th August 1941, made special reference to the 'de Wilde' bullet (the inverted commas are his). 'This was an incendiary ammunition without any flame or smoke trace,' he wrote, 'and it was extremely popular with pilots . . .' Later, in 1948, he supported an application made on Dixon's behalf for an inventor's award: 'I am very glad to record my opinion that the incendiary ammunition known as "de Wilde" was of exceptional merit,' wrote Dowding. 'It was used during the Battle of Britain and was extremely popular among the pilots, who considered it much superior to earlier types of incendiary ammunition.'

Dixon's contribution to victory was officially recognized when he was awarded the OBE 'for meritorious service', as promulgated in the London Gazette on 14th June 1945. The citation was quite specific:

> *'Colonel Dixon was personally responsible for notable advances in the design of small arms ammunition; in particular, he designed the incendiary small arms bullet used by RAF fighters during the Battle of Britain onwards.'*

Yet, with characteristic British reserve – as though keeping the secret had become ingrained – the fact that the bullet was a British invention was never adequately proclaimed, and the name of the shy but tenacious infantry officer who helped win the first decisive air battle of the war remained unknown to the general public. Histories still refer to the de Wilde bullet.

De Wilde and Kaufman did not do so badly out of their dud bullet. Although it was an unpleasant shock to them to learn after the war that it had never gone into production, and that they could not therefore claim the £1 per thousand rounds up to £35,000 provided for under their contract, they had been paid a further £10,000 (less tax) in April 1941 to perpetuate the bluff, and after the war they received an ex-gratia payment of £5,000 (again less tax) making a total before tax of £20,000 in all. This nevertheless represented a substantial saving to the Treasury.

Cajoled by friends in the RAF to put himself forward for an inventor's award, Dixon generously coupled his application with the name of J. S. Dick and they were awarded £3,000 between them, surely in all the circumstances a niggardly sum. But Dixon did not see it that way. 'Designing that bullet was part of my job,' he once said, 'and I expected no other financial reward.'

After retiring from the Army in 1950 with the honorary rank of Brigadier, Dickie Dixon was recalled for service with the Pakistani Army as Chief Inspector of Armaments, finally relinquishing his commission in 1959. He died in 1984 at the age of eighty-three.

SETTING THE SCENE

In 1939 Air Chief Marshal Sir Hugh Dowding, Commander-in-Chief of Fighter Command, was a man under notice of dismissal. Older than any of his serving contemporaries at fifty-eight, he was something of an anachronism, overdue for retirement. Once he had been heir apparent to the RAF's top job of Chief of the Air Staff, only to be passed over in 1937, a humiliation that wounded his pride but over which he disdained to show the emotion he felt, suffering it with characteristic reserve. Strict, starchy, even 'stuffy', as he appeared to some, he exuded an intellectual aloofness which acted as both repellent and carapace. It was hardly foreseeable at the time that his rejection for the leadership of the RAF would prove a lesser evil promoting a greater good – though Dowding himself may have sensed it.

After Munich, as Britain raced to rearm, air defence was accorded top priority, and Dowding's tenure at Fighter Command was extended until the end of March 1940. There was no one of comparable ability or status who might succeed him. Yet it remained a grudging, temporary reprieve. For almost the whole of that month, right up to the penultimate day, he was kept in suspense about his future, and, as he saw it, about the future of his Command. When at last the invitation came, he was asked to remain only until 14th July.

Dowding's heresy, in the eyes of his brass-hat contemporaries, had been his stubborn, single-minded absorption, throughout the 1930s, in the task of building up Britain's fighter defences, at the expense of the favoured Trenchard doctrine which saw a bomber offensive as a war-winning strategy. Resentment against him in high places, where he was regarded as rigid and opinionated, was only exacerbated when time proved him right. The summer of 1940 was half over, and the Luftwaffe's first probing attacks to test Britain's resolve had already begun, before, on 5th July, nine days before execution was due, he was asked to remain at his post until October.

In the Norwegian Campaign and in France, from April to June 1940, the RAF lost over a thousand aircraft, half of which were fighters of various types. These disastrous losses fell short of outright catastrophe only because Dowding pleaded successfully with Churchill and the War Cabinet, on 15th May, for a limit to the wastage of his front-line fighters. If it were allowed to continue, he warned, Britain would be deprived of her entire fighter force within a fortnight. Defeat in France would then involve 'the final complete and irremediable defeat of this country'.

Dowding had spent the previous four years building up the strength and effectiveness of Fighter Command, having previously given Britain's fighter defences resolute and imaginative support whilst Air Member for Research and Development at the Air Ministry. Fighter Command was essentially his creation, and he saw more clearly than anyone that the decisive air battle must be fought not over France but over Britain, where the devices and organization he had sponsored and encouraged, combined with Britain's 'moat defensive', would give the defenders the advantage.

The shambles in France, where the RAF was overwhelmed, left Dowding's squadrons reduced in number from 52 to 36, with many so depleted in material and battered in morale that a period of rehabilitation was essential. Fortunately the redeployment of the Luftwaffe on the far side of the Channel afforded a breathing space – though not before the demand for aerial protection of troops being evacuated at Dunkirk had cost Dowding another 106 fighters and 75 pilots.

The policy of intercepting German bombers before they reached the crowded beaches was inevitably misunderstood by the beleaguered troops, who looked for standing patrols overhead. The belief that the RAF had let the troops down at Dunkirk was never quite dissipated, and even before the evacuation was completed, returning troops were voicing their anger and bitterness. RAF personnel, even in remote areas, had to endure taunts in the street and boos, hisses and catcalls in the cinema whenever newsreels showed film of the RAF. Where had the Brylcream boys been when they were wanted? One example of this opprobrium will suffice. At No. 11 Flying Training School at Shawbury, in Shropshire, the station commander, Group Captain H. P. Lale, found it necessary to address a muster parade of all ranks on the station parade ground on the correct attitude to be adopted towards 'the unruly members of the British Expeditionary Force now roaming about Shrewsbury' and billeted in the town. Despite intense provocation, airmen were enjoined to avoid all forms of confrontation, and street and public-house brawls were to cease forthwith.

Lale developed his theme further in a signal, classified Secret, to his group headquarters, No. 23 (Training) Group, on 4th June, the final day of the Dunkirk evacuation:

11 F.T.S. Appendix 'B' O.R.B.
(Form 540) for JUNE, 1940
COPY OF ENCL. 39.
FILE 94/AIR (SECRET).

To 23 (T) GROUP from 11 F.T.S.. A/30   4/6/40.

Numerous reports from Service personnel have been received to the effect that the R.A.F. Section of the current NEWS REEL films now showing at SHREWSBURY are being received with hisses by the B.E.F. ARMY Troops billeted in the Town. In addition, disparaging remarks are being made in public houses which are likely to cause ill-feeling between the Services. It is felt that this conduct will not be confined to SHREWSBURY and is likely to cause a bad effect on the morale of the civilian population throughout the country if allowed to continue. It is appreciated that this attitude of troops is due to ignorance on the part of these men who do not apparently realise that much of the work of the R.A.F. is carried out behind the enemy's lines, nevertheless it is felt that some action should be taken to offset this present position. It is recommended that any ill effect on the morale of the country be counter-acted by a B.B.C. Broadcast giving details of the number of enemy Aircraft destroyed by the R.A.F. to date, together with some indication of the odds encountered. A further broadcast by an Army officer of high rank in appreciation of the work of the R.A.F. is also suggested. The question could also receive the attention of all army commands at home. Local action has been taken to inform O.C. N.WALES AREA of the conduct of troops in SHREWSBURY, and he is dealing with the matter.

(Signed)   H. P. LALE G/C.

The restraint imposed by Dowding and Park undoubtedly left our fighters more heavily outnumbered than they need have been, and to this extent they were culpable. But Dowding was still intent – justifiably – on husbanding his forces for the crucial battle. Nevertheless a massive effort was made, 2,739 fighter sorties being flown over the evacuation area, and whenever pilots met the Luftwaffe on anything like equal terms they found their enemy far from invincible. Indeed the RAF as a whole was heavily involved throughout, the bomber and reconnaissance effort also being substantial, making a worthy and effective contribution to the miracle of Dunkirk. But how to convince the doubters? Churchill himself, speaking in the House, did much to dampen criticism by attributing to the RAF at Dunkirk a glorious victory. 'Unhappily', he wrote afterwards, 'the troops on the beaches saw very little of the epic conflict in the air, often miles away and above the clouds . . . In Parliament I took pains to spread the truth.'[1] This was vindication from the top, far beyond the expectations of the station commander at Shawbury; yet resentment died hard.

For Dowding, then, the performance of his pilots over

1. Winston S. Churchill, *The Second World War: Vol. II, Their Finest Hour* (Cassell, 1951).

Dunkirk, although serving to re-emphasize the disadvantages of operating, as it were, away from home, had its positive side. On the debit side, the pilots he lost were highly-trained pre-war regulars, reserves and auxiliaries, the cream and nucleus of his force.

Withdrawal from Dunkirk lasted from 28th May to 4th June; and on 17th June France asked for an armistice, leaving Britain to continue the war alone, or to surrender. Even before the anticipated directive from Hitler for a landing operation against Britain was promulgated, the Luftwaffe began moving into position in the newly-occupied countries, where they stood within an hour's flight of London. Convinced that Britain's position was impossible, Hitler began working on a peace offensive; but in case this should fail he ordered his fighting services, on 2nd July, to produce contingency plans for an invasion.

With Britain showing no signs of surrendering, Hitler's military and naval advisers recommended that intensified naval and air attacks on Britain's ports and centres of distribution might encourage a more realistic response. This, they urged, would be a safer and sounder policy than invasion. But it would be attritional and long-term, and Hitler was impatient to neutralize Britain before turning east. Thus, in his Directive No. 16, dated 16th July, he wrote:

> As England, despite her hopeless military situation, still shows no sign of willingness to come to terms, I have decided to prepare, and if necessary to carry out, a landing operation against her.
>
> The aim of this operation is to eliminate the English motherland as a base from which war against Germany can be continued, and if necessary, to occupy the country completely.

The annihilation of Fighter Command, which was seen from the first as the essential prelude to invasion, was estimated to take from two to four weeks. 'The English Air Force must be eliminated to such an extent,' said Hitler, 'that it will be incapable of putting up any substantial opposition to the invading troops.' Plans for the occupation, clearly intended to be punitive, were put in hand.

Meanwhile, in early July, the three Air Fleets available to Goering, No. 2 based in Holland, Belgium and north-east France under Albert Kesselring, No. 3 in north and north-west France under Hugo Sperrle, and No. 5 in Norway and Denmark under Hans-Jurgen Stumpff, mustering over three thousand aircraft in all, had begun a preliminary offensive in the English Channel aimed tactically at our coastal convoys and naval installations, but designed strategically to bring Fighter Command into action at a disadvantage and weaken it substantially before the main battle was joined.

This preliminary phase lasted for six weeks, from 1st July through to the final build-up to Goering's *Adler Tag* or Eagle Day, scheduled for 10th August. In the course of it, Fighter Command suffered further serious losses, particularly among squadron and flight commanders whose leadership was such a vital factor in restoring and maintaining morale. Although neither side committed its full strength, coastal convoys and naval installations were persistently attacked and had to be protected, and aerial dogfights sometimes involved up to 100 aircraft, with the defending pilots often flying between five and seven hundred sorties in a day. RAF losses, although greatly exaggerated by the Luftwaffe, reached a point by 18th July when had they continued at the same rate the Command would have been wiped out within weeks.

On 19th July, Hitler, speaking as though the war was already won, made what he called his 'last appeal to reason'. In a farrago of blandishments and threats he 'saw no reason for the war to continue'. The alternatives for Britain were to surrender or to be destroyed. The speech coincided with another gloomy day for Fighter Command; but heavy proportionate losses for the Luftwaffe in the next forty-eight hours lent substance to Foreign Secretary Lord Halifax's unequivocal rejection, on the 22nd, of Hitler's so-called peace offensive. Even more reassuring, a dynamic Canadian newspaper proprietor named Lord Beaverbrook, appointed Minister of Aircraft Production by Churchill in mid-May, so galvanized the aircraft industry that planned production began to be substantially exceeded, and Dowding's fighter strength, which had fallen to 331 after Dunkirk, rose to more than 600 within a month. Over 1400 fighters were built in the three-month period from June to August, against a planned production of 900, the repair of damaged planes was vigorously accelerated, and the supply of fighters – Spitfires and Hurricanes – was scarcely a problem throughout the Battle. The shortage, escalating to crisis point in September, was not of machines but of men.

In that preliminary phase, Britain's whole complex defence system, including early radar warning, ground/air observation, reporting, filtering, plotting, and the dissemination of information, was overhauled, expanded, and tested, while new squadrons were created, reserves increased, and deficiencies made good. When, in the first ten days of August, it became apparent that the Luftwaffe was conserving its strength for an all-out effort, Fighter Command was ready.

Dowding had split his forces geographically into four groups, two of which, Nos 11 and 12, were the most important, though 12 Group was assigned a secondary, supporting role. No. 11 Group in the south-east, under Air Vice-Marshal Keith Park, was by far the biggest and most active, facing as it did the bulk of Air Fleets 2 and 3 with the shortest period of warning, liable to be as little as twenty-five minutes. No. 12 Group, under Air Vice-Marshal Trafford Leigh-Mallory, lying farther back from the enemy bases, was responsible for the defence of the eastern counties and the industrial Midlands and for acting in support of 11 Group. No. 13 Group covered north-east England and Scotland. Congestion in the south-east prompted Dowding to form a fourth group, No. 10, in the south-west.

Each group was divided into sectors, each sector controlling a clutch of airfields within its boundaries. There were seven sectors in No. 11 Group alone. Information from some fifty coastal early warning radar stations and from the Observer Corps, a band of volunteers 30,000 strong sited inland who plotted enemy air movements and reported to their own Centres, was passed to a Filter Room at HQ Fighter Command at Bentley Priory by landline, where it was plotted centrally and disseminated to operations rooms at group and sector level. Fighters 'scrambled' under group orders and were controlled and 'vectored' via voice radio by sector stations.

Thanks to Park's cautious and restrained strategy under Dowding (in defiance of ill-judged pressure from the Admiralty and the Air Ministry to meet force with equal or superior force, which was precisely what Goering wanted), and thanks to Beaverbrook's dynamism, Fighter Command's Order of Battle and Pilot State at the beginning of August was substantially the same as at the beginning of July: in round figures, 650 aircraft, mostly Hurricanes and Spitfires, and 1100 pilots. Goering's objective of weakening Britain's fighter defences in a preliminary phase had been largely frustrated, while remedial action had corrected many shortcomings.

In the month preceding Goering's much-vaunted Eagle Day, the Luftwaffe lost nearly 300 aircraft, against Fighter Command's 150; but on both sides the losses were made good. Dowding, always far from complacent, nevertheless believed that time was on his side if only his pilots could hold out. On 8th August, in a resounding Order of the Day, he proclaimed: 'The Battle of Britain is about to begin. Members of the Royal Air Force, the fate of generations lies in your hands.'

Dowding's squadrons, on the eve of this Second Phase of the Battle, were more battle-hardened than battle-weary. But that, as already indicated, had not always been so.

DOWDING, PARK AND LEIGH-MALLORY

When Air Vice-Marshal Leslie Gossage (see Chapter 5) was posted from command of 11 Group in the Spring of 1940 to become Air Member for Personnel, Trafford Leigh-Mallory, who had commanded 12 Group since 1937, seemed the obvious successor. Instead, Dowding appointed his senior air staff officer, Keith Park, leaving Leigh-Mallory where he was. Since 11 Group, as the nearest both to France and to London, was much the largest and most important of the Fighter Command groups, the preference for Park was inevitably something of an affront to an able and ambitious career officer like Leigh-Mallory. He did not hide his resentment, and as he also had a reputation as an intriguer, a stormy meeting that he had with Park soon afterwards, when he vowed that one day he would get Dowding sacked, may have had relevance later that year.

Park, as already related, had to resist continual pressure, in the preliminary phase, to meet the German assaults on at least equal terms by concentrating his forces against them. But, with Dowding's unqualified approval, he favoured a more flexible response, thereby always keeping a strong reserve in hand. The RAF's numerical inferiority dictated this: it could not stand a war of attrition. The 'big wing' strategy, in which three, four or five squadrons operated as a single unit, was proselytized by Douglas Bader in 12 Group, and backed up, after some persuasion, by Leigh-Mallory. But it was never a starter in 11 Group, where warning was short, scramble meant scramble, and there was rarely enough time in which to assemble a composite force. Congestion on airfields, and the overloading of communications and ground control, were other problems peculiar to 11 Group.

Leigh-Mallory's squadrons were rarely subjected to the

incessant raiding and repeated scrambling, four or five times a day, that afflicted the south-east. Any attempt by Park to operate big wings and the next wave of bombers might have caught half his squadrons on the ground refuelling, with disastrous results. To the suggestion that it didn't matter whether intruders were shot down on the way in or on the way out, as long as they were destroyed in sufficient numbers, Park could reply that the destruction of his sector stations, all well within the reach of the Luftwaffe, would gravely hamper his squadrons if it did not put them out of action altogether. Also there might come a time when the target would be London.

Any controversy on this subject should perhaps have been silenced by Dowding, with an insistence that the two subordinate commanders co-operate. Here Dowding's natural aloofness may have proved a weakness. 12 Group's responsibilities in support of 11 Group, particularly in protecting Park's airfields when his squadrons were airborne, called for swift reaction, and this led to bitter recriminations when the forming-up process delayed despatch and 12 Group squadrons reached the scene of the action too late. Park was bound to contrast the prompt support he got from 10 Group, to the west, with what he regarded as the unwieldy manoeuvres of 12 Group to the north.

It was part of Dowding's strategy to keep all his groups intact as far as possible, rarely committing more than a minority of his force, rotating squadrons regularly but never denuding any one group. The bigger the force despatched, the greater the risk of catastrophe. It was Dowding's ability to call up reserves when they were needed that continually bewildered Goering: just when he thought he had gained a decisive advantage, back would come the defenders with renewed strength.

The quality of Leigh-Mallory's squadrons, and of Bader's leadership, was never in doubt, and they enjoyed some spectacular successes. But it has to be said that their victory claims, when operating as wings, were often wildly exaggerated. It was on these claims, at a later date, that Dowding's handling of the campaign was to come under critical scrutiny, perhaps influencing his summary dismissal in November 1940, which upset so many. Later still, in the light of post-war research, he and Park were vindicated.

GEORGE DARLEY AND JOHN DUNDAS

The story of 609 (Auxiliary) Squadron is in many ways microcosmic, representative of the Battle as a whole. First came the depletion of resources, moral as well as physical, before and during Dunkirk. Then came a hurried renaissance under resolute leadership, purposeful if not always popular. Finally, the hard school of experience that characterized the preliminary phase in July, when individual faith was restored, bonded the squadron into a formidable collective force in time for Eagle Day and the second and subsequent phases, right through to the end of October and beyond.

At the centre of this microcosm stood two contrasting characters: George Darley the orthodox regular airman, and John Dundas the flamboyant auxiliary. How, in the weeks that followed, they turned conflict into consensus provides one of the outstanding success stories of the Battle.

2

The Salvation of 609 Squadron

THE ELLIPTICAL WINGS of the Spitfire, glinting in the summer sunshine, added an aesthetic dimension to the perfectly executed victory roll. John Dundas, twenty-five years old and one of No. 609 Auxiliary Squadron's most gifted and aggressive pilots, had claimed another victim, and the squadron got ready to cheer. They had had precious little to celebrate since their losses over Dunkirk in May and June had obliged Dowding to send them back to Yorkshire to recuperate.

One man, however, was not amused. George Darley, the new squadron commander, a year older than Dundas, had made a mental note that this flamboyant individualist needed, like the rest of the squadron, to be brought into line. A quiet word had failed to do the trick. A publicly witnessed rebuke, decided Darley, was needed, and for this he had to choose his moment. Something of a man apart though Dundas was, he was liked and respected by everyone. In contrast, Darley, operationally, had yet to prove himself.

As Dundas approached the other pilots at dispersal after landing and parking his Spitfire, Darley, his face like thunder, walked down the perimeter track to confront him in full view of the squadron. 'How did you know,' he asked, in his rather precise, stilted voice, 'that you didn't have half a dozen bullets through your main spar? Or two or three through your control wires?'

It was a fair question. The tall, aristocratic Dundas, towering above the medium-sized Darley, was known to press home his attacks more closely than anyone; he often brought back the evidence, in the shape of cannon and bullet holes, to prove it.

As Dundas hesitated, Darley followed up his advantage. 'Are you certain you hadn't?'

Dundas gave a rueful smile. 'No, I suppose not.'

'Then you're a bloody fool, aren't you? If you want to break your neck you can do it, but not in one of my aircraft on my airfield.'

For 609 Squadron, recruited in peacetime from the West Riding of Yorkshire, this was one of the many reprimands administered by Darley within a few days of his arrival. This surprisingly boyish-looking regular officer with the southern accent was making his presence felt. There would be no more victory rolls.

Although Darley might seem a conventional personality compared with the colourful Dundas, he knew what he wanted, and he didn't care whom he antagonized to get it. He had got their backs up pretty effectively with his opening address, delivered at dispersal, which had gained him the reputation of being the bluntest, rudest man they had known.

'You are a miserable, ignorant, self-pitying lot,' he had told them. 'But you're not going to stay that way, not if I have anything to do with it. And I'm going to have a lot to do with it.

'I know you lost half the squadron over Dunkirk. But you're not the only ones. And it's an experience you've got to learn from. It's your lives that are at stake.'

Who was this overblown upstart whose clipped, affected mumblings they had to strain their ears to decipher – only to boil with indignation at his insults? Promotion in auxiliary squadrons traditionally came from within. What had they done to have this plum-in-the-mouth interloper thrust upon them?

In a brief appraisal on arrival, Darley had judged that the pilots lacked nothing in individual courage. Their malaise lay in something less tangible. These week-end volunteers from the West Riding had joined up to shoot down Germans, not to be shot down themselves. Due to inexperience and the loss of their leaders they had taken a thrashing over Dunkirk. That, in an auxiliary unit, meant the loss of their friends, the people they had grown up with. For some it meant losing a sister's husband or boyfriend, so close were the family ties. But July 1940 was no time for lamentation or for long convalescence. Someone had to take the squadron by the scruff of the neck and shake it out of its despond.

Darley then produced the gesture, both dynamic and symbolic, which quelled the mutinous mutterings that his invective had provoked. He took off his jacket.

'We're going to take off our jackets and fight. I'm going to fight, and you're coming with me.

'We're going to fight together as a squadron. I don't want any heroes. I don't want any aces.

'We shall be fighting against odds. Every man who goes off on his own to chase personal glory increases the odds against the rest of us.

'We shall still have our losses. That's inevitable. But I'm going to keep those losses to a minimum. It's the kill/loss ratio that I'm going to change.'

The abrupt, unemotional, indistinct monotone in which this peroration was delivered, untheatrical except for the removal of the jacket, somehow magnified its effect. They were not being harangued. But there was a hint of pugnacity in Darley's final sally. 'If anyone doesn't want to stay and fight, now's the time to say so. And if anyone wants to argue, now's the time to do so, while I've removed my badges of rank.' There were no challengers, and the meeting broke up.

Darley's subsequent admonishing of Dundas had more to it than vexation at the victory roll. It had seemed to Darley that he had won over most of the squadron, but not Dundas. He had to mould and redirect the World War I 'ace' mentality that Dundas radiated.

Darley had served in auxiliary squadrons in peacetime as adjutant, a post generally assigned to a regular, and he knew well enough that their 'rich playboy' image was superficial, and that their dedication and work-rate could be second to none. He understood, too, the territorial and family ties that bound them. He was no martinet, but the pilots had been leaderless for too long and had been doing very much as they liked. They needed discipline.

Curbing a man like John Dundas was difficult, and not

always wise. The right balance had to be struck. Most of the time he sat at dispersal sucking his pipe and reading a book, the picture of docility – until he got in the air. Although he enjoyed a reputation as a raffish gadabout, and a first-nighter who numbered famous actresses among his friends, he was also an intellectual. A scholarship to Stowe, a place won at Christ Church, Oxford, and a first-class honours degree in Modern History before he was twenty-one, had been topped off by a year shared between the Sorbonne and Heidelberg. He had then joined the editorial staff of the *Yorkshire Post*. Meanwhile he learnt to fly with 609. All this might suggest a wealthy background. But the family, although well connected, and playing a full part in Yorkshire sporting and social life, was modestly endowed, and John Dundas's tastes proved expensive. When it came to younger brother Hughie's turn he was articled to a firm of family solicitors in Doncaster. Hughie, five years younger than John, resented this not at all; it gave him, in turn, what he wanted above all else, the time and opportunity to fly.

In any case, John's academic honours had been achieved with what, to Hughie and to others, seemed ridiculous ease, and Hughie did not expect to be able to emulate him. He could never understand how John could study perfectly happily with a portable gramophone beside him going full blast.

The contrast, then, between the patrician John Dundas and the homespun George Darley could hardly have been sharper. Darley had joined the Air Force straight from school. If Dundas was the gifted amateur, Darley was the plodding professional. Yet it was Dundas who had been fighting since the outbreak of war and who had survived the skirmishes over Dunkirk, where Hughie, too, following in his brother's footsteps, had fought with another auxiliary squadron, 616. And it was Dundas whose experiences had bred a philosophical outlook. Distress at his squadron's losses had been accompanied by a fatalistic view of his own chances of survival. When an unexploded bomb fell near his sleeping quarters he refused to move out. 'If it goes off, it goes off,' he told his vanishing room-mate.

Darley, for his part, had no practical experience of air

fighting, had never aimed a forward-firing gun or a camera gun, and had never fired any kind of gun in anger; so it was not altogether surprising that Dundas found his authority hard to accept. This was Darley's first command ever, and with the decisive air battle likely to begin at any moment he was nothing like so sure of himself as he tried to appear. Prudently, he kept his deficiencies to himself.

In his favour was the fact that although not perhaps a brilliant pilot he was a thoroughly competent one, and a fully qualified instructor. The squadron discovered these things in the first days of July as Darley organized a programme of combat simulation, with himself as the tantalizingly elusive target. 'Come in closer!' he called to them on the radio. 'You're not shooting me down!' Here, it emerged, was a man who could teach them something.

Darley had other assets in addition to his flying expertise. He had rented a house on the edge of the airfield, not more than a hundred yards from dispersal, where his young and gregarious wife Marjorie dispensed morning coffee, afternoon tea with cakes on the lawn, and in the evenings the contents of a barrel of beer; all flying was restricted to daylight. A tacit agreement that 'shop' should never intrude was readily honoured under the charm and magnetism of Marjorie Darley, while her husband, apparently relaxed without ever letting his hair down, presided. For a man who would have to act ruthlessly on occasion, a degree of remoteness had to be preserved.

Darley weeded out the only pilot whom he regarded as unsuitable and recommended some of the older auxiliaries for instructor duties. He had no thought of parting with Dundas. Every squadron had its mainstays, the men who inspired the others, and he recognized that Dundas was one of them. Of the pilots posted in as replacements, three were American volunteers who delighted Marjorie and everyone else with their breezy, wisecracking manner. They were 'Shorty' Keogh, Andy Mamedoff and 'Red' Tobin. (Sadly, all three were killed later with the Eagle Squadron.) There were also two Poles, Nowierski and Ostaszewski; it was a long time before Marjorie could get them to relax completely, but their manners delighted her.

They always greeted her with a bow, a click of the heels, and a kiss of the hand.

Darley's avowed intention of leading the two flights together as a squadron was frustrated in those early weeks of July by orders from Fighter Command. While one flight was to operate from the home base at Middle Wallop, near Stockbridge, the other was to operate from an advanced base fifty miles away at Warmwell, near Weymouth, in order to defend the Portland area. This, the Royal Navy's principal Channel base, was a major target of German bomber raids, and it was also one of the areas which the Germans were believed to favour as a potential site for their invasion landings. The two flights, A and B, would take turn and turn about.

Conditions proved to be primitive at Warmwell, and it was Darley who got up at three o'clock on the first morning to get the kitchen going, so that the flight could come to readiness at dawn on a full stomach. He personally served everyone with eggs and bacon and tea. For this he was hauled up before the station commander, a veteran of World War I, for making free with his kitchen.

'I once commanded a fighter squadron myself,' said the station commander, 'and we always had our meals at fixed times. I fail to see why 609 Squadron shouldn't do the same.'

Darley's riposte that the meal-times of the Luftwaffe might not synchronize with 609 Squadron's was not well received. But Darley could be as blunt with his seniors as with his juniors when occasion demanded, and he told the station commander what he thought of him and his kitchen, then went over his head to higher authority to get what he wanted.

There were no such problems back at Middle Wallop. From his deckchair in the garden of his rented house, Darley had his own private line to the Middle Wallop sector controller, and when the squadron was called to readiness he simply ducked through a gap in the hedge to dispersal and waited for the rest of the squadron to arrive by truck from the Mess. Sometimes many of the pilots were sitting in the garden with him when the telephone rang, and they would race to dispersal together.

Marjorie Darley, the only woman amongst these high-spirited young men, was deliberately shielded by them from the harsh realities of war. Gallantly considerate, they left the horrors on the far side of the hedge. Her naivety, her sparkle, and her unspoilt happiness, were just what they needed.

Yet she did not worry unduly. She had led a sheltered life, the atmosphere of these summer days was intoxicating, and she was young. Of course she knew it wasn't a game, but George seemed so calm, so sure of himself, and the others so light-hearted, it scarcely occurred to her that anything could go wrong.

All the pilots in their way were special to her, but her favourite, her heart-throb, was Frankie Howell, a regular, one of the flight commanders, tall and fair-haired, blue-eyed and clear complexioned, with the pale blue squadron scarf carelessly bunched at his throat. Faintly amused and disarmingly casual, he was the perfect image of the fighter boy.

Another favourite was Noel Agazarian, of French and Armenian extraction, sent down from Oxford, yet so gentle and unassertive that she couldn't imagine how he could ever shoot anyone down.

When she heard the planes coming back from a patrol she would run to the top of the air raid shelter in the garden, or slip into the house, climbing the stairs to a side window from which she could watch them banking and side-slipping as they came into land. For all her flirtations, it was George's plane that she looked for. He was leading them; he would be the first to attack; therefore he would be the first back. That was her simple logic.

As soon as George landed she would start cooking – or more often re-heating – a meal. Then, peeping through the gap in the hedge, she would watch them taxi to dispersal, leap out of their cockpits, and form an animated group from whose whirling dumb-show she could judge their success. Individual and collective experience was described in a wealth of extravagant gesture and mime – especially by the Poles. It was almost as good as seeing the scrap.

Once, when George came in cool and unflurried as usual, he found her in a state of excitement. 'He waved to me!' she said.

'Who did?'

'Frankie Howell! My heart-throb!'

He asked her how she knew it was Howell, and she told him: by the identifying letters on his plane. 'I was flying Frankie's plane today,' he said.

What a let-down! It had been her husband who waved.

The splitting of his force between Middle Wallop and Warmwell meant a penny-packet operation which Darley detested. It led to the squadron's first losses under his command. Tuesday 9th July was a wet day, and after a false alarm in the morning two of the pilots on stand-by at Warmwell, Peter Drummond-Hay and David Crook, both auxiliaries, sat for much of the afternoon planning the trip they were to make next day, when, being off duty, they would be meeting their wives in London. Then at 6.30 pm a section of three Spitfires was ordered up to patrol off Weymouth.

Spotting some Junkers 87 Stuka dive-bombers attacking a convoy, they raced after them. Then Crook, the last in line, glimpsed a formation of German fighters overtaking them rapidly. After shouting a warning he shot down one of the Stukas and made his escape. He nearly crashed his Spitfire when he got back to Warmwell, and when he got out of the cockpit he noticed his hand was shaking and his voice was unsteady. It was the first time he had been in action, he had almost certainly killed someone, and he felt both scared and exhilarated. Since the attack he had seen nothing of the others.

One of them, in fact, was missing. It was Crook's friend Peter Drummond-Hay. He had shot down a Messerschmitt 109, as was later confirmed, then been shot down himself.

Returning to Middle Wallop that night, Crook, who had been rooming with Drummond-Hay, moved into the cubicle next door. The vision of his friend lying in his cockpit at the bottom of the Channel haunted him all night.

Next morning Drummond-Hay's wife was on the phone, wondering why her husband hadn't confirmed their meeting. The telegram announcing that he was missing had not yet reached her. Darley, scarcely knowing the man, and knowing nothing of his wife, sought help from Crook in writing the letter of sympathy.

Crook went on his short leave alone. When he came back, two more pilots had been lost. One of them, flight commander 'Pip' Barran, had held the squadron together before the arrival of Darley. If Barran could go, thought his colleagues, what chance was there for them?

In a vehement protest to the controller of the Middle Wallop sector, Darley complained of the criminal futility of sending small sections of fighters to cope with the intense air activity that was developing in the Portland area. Instead of doing their job of destroying the bombers they were being compelled to fight for their lives against the odds.

Darley shocked the authorities still further by querying whether the convoys they were trying to protect were necessary at all. Could their cargoes not be transported by alternative means? Were we not playing into the enemy's hands by frittering away our best pilots on these suicidal missions when the crucial air battles were yet to come?

Stunned by these additional losses, the squadron seethed with resentment. No one blamed Darley, but all his previous work was being undone. Fortunately the force of Darley's arguments was belatedly recognized. By the end of July, reinforcements to the sector enabled 609 to operate together as a squadron; and in August, sailings were reduced to a fraction.

Meanwhile Dundas's brother Hughie, sent north with 616 Squadron for what was virtually a rest, thought it grossly unfair that 609 had not been similarly relieved. Darley was asked if he thought the squadron should be rested but answered firmly 'No!' Action was part of the therapy.

A lull in the first week of August ended dramatically on Thursday the 8th when the Germans mounted their biggest anti-convoy strike yet. Twenty merchantmen sailing through the Channel under naval escort came under ferocious attack, and as the ships neared Swanage, 609 was called to their defence.

Heading the full squadron into action for the first time, Darley found his natural emotions of fear and nervous anticipation greatly attenuated by his responsibilities as leader. Checking that the squadron was with him, searching for the protective balloons known to be suspended above the convoy, flying a course, and above all watching for enemy fighters, gave him too much to think about to be frightened.

It was a clear day, with brilliant sunshine, just the sort of weather that suited the high-flying German fighters, who could approach from the south and dive out of the sun. Darley therefore treated the vector given him by the ground controller as no more than a guide. Making continual adjustments, he climbed through clear patches rather than ascend through cloud, lest their silhouettes be limned against the cloud-tops when they emerged, and led the squadron in a wide sweep seawards so as to beat the Germans at their own game and come at them out of the sun.

Like the rest of the squadron, Darley was learning all the time. He believed above all in the virtues of flexibility and surprise. His instructions to his pilots, so unlike some of his earthbound mumblings, were crisp and crystal clear.

Fifty-seven Stukas, escorted by fifty Messerschmitts, 109s and 110s, were converging on the convoy. Eighteen Hurricane fighters, together with Darley and his twelve Spitfires, were manoeuvring to fend them off. The scene was set for the first great dog-fight of the Battle of Britain.

Outnumbered though they were, Darley's down-sun approach gave 609 the initial advantage, and it was Darley himself who drew first blood, sending a twin-engined Messerschmitt plummeting into the sea. Several of the ships below him were already on fire, their protective balloons adrift and ablaze, and with great geysers of water erupting as though from the sea-bed Darley burst through the cordon of fighters and blasted away at the Stukas.

A hundred planes were darting in and out of a space as confined in its way as a goldfish bowl, but Darley held on. Three of the Stukas, mortally hit, fell to the guns of 609, together with three more fighters, and others were so badly crippled they were written off after limping back to France. Seven ships were sunk, and in the day's fighting the RAF lost twelve pilots killed.

But the Luftwaffe suffered even heavier losses, and apart from a few stray bullet-holes 609 came through unscathed.

To the rest of the squadron Darley's cheerful, imperturbable leadership was a revelation. He had shown he could bring them through heavy fighting without loss, while inflicting severe damage on the enemy. Whatever they had felt beforehand, the squadron would go along with him now.

The commanders of the German air fleets in France now reported to Goering that they were ready for *Adler Tag* – Eagle Day, the day when the massive assault which Goering had promised would clear the skies within four days was to be launched at last. The first blows were to be struck on August 10th, but bad weather dictated a reprieve. When the sun shone unexpectedly on the 11th, however, the Luftwaffe staged a dress rehearsal of the extravaganza planned for Eagle Day, launching synchronized attacks on the Fighter Command Groups in their biggest raid yet. Their main target, though, was again Portland.

This time the German horde consisted of 75 bombers escorted by 90 single- and twin-engined fighters, 165 aircraft in all. By ten o'clock that morning coastal radar stations were forecasting a raid of a hundred plus, and 609 Squadron were ordered aloft.

The Germans sent in the Messerschmitts first, in a feint attack intended to draw off the intercepting fighters, and in this they had some success. But they paid dearly for it. George Darley, leading twelve Spitfires of 609, saw one of the Messerschmitt legions, of the twin-engined variety, forming a classic defensive circle five miles south-east of Portland at 23,000 feet, orbiting continually, protecting each other's tails. This manoeuvre made it impossible to get astern of one of them without point-blank exposure to the guns of another. An attack from abeam, too, could be fiercely contested, but this, without a moment's hesitation, was the route Darley chose. He simply led the squadron straight at the circle.

By aiming full deflection shots at the orbiting Messer-schmitts, then breaking away and diving on the far side, Darley's Spitfires shot down five of them, Dundas claiming one, and of the ten German crew-men there was only one survivor. The umbrella of Me109s, caught on the wrong foot by Darley's deliberate impetuosity, was slow to react, and when the ammunition of the Spitfires ran out the entire squadron escaped back to base, only one plane having sustained serious damage. After so fierce a scrap it seemed almost miraculous.

This spectacular five-nil victory chalked up the best kill/loss ratio yet. Darley was proving his point.

Next day the Luftwaffe bombed Portsmouth, the docks and the city, this time in such strength that one astonished 609 pilot described it as 'the whole German Air Force bar Goering'. In spite of themselves they were shaken by the density and symmetry of these armadas, which were virtually impossible to turn back.

Once again 609 were confronted by an orbiting multitude of Me110s, and again, by correct positioning and well-timed aggression, they knocked several down. Then, as the high-flying Me109s dived to the rescue, they turned to repel the new threat, and the dog-fight that developed over The Needles resulted in at least two more Messerschmitts being shot down. Dundas got a 'probable', its falling-leaf descent being watched by a colleague, and again the squadron suffered no loss.

Despite these successes, by the dawn of Eagle Day, Tuesday 13th August, Goering believed his pilots had the measure of Fighter Command.

Of all the Luftwaffe units engaged in the battle, none had a more significant task than the phalanx heading for Middle Wallop, intent on dive-bombing the airfield and hangars and wiping the station off the map. This was to be retribution for the toll 609 had taken in the previous days.

Sighting Lyme Regis in the distance, and using it as a pin-point, the Stuka crews turned north-east while they were still out to sea and set course for their target. The time was four o'clock. Half an hour earlier, flaunting superstition, Darley had taken off with thirteen Spitfires to keep a radar-assisted tea-time appointment somewhere west of Weymouth.

There were twelve names on the squadron board, comprising four sections of three, with John Dundas relegated for once to reserve, standing by with a spare aircraft. But no one dropped out, and when Dundas pleaded to be allowed to come along, Darley, recognizing that he could hardly keep a man like Dundas out of this particular scrap, signalled to him to join his own section as Red 4.

Climbing rapidly after take-off, with Darley leading, the squadron was ordered to patrol over Weymouth at 15,000 feet. Presently they began to hear German voices in their earphones. By a freak coincidence the wavelength being used by the Germans was overlapping with their own.

They were above cloud when Dundas, tucked in astern of Darley, sighted enemy fighters overhead. He called Darley, and Darley, not being able to see them, told him to take over the lead.

Climbing into the sun, with the rest of the squadron following in line astern, Dundas had reached 18,000 feet when he saw, silhouetted against the cloud below, three huge arrow-head formations of Stukas, eighteen in each block, sweeping north-east. Someone was in for it if they were not broken up. It did not occur to him that the target might be Middle Wallop.

Above them the umbrella of German fighters was coming under pressure from three Hurricane squadrons. All they needed to worry about was the close escort.

While Dundas dropped back into line as Red 4, Darley led the squadron round in a wide semi-circle so as to approach with all possible stealth from the south-west. For once his throaty voice betrayed his excitement as he gave what to the others seemed an unusually tremulous 'Tally-ho!'

'*Achtung! Spitfeuer!*'

To hear this phrase reverberate in their own earphones from a dozen guttural voices gave them an added impetus. Flight commander 'Butch' McArthur, Nowierski the Pole, and David Crook, were guarding the squadron's rear, keeping slightly above the others. Seeing some 109s pass underneath they dived after them, pouring a torrent of fire into them from close range. Two of them burst into flames and spun crazily down, leaving spiralling smudges of smoke. A third staggered uncertainly away.

By approaching out of the sun Darley had adroitly slipped the leading sections through the escorting screen. He was content for McArthur's section to fend off the fighters. He himself was after the bombers.

Given the advantage of position, altitude and surprise by their leader, the men of 609 used them to deadly effect. As Darley took pot shots at the Stukas without throttling back, so as not to impede his section, the rest of the squadron pounced. Every single pilot fired his guns, and almost immediately, in a rigid, grotesque formation, five of the luckless Stukas fell from the sky.

On the cliffs above Portland, Winston Churchill, along with Generals Alan Brooke and Claude Auchinleck, and a little-known corps commander named Bernard Montgomery, broke off their survey of coastal defences to marvel at the spectacle.

Later, back at Middle Wallop, every 609 pilot engaged in the action claimed victories – some more than one – except the unselfish Darley, the man who had master-minded the massacre.

For once the claims were not greatly exaggerated. Six Stukas were afterwards confirmed as having been destroyed by 609 Squadron, Dundas got one and a probable, and Crook and Nowierski, too, had their Me109s substantiated. A third 109 managed to limp back to France with its pilot wounded and its airframe a write-off. This made 609 Squadron Dowding's star performer that day.

There were still auxiliary pilots on the squadron with nostalgic memories of the 'Glorious Twelfth', the first day of grouse shooting on the big Yorkshire estates. They called Goering's Eagle Day the 'Glorious Thirteenth'.

It hadn't occurred to Darley and his pilots that they had, in effect, been defending their own base; they did not know that because of their recent successes Middle Wallop had been singled out for destruction. The realization came within twenty-four hours.

Marjorie Darley, watching what she thought was a friendly Blenheim twin-engined bomber from her favourite vantage point on the top of the air raid shelter next day, suddenly saw its bomb-doors open and a clutch of black eggs fall away. She rolled down the side of the shelter and threw herself inside, banging the door as the blast of the bombs rattled the structure. It was unbelievable. Until that moment, everything had been as tranquil and rural as usual.

At the northern end of the field, four airmen, having first taken refuge in a slit trench, noticed that the huge steel-plated doors of the 609 Squadron hangar were open. They were squadron men, and they knew Darley's orders. Those doors must be closed in the event of a bombing attack. Inside were a number of Spitfires, under repair.

Led by Corporal Bob Smith, a trusted auxiliary, they raced to the hangar and began winding the ratchet handles that operated the doors. They had scarcely begun when a 500-kilogram bomb from the raider crashed through the hangar roof, blasting the doors outwards. Thirteen tons of steel toppled over on top of them, crushing three of the four airmen to death. The victims were two leading aircraftmen, Henry Thorley and Ken Wilson, and auxiliary Bob Smith.

Darley had deliberately rejected heroics as a recipe for victory. Yet by his leadership he had turned the whole squadron, pilots and ground crews alike, into heroes.

It was another airman, Sergeant Alan Feary, twenty-eight years old and the only NCO pilot on the squadron (rejoicing in his role of odd man out), who avenged their deaths by shooting down the intruder. Airborne at the time of the attack, he fired all his ammunition into the bomber at close range and it crashed in flames five miles away, killing the crew.

After initially seeming intent on setting the whole squadron against him, Darley had proved himself to be the right man in the right place at the right time. He had given 609 Squadron back its proper conceit, its swagger and its pride.

Hugh Dundas was now back in action with 616 at Kenley, and on 22nd August John flew over to have lunch with him. 'John looked surprisingly well,' noted Hugh, 'and was full of life.' It was very nearly their last meeting, as Hugh was shot down over

Dover that evening. Wounded and with his plane on fire, he only just got out in time.

'Very sorry to hear that a 109 – or rather, twelve of them – inflicted grievous bodily harm on you over Dover,' wrote John. There was a wistful note in his ensuing comment. 'Anyhow you'll now get a nice spell of leave, which I rather envy you.' This admission, which he made to no one else, was a clear indication of the onset of fatigue.

He had just had a shattering experience. The squadron, sent off by the controller too late and too low, had been jumped by 'myriads of 109s. The result was that one of our machines was shot to hell, two more were damaged, and not one succeeded in firing a round. I was reduced to the last resort of the harassed pilot – spinning. It was most humiliating. But fortunately we didn't lose any pilots. Before long we'll get our revenge, I hope.'

It came quickly, within twenty-four hours. 'We got in among a gaggle of Me110 bombers and shot them down in considerable numbers,' wrote John. 'I felt pleased about it as (a) we lost no one, and (b) I was leading that time and managed to bring the chaps in against the leaders of the Jerry formation, which broke up the raid completely.' Darley had handed over to him at the start of the action because, as on a previous occasion, he had seen the enemy first and was in a better position to lead. 'It was most gratifying,' concluded John.

When Hughie and 616 moved up to Kirton-in-Lindsey in Lincolnshire to re-form, and later join a wing of five squadrons under Douglas Bader operating from Duxford, John had even more reason for envy. 'It's the best thing I've seen since the war started,' Hugh told him. 'Instead of being almost invariably practically alone among many Huns, we are a large, concentrated and formidable-looking force.' John was trying to entice Hugh to 609, but Hugh was too excited by the 'big wing' experience to leave. In any case 616, like every other squadron, was becoming desperately short of pilots.

Leading 609 throughout August and September, Darley established a kill/loss ratio second to none. For the whole of that time they were in the thick of the fight, yet only three pilots were lost. During October the squadron claimed its hundredth victory.

On 6th October, after a short leave, John Dundas wrote home: 'Good news. When I got back I found I'd got "B" Flight and have been given the DFC, so I'm now wearing it and feeling rather a fool.' Promotion to flight lieutenant was shortly to follow. Only one man could have put him up for these honours, he knew. It was a far cry from the day when Darley had called him a 'bloody fool'.

Four days later he was back in Yorkshire on sick leave after being 'mildly peppered by an Me 110' according to Hugh, whom he visited at Kirton-in-Lindsey. 'As usual when he visits the squadron,' wrote Hugh, 'the evening developed into a party. Much sherry, claret and kummel were consumed.' Mess parties usually meant Mess games and the rough and tumble they entailed. An insight into how these young pilots coped next day is given by Hugh in his diary. '11th October – Woken up at 6.15 – early start.' He needed a draught of Eno's Fruit Salts before coming to readiness. 'At 8 o'clock Mac, John and I took off and had a tremendous triangular dogfight. It started at 10,000 feet and ended up between the hangars; the troops were impressed, but the CO wasn't.' His reaction was much the same as Darley's had been three months earlier. But Hugh was unabashed. 'It was colossal fun.'

Later that day, to keep themselves fit, John and Hughie played squash, John winning 3–2. 'The evening ended,' noted Hugh, 'with the customary roughhouse at Wortley.' This was the home of the Earl and Countess of Wharncliffe, near Sheffield, and their daughters, frequently visited by John and Hugh. It was a place where they were accustomed to letting off steam.

Meanwhile George Darley had been awarded the DSO, promoted, and posted elsewhere. He left the squadron to a spontaneous valedictory ovation, which by popular request climaxed in the ceremonial removal of his jacket. The singing of 'For he's a jolly good fellow' was unusually emotional, provoking genuine tears of gratitude and affection from the men he had led. Gratitude because he had guided them out of the shadows to sunlit uplands. Affection because, in his formal, imperturbable way he had shown them, beneath the mask of reserve, that he cared.

In answer to a congratulatory signal from the squadron on his decoration, Darley wrote: 'Your congratulations are entirely misdirected. That award is due to the whole squadron. Please convey my congratulations to them all.' Copying this message into the squadron record book, an anonymous diarist wrote:

Darley's honour was nevertheless well earned. If the squadron had indeed played up to him, this was a natural response to first-class leadership and personal example.

Darley assumed command of the squadron just after it had gained moderate success at rather heavy cost in the Dunkirk evacuation period, and morale was none too good.

Darley had none of the physical attributes of the natural leader of imaginative fiction. At a first glance he could pass for a wizened schoolboy . . . But he demonstrated from the very first that he was a master of his calling.

During his command if the morale of the squadron could be plotted as a graph, it would describe a rising parabola. Darley left the squadron with a rare spirit of 'tails up'.

According to surviving squadron members, the anonymous diarist was former journalist John Dundas.

Sadly, when the time came, seven weeks later, for the diarist himself to be eulogized, the circumstances were less congenial. The Battle of Britain, so far as action in daylight was concerned, was theoretically over. Yet like a firework that is all but spent, one last coruscation was to come.

The combatants were the famous Richthofen Squadron, led by the high-scoring German fighter leader Helmuth Wick, and 609 Squadron, under its new commander Michael Robinson. The date was 28th November.

A misty late-autumn morning had given way to a fine, cloudless afternoon when 609 were scrambled for the fourth time that day, with Robinson leading the squadron and John Dundas leading the second flight of six. They began climbing to 25,000 feet on orders from control and had reached 23,000 when they spotted a gaggle of Me109s at exactly the same height. The German pilots, instead of engaging, retired.

After a lapse of ten minutes they reappeared, but at a much greater height. As they passed directly above 609, the leading section dived at the Spitfires out of the sun. 'Break round towards them!' ordered Robinson. The result was that the 109s, guns firing, passed harmlessly by.

'Re-form!' called Robinson. But already one section of Spitfires, led by Dundas, was clashing directly with three of the leading German section. Suddenly the whole squadron heard an excited shout.

'Whoopee! I've finished a 109!' It was, unmistakeably, the voice of John Dundas.

'Good show, John!' called Robinson. 'Re-form as quickly as possible.'

When he got no answer, Robinson called again. Perhaps John was out of range, chasing a 109 back to France. He continued to call for the next few minutes, but there was still no answer. There never was any answer. The voice of John Dundas had been stilled.

One of Robinson's pilots saw a torn parachute going down off The Needles. When they landed back at Middle Wallop, two pilots were missing, John and his No. 2, Pilot Officer P. A. Baillon. Robinson took off again with a colleague and made an intensive search of the sea over which they had fought. But when darkness overtook them they were forced to return. Naval launches too were alerted, but in the failing light they found nothing.

That evening a Luftwaffe-inspired signal reached the RAF appealing for news of a Major Helmuth Wick, leader of Jagdgeschwader 2. He too, it seemed, was missing. Perhaps there was a connection.

Several days later a body was washed up along the coast. A torn parachute was attached to it. But it was not John Dundas. It was the body of Helmuth Wick.

Dundas, it seemed, had indeed got his man, as his last radio call had indicated, no doubt supported by Baillon. Almost simultaneously, Wick's section had avenged their leader's death, more than levelling the score. Since this was the only contact between the two air forces that day, and Wick, Dundas and Baillon were the only casualties, conjecture that they might have clashed became certainty.

As on so many previous occasions, Dundas had gone right in for the kill. Inevitably the time had come when he hadn't got away with it. Baillon, too, young and recently married, with a wife expecting a baby, had perished.

The fate of John Dundas, after many months of air fighting, was to be killed at the moment of his greatest triumph, in the last great dogfight of the Battle. 'So it has happened at last,' wrote Hugh in his diary. 'I suppose it had to happen. I suppose we were inordinately lucky to have survived intact as long as we did.'

A month later he wrote: 'Unhappiness about John is gradually growing on me. For the first time I have felt a sickening desire to be away from aeroplanes and pilots: I suppose it will wear off. It's got to, if I am going to be any good again.' Eventually it did.[1]

There were no more great trials of strength between RAF and Luftwaffe, between Spitfire and Messerschmitt, that year, and indeed this combat was almost an anachronism, since the Battle had already been won. A bar to John's DFC was in the pipeline, and his station commander wrote that he was 'undoubtedly one of the best air fighters this war has produced.' So 'what good came of it at last?' The clash, as Hugh wrote recently, 'certainly contributed nothing, one way or the other, to the course or outcome of the war.' Yet enemy raiders still had to be challenged, and a bitter and protracted air war still had to be fought if victory was to be gained. Hugh Dundas was one of those who fought it, in Western Europe, in Africa, and in Italy, his fame, as 'Cocky' Dundas, eventually surpassing John's. But

1. See *Flying Start: A Fighter Pilot's War Years*, by Hugh Dundas (Group Captain Sir Hugh Dundas, CBE, DSO, DFC), published by Stanley Paul, 1988.

the loss of his brother, as he has written, 'affected my life deeply. I think that hardly a day has gone by since then when I have not thought of John.'

This would be echoed by countless of the bereaved. Yet such losses affected many more lives than those of sorrowing relatives. 'John', reflected a contemporary, 'was one of the rising generation whom post-war Britain could ill afford to lose.'

· For Marjorie Darley, who had fallen just a little in love with all the young pilots she had entertained so gaily in the house at Middle Wallop, the moment of truth came in 1941, after George had been posted overseas. Then, living in the West Country, she volunteered to make up a party to entertain convalescent airmen at a hotel in Torquay.

It was not until then, dancing with one of the pilots, looking him fixedly in the eye, and determined not to flinch at the terrible burns that disfigured him, that full cognition came and she understood that the Battle of Britain had been for real.

THE BOMBERS – RARE SUCCESS AND TRAGIC FAILURE

'Much has been written about the conduct of the Battle from the fighter point of view, but the contribution of the bombers to victory is less well known.'[1]

'The RAF bombing raids of 1940 have seldom been accorded due recognition for their morale benefit or for the great skill and bravery involved. Furthermore it must be recorded that Bomber Command suffered far greater casualties in flying personnel during the Battle of Britain than did Fighter Command.'[2]

The story of British bombing in the early years of the war is a melancholy one, with only the occasional success to balance against the overwhelming weight of abject failure. Air Ministry policy was clear and unequivocal: strategic bombing of selected precision targets was to be the objective, aimed at the progressive weakening of the Nazi war machine. But, after Dunkirk, although a strategic role was still attempted, Bomber Command became increasingly involved in the tactical bombing of targets directly related to the forthcoming air Battle.

At first the intention was to reduce the potential weight of German air attack against Britain by the bombing of related industrial plant by night and the newly occupied air bases in France and the Low Countries by day. While these remained prime objectives, the top priority passed in July, as invasion became a self-evident threat, to enemy ports and shipping, backed up by the sewing of mines in coastal waters. The effectiveness of these routine raids was severely

1. *Air Bombardment: The Story of its Development*, by Air Marshal Sir Robert Saundby, KCB, KBE, MC, DFC, AFC, DL (Chatto and Windus, 1961).
2. *Battle Over Britain*, by Francis K. Mason (McWhirter Twins, 1969). The statistics have been amended many times but the premise holds good.

limited by the size and capacity of the available bomber force, but they were persisted in, while opportunities for delivering destructive precision blows in set-piece attacks were continually sought. Attacks on air bases, too, despite their proliferation and comparative immunity, were stubbornly pursued.

Failure, often tragic failure, attended these efforts all too often during these grim early years, while success when it came was fleetingly savoured as fresh disasters befell.

The Last Man In:
'Babe' Learoyd, VC

'BABE' LEAROYD, they called him, after Baby Leroy, child star of a 1930s Maurice Chevalier film.[1] And as nicknames are often born of incongruity, 'Babe' had just the right tinge to stick to RAF pilot Roderick Learoyd. Now twenty-seven, he was over six feet tall and powerfully, even ruggedly, built. Yet 'Babe' was not altogether inapposite for so gentle a giant.

Something more than soft-spoken amiability, however, was going to be demanded of Rod Learoyd on the night of August 12th/13th 1940 – as indeed it had been for many nights past. Next day was to be Goering's Eagle Day, when the Luftwaffe would set out to eliminate the RAF from the skies.

Learoyd was not a fighter pilot, but he was inextricably involved, as were all bomber pilots, in the Battle. From the two twin-engined Hampden squadrons based at Scampton in Lincolnshire – Nos 49 and 83 – five four-man crews had been selected to attack and destroy a special target. Learoyd's crew was one of them.

The target had been attacked before, the Germans had concentrated guns and searchlights to defend it, and opposition would be intense. The nature of the target meant that each aircraft would have to attack individually from low level, which meant a separation, to avoid risk of collision, of two minutes

---

1. In addition to the 1933 film *A Bedtime Story* with Maurice Chevalier, Baby Leroy made a number of films, notably with W. C. Fields, before retiring in 1936 at the age of four.

between planes. And the nature of the weapon to be dropped made the timing even more critical.

The target was the old aqueduct where the Dortmund-Ems canal passed over the top of the river Ems, six miles north of Munster. Only a low-level precision attack stood any chance of success. The weapon, to be aimed into the canal at the point of the aqueduct, was a 1,000-lb. delayed-action mine. The delay chosen, to give the Germans no chance of neutralizing the mines before they exploded, was ten minutes.

The first mine was due to be dropped at 23.15, the other four at 23.17, 23.19, 23.21, and 23.23 respectively. Each succeeding plane was likely to attract a progressively more fearsome and accurate barrage, threatening the schedule. But if the timing was right, even the last man in would have a two-minute safety margin before the first of the mines exploded. *If the timing was right.*

Learoyd was the last man in.

One hundred and sixty-eight miles long, and running approximately north/south, the Dortmund-Ems canal linked the industrial Ruhr with the northern port of Emden, giving access from the Rhine to the North Sea, and vice versa, entirely on German soil. It also linked the Rhine with the Mittelland Canal, which in turn connected it with the developing industrial areas in east and central Germany. Using barges big enough to carry two train-loads of freight, the Germans substantially eased the strain on their overloaded railway system. If traffic on the canal could be interrupted, Hitler's plans for the invasion of Britain might be seriously hampered.

Harassment of the German transport system was one of the few aggressive acts of which the RAF was capable at this time. The important thing was to strike at a vulnerable point, thereby producing a bottleneck, and as a result the eye of the planners fell on the aqueduct over the river Ems. But the Germans were alert to the danger, and they doubled the RAF's task by splitting the canal into two lanes north and south of the old aqueduct and building a new one, a few hundred yards upriver from the old. This gave them an alternative if one or other of the aqueducts was damaged.

By mid-June 1940, photographic reconnaissance showed that the new aqueduct was complete and in the process of being filled with water. Soon it would be open to traffic. Simultaneously, the planners noted that a new type of bomb or mine would shortly be available, which could be dropped successfully in eight feet of water at low level and at a reasonable speed, with a delay fuse substituted for its standard magnetic mechanism. The operational intention to destroy the two aqueducts with these mines was formulated.

The commander of the Group entrusted with the task believed he had about fifteen crews on whom he could rely to plant the mines accurately, provided there was not too much interference from searchlights. He did not think his crack peacetime crews would be deflected from their purpose by guns. His name was 'Bert' Harris, Air Vice-Marshal Arthur Harris, better known later as 'Bomber' Harris, C-in-C of Bomber Command.

Meanwhile a series of more orthodox attacks in July emphasized the difficulties of inflicting significant damage on the canal. Precision bombing from high level, with the bombsights then available, was not feasible, and the damage caused by near misses was easily repaired. Nevertheless, one of many gallant attacks, in which Learoyd took part, succeeded in putting the new aqueduct out of action. By the first week in August, the need to halt traffic on the old aqueduct had become urgent.

This was when the decision was taken to send in five Hampdens at low level with the new 1,000-lb. mine. As on previous occasions, diversionary attacks with the object of drawing searchlights and flak away from the aqueduct were to be made simultaneously.

The crews selected for the attack began intensive training in the second week of August, dropping practice bombs from low level on simulated targets in nearby rivers and canals. But the target itself was kept secret. The Germans were known to be strengthening their defences alongside the canal, and the smallest Intelligence leak might bring disaster.

On the afternoon of 12th August the crews were told they would be going that night, but not until briefing at 19.30 were they shown target maps, photographs of the target area, and models of the aqueduct. Such meticulous preparation was unique in 1940, pre-empting the dam-busting of 1943.

First man in was to be Flight Lieutenant James Pitcairn-Hill, known as 'Pit' or 'Jamie', a dedicated war pilot with a reputation for fearlessness. Some of the bravest pilots were sometimes content to live to fight another day; 'Pit' would go in whatever the odds.

Second and third would be two stocky, high-spirited Australians, Flying Officer Ellis Ross and Flight Lieutenant Allen Mulligan, in that order. Ross was twenty-six and Mulligan twenty-five, and they had come over together from New South Wales seeking adventure before the war. In their dark-blue uniforms they were unmistakeable and inseparable.

No. 4 was the newly-commissioned Pilot Officer H. V. Matthews, a peacetime sergeant pilot, equally experienced. And finally came Learoyd. Unknown to him he had just been recommended by Harris for the DFC – for mining operations in enemy waters, and for a determined attack on the safety gates of the new aqueduct the previous month.

Six other Scampton crews were briefed for diversionary bombing attacks, their initial task being to give the impression that bombing not mining was the intention. Afterwards they were to fly round the target at 2,000 feet to distract the defences and draw their fire.

Briefing took forty-five minutes, and at 20.15, after all watches and clocks had been synchronized, the crews were driven out to dispersal. At 20.30 the flare path was lit, but it was still barely dusk when, twenty minutes later, the last of the eleven Hampdens climbed away into the evening sky. Learoyd, in Hampden P4403 – which he had nicknamed Pinocchio for luck, though he could never be sure how to spell it – was last off.

As he accelerated across the grass field Learoyd glimpsed one of the other Hampdens in the circuit, but after climbing through cloud to 8,000 feet he found himself alone. Soon he had a call from his under-gunner, Leading Aircraftman W. R. Rich, from the infamous 'tin', the claustrophobic gun-mounting in the belly of the Hampden.

'We've got a leaking exhaust manifold. There's flames shooting out of it.'

This was a fault they could do little about. It would act like a beacon if there were fighters around, and on any normal mission Learoyd would have turned back. But he couldn't help thinking what might be said if he did. On a night like this, it needed more courage to turn back than to press on. He held his course.

All three crew-men, navigator Lewis down in the 'birdcage' nose, Ellis at the radio amidships, and under-gunner Rich, went through the same thought processes and shied away from the shame of turning back. By tacit agreement the tell-tale torch was forgotten.

After two hours' flying on an east-south-easterly course the cloud cleared, and soon, in the light of a half-moon, ground features gleamed. Learoyd began to lose height, and by 23.03 he was circling at 4,000 feet north of the target, waiting for zero hour.

Everything was going as planned. It was almost uncanny. Four miles to the south he could see the fork where the canal divided. The left-hand fork would take him to the old aqueduct. Beyond it, perfectly placed to light their way in and illuminate the target, was the moon.

Zero hour came, and the night was still quiet. Then, with the theatrical brilliance of a military tattoo, a hundred guns exploded in the middle distance and searchlights probed. That would be Pitcairn-Hill.

One hundred and fifty feet above the silver ribbon of water, scorning evasive action, Pitcairn-Hill kept his Hampden rock-steady through a curtain of tracer and shell-fire. Half-blinded by searchlights beamed along his line of approach, but guided by his navigator from the nose, he forced his Hampden through the holocaust despite numerous hits and succeeded in planting his mine before climbing away. None of his crew, two of whom were wounded by the barrage, saw the mine fall, but they hoped at the very least for a near-miss.

The time of the drop was 23.16. One minute late. At 23.26 the mine would explode.

Next man in was the Australian Ross. His crew, two sergeants and a leading aircraftman, were British. To the dismay of those waiting to go in, and of those circling above trying to distract the defences, Ross's Hampden never reached the aqueduct. It was still some way short when it blew up.

Having seen his compatriot obliterated, Mulligan was next. He too had a British crew. Barrage and searchlights converged on him as it had on Ross, and before he reached the aqueduct two of his crew were mortally wounded, while his port engine burst into flames. Jettisoning his mine in a desperate effort to regain control, Mulligan headed forlornly for base. He had got almost to the Dutch border when he crashed near Rheine. He and his navigator survived to be taken prisoner.

Somehow the fourth Hampden – Matthews' – unloaded its mine at 23.22 and was still flying when it emerged on the far side of the aqueduct, but one engine was a heap of buckled metal and only the resilience of man and machine saw the crew home. Although they believed they had dropped their mine accurately they could only guess where it had fallen.

Everything now depended on the last man in.

One minute earlier, Learoyd had descended to three hundred feet, but he had sensibly kept well north of the barrage. He had some way to go to the target, and he knew Pitcairn-Hill had been a minute late with his attack, but he reckoned he would just about get through in time.

Banking round from the east in a diving, left-hand curve, building up as much speed as he dared, he flattened off at 150 feet as he lined up on the canal. 'Can I fire at them?' asked Rich, and Learoyd answered 'OK'. There was no need to conserve ammunition – they were in no danger from fighters here.

All was quiet after the fusillade of earlier minutes, but the defenders had the range and height, and as Learoyd reached the canal fork his machine, caught in the searchlights, came under withering fire.

Up to this point Learoyd had been controlling the run. Now, dazzled by the lights, he just had time to take the left fork before ducking into the cockpit to recover his vision. He knew the heading of the canal, but he called to Lewis to give him corrections on the final run in.

Staring down from his birdcage, Lewis soon realized they had over-corrected at the fork and were drifting too far to the left. 'Right, right!' he called, and then 'Steady!' Learoyd, shooting a glance out of the cockpit through narrowed eyelids, saw the ribbon of the canal stretching ahead and knew they were back on line.

Above the duet of the Pegasus motors the barrage was a staccato accompaniment. Suddenly a pom-pom shell, fired from point-blank range, passed straight through the outer starboard wing, sending chunks of metal spinning into the canal. Learoyd felt the plane lift with the shock of it and fought to hold her straight and level.

The Hampden was being hit repeatedly now, and another shell in the same wing, this time between fuselage and engine, forced another correction from Learoyd as the plane lurched to the right. But when he shot another glance forward he was staring straight at the aqueduct, bang on line.

'OK!' called Lewis, and then 'Finish! Bomb gone!' The crew felt the thump underneath as Lewis, judging his moment, released the mine. The time was 23.25. One minute to spare.

'Got it! Right in the middle!' The shout came from Rich as they passed over the top. From his vantage point under the belly he saw the splash as the mine hit the water. Learoyd immediately swung the Hampden to starboard and made full use of its manoeuvrability in an effort to escape. Despite the punishment the airframe had suffered, the engines kept going, and gradually the flak and the tracer fell behind.

Could they coax the crippled Hampden home? First Rich reported that oil was seeping into the 'tin'. Then Ellis, from the dorsal gun position, noticed the landing flaps were drooping. The hydraulic system had been damaged, the flaps (air brakes) were useless, and the undercarriage indicators had gone blank. It looked as though they would face a 'pancake' landing at base. If they could get there.

Sluggish though the Hampden had become, it was a robust machine and was still flying. They set course for Scampton.

After three hours of nail-biting tension, they finally reached the circuit at Scampton. Their relief was palpable, yet Learoyd, with a doubtful undercarriage and drooping flaps, resisted the urge to get down quickly and elected to wait for daylight. At the same time he would be burning off fuel to reduce the fire risk in a crash-landing. This meant another two hours of hazardous flight.

Pitcairn-Hill and the others were all safely down; only the Australians Mulligan and Ross were missing. But it was 04.53, after more than eight hours in the air, before Hampden P4403 came in to land. The undercarriage mercifully stayed down and locked.

Photo reconnaissance later that day confirmed that the aqueduct had been breached. Learoyd's mine had landed squarely on target, exploding in the north-east corner of the aqueduct and blowing a sizeable hole, draining the canal. Ten days later the canal was still blocked, with the movement of barges and motor-boats from the Rhineland to the invasion ports substantially delayed. This was extremely frustrating for Hitler, who, despite the threat of deteriorating autumn weather, was shortly afterwards obliged to postpone his invasion D-day from 15th to 21st September.

For the second time in a fortnight, Bert Harris sat down to write an encomium on Learoyd. '*Nothing can deter this pilot,*' he concluded. And Charles Portal, then C-in-C Bomber Command, wrote:

> '*It is difficult to find words to express my admiration for this officer's courage, and I will merely add that in my opinion the odds were strongly in favour of F/L Learoyd meeting his death in the course of the operation, and that before he started he was well aware of this.*'

Much the same might have been said of any one of the twenty regular airmen who flew on that perilous raid, and several of them were decorated, among them Pitcairn-Hill and Matthews, also Mulligan when it was known he was a prisoner, together with several crew members. Sadly, very few of these men survived the hectic weeks that followed.

Curiously enough Babe Learoyd never did get the DFC for which he had earlier been recommended, something that even today, in his home on the Sussex coast, he mildly regrets. They gave him the VC instead.

4

The Doomed Squadron

THE NEW SQUADRON COMMANDER was an unknown quantity. The squadron much preferred the old one.

They had learned to love the irrepressible Irishman Paddy Bandon, Wing Commander the Earl of Bandon, known throughout the Air Force as the Abandoned Earl. He was a hard act to follow: extrovert, gregarious and party-loving, his deep-throated laugh penetrated the farthest workshop and store. The squadron, which had been through difficult times under his leadership, resented his going.

His successor, Edward Lart — Edward Collis de Virac Lart, descended from a line of French noblemen who traced their ancestry back to the eleventh century — was an introvert and a loner, reticent and withdrawn, desiccated by long service in India, with a dry, sardonic sense of humour to match. Max Hastings, writing about him in his book *Bomber Command*, called him 'a chilly, ruthless officer who feared nothing and had no sympathy for others who obviously did'.[1] Yet he had two things in common with Paddy Bandon. He was dedicated to moulding an efficient squadron. And he was determined to lead from the front.

After tragic losses during the Battle of France, Bandon's mission had been to ease No. 82 Squadron, based at Watton in Norfolk, back to self-confidence in time for the next German assault. Lart, as this assault developed into what was to become the Battle of Britain, was not so considerate.

To the squadron Ted Lart was an enigma, and rumours about

---

1. Max Hastings, *Bomber Command* (Michael Joseph, 1979).

him proliferated. Among the more colourful were that he had been despatched in disgrace to India and that while serving there he had lost his wife and children in the Quetta earthquake of 1935 – an experience, it was thought, that accounted for an aggressive bravery that some saw as recklessness and bravado. He didn't care, it was said, whether he lived or died. However, the facts were that he was not in India at the time of the earthquake and that, although no misogynist, he was and always had been a bachelor.

Other rumours – that'he had come to the squadron straight from overseas, sent home, because of some social indiscretion, as abruptly as he'd been sent out, and that he had no war experience outside the bombing of recalcitrant tribesmen – possibly held more substance. He does seem to have been despatched overseas in a hurry, and he had been back in Britain no more than a month. But in that short time he had learnt to fly Blenheims with one squadron and done four raids over enemy territory in a week with another.

Of scarcely average height, slim and physically fit, Lart in his fortieth year retained a luxuriant head of chestnut hair which was the envy of many younger men on the squadron. He retained, too, a youthful capacity for risk-taking. Whether peace-keeping from the air on the North-West Frontier, where he had twice been mentioned in despatches, or hunting big game on lone forays into the hills, he was accustomed to physical danger. Indeed it might be said that he looked for it and thrived on it. Thus his allegedly hurried return from India seems more likely to have been stimulated by his own anxiety to get into the fight.

If there was any man in the Air Force likely to take on an impossible mission and make a success of it, Lart was that man.

82 Squadron formed a part of No. 2 Group, the light bomber group of Bomber Command. From 1st July 1940, when Lart took over the squadron, the crews operated individually, bombing airfields in France, Germany and Holland, though in daylight they were required to stick rigidly to their brief to turn back without adequate cloud cover. 'Tasks', ordered Bomber

Command, were 'to be carried out only to the extent which is rendered possible by the conditions prevailing at the time.' This was in consideration of the extreme vulnerability of the twin-engined Blenheim to German fighters, which had been pathetically proved in the Battle of France. The result, for many of the pilots, and especially for Lart, was frustration. 'I'm sick of all this turning back,' said sergeant pilot John Oates, thirty-two years of age and a Yorkshireman. A fellow pilot reacted differently. 'Look, Johnnie – the blokes who didn't turn back are nearly all dead.'

Lart took a cynical view. Once, when a pilot who had forfeited his confidence was taking off on a bombing mission Lart was heard to mutter: 'I suppose he'll find some excuse to creep back – probably before he's half-way across the Channel.'

The crews were all peacetime regulars or reservists – professional airmen to a man, but under severe nervous strain. Their courage was not often in question, but they were mostly content to stick to the book, happy, when vindication seemed certain, to live to fight another day. Lart, privy to a deeper insight into the course of the Battle, knew that 'another day' might be too late.

On raid after raid it was Lart who pressed home the attack. On 7th July he penetrated 300 miles into enemy territory alone and in daylight to attack Eschwege airfield. Invariably he followed up his incursions with a vital reconnaissance, noting Luftwaffe dispositions. Of ten crews operating on 18th July, eight turned back, but Lart attacked canal barges assembling for the projected German invasion, and so did one of his senior pilots, the lean, balding Flight Lieutenant Ronald 'Nellie' Ellen. Ellen found Lart ascetic and uncommunicative, but he fully supported his efforts to revitalize the squadron.

On 28th July Lart's was the only one of seven crews to bomb the Dutch airfield at Leeuwarden. Three days later, on 31st July, Air Commodore James Robb, Air Officer Commanding 2 Group, recommended Lart for the award of a DSO. The citation concluded: 'By his courage, devotion to duty and skill as a pilot he has set an inspiring example which has more than maintained the excellent *esprit de corps* of all ranks under his command.'

When thirteen out of fourteen aircraft returned for lack of cloud cover early in August, Lart attacked Boulogne airfield from low level and suffered superficial damage from his own bombs. He used this as a stick to beat his crews with. *'That,'* he said, pointing to the damage, *'is the level I expect you to bomb.'*

In one crew, a dilatory gunner was left behind because Lart wouldn't countenance further delay. Some said he was mad. Others noted a dramatic improvement in time-keeping.

Meanwhile the inability of the daylight Blenheims to play a significant role in the Battle was worrying commanders and Air Ministry alike. Spitfire and Hurricane pilots were locked in a fight to the death with the Luftwaffe in those first days of August, and Air Marshal Charles Portal, C-in-C, Bomber Command, ordered daylight precision attacks on enemy airfields, aimed at harassing concentrations of German air strength. But he did not change his opinion that such attacks without cloud cover would prove disastrous, and the insistence on such cover remained. Under this embargo, pilots were again and again forced to turn back.

Yet the Blenheims could not be left to stand idly by while Fighter Command was overwhelmed, and 82 Squadron were ordered to practise formation attacks at high level. Judging from experience in France, these too seemed doomed to failure. At 20,000 feet the Blenheim was sluggish and sloppy, inviting attack, and making close formation flying an additional strain for the crews. When the revised tactics were tried out on 7th August there was an ironic twist. From 20,000 feet the target was cloud-covered and the raid was aborted.

On the afternoon of 12th August, Lart received orders from 2 Group for a high-level formation attack on the bomber airfield at Aalborg West in Jutland by twelve Blenheims. It was a grass field, but since occupying Denmark the Germans had refurbished it, though the work was not yet completed. Targets to aim at would be parked aircraft, dispersals and airfield buildings. British Intelligence had wind that some fifty Junkers 88 bombers were massing there for 'Eagle Day', together with

Junkers 52 troop transports for the invasion. The pressure on Portal was mounting.

Aalborg was at the limit of Blenheim operational range. The bombing height was to be 20,000 feet 'if possible', in the hope of escaping the defences, but Lart doubted whether this was feasible or even desirable. It was doubtful whether, with the aids then available, they could bomb accurately from that height, and they would probably be equally vulnerable. In any case such an attack would depend on clear skies.

Meanwhile a significant phrase had begun to appear in group orders: *'irrespective of cloud cover'*. And '20,000 feet if possible' gave formation leaders considerable latitude.

Even at 20,000 feet, however, the Aalborg plan, without fighter cover and in daylight, looked suicidal. But the orders and the implications were clear; it would be useless to argue. Lart would simply be told that either he led the raid or made way for someone who would. Even if he had a mind to protest, he would not save a single one of his crews. All he would achieve would be personal ignominy and the saving of his own skin. There is no indication that he resisted.

Late that afternoon he drew Ellen aside. 'Take the chaps into Norwich this evening. You can use squadron transport. But don't be late back. It'll be an early start tomorrow.' The condemned men were to be given a hearty supper.

At 5.30 next morning, 13th August, the crews were awakened. They were due to take off at 8.30. When they learned the target, most were resigned to their fate. They just hoped for a miracle, or to survive as prisoners. Many found a quiet moment to write letters to loved ones, to be posted if they didn't come back.

Briefing was tense and succinct. The load was to be four 250-lb. high-explosive bombs and eight 25-lb. splinter bombs to disable parked aircraft. Flak and fighter opposition must be expected, but the aim was to put aircraft and support buildings out of commission, and the attack was to be pressed home at all costs. The importance of destroying the Junkers 52 transports, which it was thought would be obvious targets, was stressed. All crews were to co-ordinate their actions with Lart's, opening their bomb-doors and releasing their bombs simultaneously so far as was possible. They were not to attempt to get back to their base in East Anglia, which would be out of range, but were to take the shortest route back to Britain and put down where they could in the north-east of England or in Scotland.

When Ellen's navigator, Sergeant John Dance, climbed into his Blenheim, the D-ring of his parachute snagged on an obstruction, exposing the canopy. 'I'll have to manage without one,' said Dance. But Ellen, standing up to an impatient Lart, insisted that Dance go back to the parachute section for a replacement.

Other minor delays had already proved sufficient to allow one crew, whose posting notice had just been opened in the orderly room (they had been flying operationally since September 1939), time to be recalled, their place in the formation being taken by the stand-by crew. Thus the experienced Flight Lieutenant D. M. Wellings, a brother of E. M. Wellings, cricketer and cricket writer, gave way to newcomer Pilot Officer E. R. Hale. Hale had been on the squadron a fortnight.

Irishman Bill Magrath, a navigator with sergeant pilot Don Blair, often had premonitions about others, but never about himself. Today his mind was a blank. Was it his turn? Just in case, he took care, as was his habit, to eat the whole of his chocolate ration before take-off. No one else was going to get that. He and his pilot and gunner were all aged twenty.

The morning was fine, but after they crossed the Norfolk coast the sea was hidden by a layer of cloud. Lart led them up to 8,000 feet, then levelled off. They had formed up into two flights of six, each flight split into two vics (V-formations) of three, the whole stepped down from the front like a ladder. Lart was leading A Flight, while leading B Flight, which had taken off from the nearby satellite airfield at Bodney, was a ginger-haired squadron leader named 'Rusty' Wardell.

Ahead lay a flight of exactly four hundred and fifty miles, stretching the Blenheims to the limit of their endurance. Throttle manipulation to maintain station at high altitude would have reduced their margin still further, and it became plain that Lart intended to stay at 8,000 feet. Reflecting on this,

Rusty Wardell twisted the ends of his incipient handlebar moustache even more fiercely than usual.

Lart faced an impossible dilemma. If they stayed at their present height, and the cloud evaporated, they would get the worst of both worlds. But 20,000 feet he dismissed as impracticable. Better to fly at heights to which they were accustomed. Rather than be frustrated by cloud, as had happened six days earlier, and having regard to the phrasing of his orders, he elected to stay where he was.

Two hours later, as they approached the Danish coast near Ringkobing (Lart was taking a more direct route than the one originally planned, to conserve fuel), the crews saw with alarm that the cloud was dispersing. Suddenly Magrath realized that he had a premonition after all. He wouldn't get back from this one. He had bought a one-way ticket.

None of the pilots expected Lart to turn back, though one was about to do so. This was a Sergeant Baron, No. 6 in the second section. Baron's fuel gauges were playing up, recording an excessive consumption. At first he thought it might be the gauges, but he became convinced that the gauges were right. They were still some way short of the Danish coast when he broke radio silence to tell Lart of his problems, then tailed off. Lart's comments are not recorded. He continued on course.

That Lart was interpreting his orders correctly was underlined when, after Baron's problems had been provisionally diagnosed back at base as a 'supposed fuel shortage', he was placed under open arrest awaiting court martial.

Meanwhile a German observation post on the Danish coast at Sondervig, near Ringkobing, had reported the airborne invasion. From its estimated heading the target looked likely to be Aalborg. Soon afterwards the air raid alarm was sounded in Aalborg and the crews of the anti-aircraft gun emplacements there were alerted.

British Intelligence had been accurate about the positioning of the Ju88 bombers – they had recently been flown down from Stavanger. What was not known was that, to support them in their bombing of Britain, nine Messerschmitt 109E single-engined fighters of Fighter Geschwader 77 had been switched

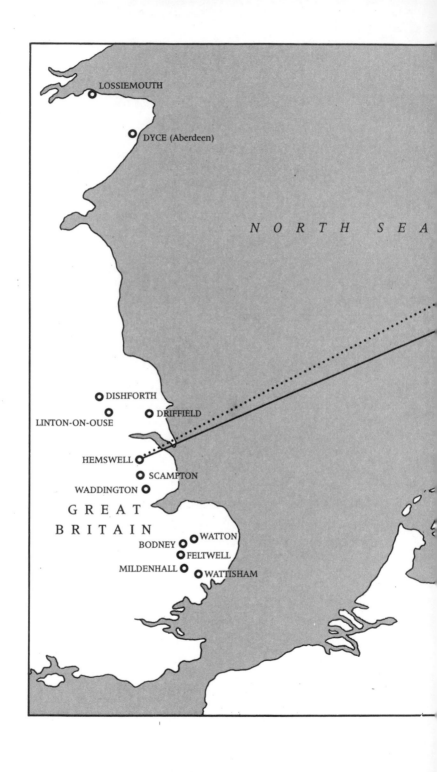

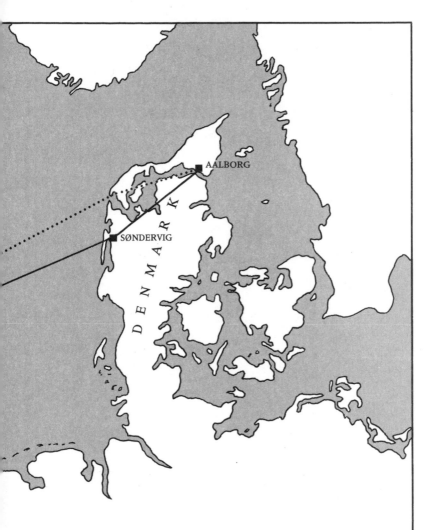

'The Aalborg raid was mounted by Blenheim IVs of 82 Squadron from Watton and its satellite airfield Bodney on 13th August 1940. The dotted line indicates the planned route, the unbroken line the actual route, a few miles shorter, taken by Lart'.

```
0                    100                    200 miles
```

south from Norway to the fighter airfield at Aalborg East and another twenty-five – the remainder of the Geschwader – had been posted to Jever, near Wilhelmshaven in North Germany, in preparation for Eagle Day. The smaller Aalborg section had just arrived when news of the Blenheims came through, and the pilots, with their engines still warm, were immediately scrambled.

As the eleven remaining Blenheims motored at 8,000 feet and at 180 miles an hour across the flat Jutland landscape in bright sunshine, a veritable hornets' nest was being stirred up to receive them.

Lart, continuing on a north-easterly course, doubted his own and anyone else's ability to hit specific targets from 8,000 feet, and he began a shallow dive down to 3,000, intent on plastering the best targets before swinging left towards the North Sea and Scotland. The others in A Flight followed in close formation. Rusty Wardell, however, leading B Flight, elected to vary the direction of his attack, hoping to confuse the defences, and he started a detour to starboard, planning his attack from that angle. His flight, reduced to five, kept in close.

When the alarm at Aalborg was followed by the staccato detonation of guns, the townsfolk began hurrying for shelter. But some stayed to see what would happen. 'I looked up and saw about ten English bombers,' said one eye witness. 'They seemed to be in two different formations, flying in finger formation at about 3,000 feet.' Long before Lart's flight reached the airfield, the guns on the shores of the fjord were probing for their range.

The German tactics were to hold their fighters off until the target was positively identified, relying on the ground gunners, if it proved to be Aalborg, to put the bombers off their aim. The airfield was surrounded by guns. Puffs from a random succession of explosions curtained Lart's flight as they swept on in tight formation towards the airfield. Several of the Blenheims were hit by shell fragments on the run in, making pinpoint accuracy impossible, and one crew, on the port side of Lart, piloted by Yorkshireman Johnny Oates, forgot all past frustrations as direct hits in the turret and an engine somersaulted their plane. Diving steeply, the Blenheim seemed certain to crash, but miraculously Oates retained some measure of control. Flattening off but letting the dive continue to low level, he jettisoned his bombs on the airfield and hedgehopped north-west as best he could on one engine.

The rest of Lart's flight suffered further hits and all dropped their bombs under pressure. They caused only minor damage and inflicted few casualties, the only fatal ones being three Danish airfield workers. As they veered to the north-west, the fighters moved in for the chase.

The crews of Lart's flight had seen four German fighters taking off as they approached the airfield to bomb. Now others were joining them. Meanwhile those Danes who had stayed above ground to watch saw five more Blenheims approaching in impressive but vulnerable formation, presenting what looked like an unmissable target to the German guns.

First of Wardell's flight to suffer serious damage was Blenheim C for Charlie, flown by a young pilot officer named Douglas Parfitt. Forced to release their bombs over a farm short of the target, killing some cattle, Parfitt and his crew, Sergeants Youngs and Neverson, were already struggling to stay airborne when their plane received a direct hit that severed the tail. Eye-witnesses saw the plane pirouetting down in two pieces, with little hope for the crew. In fact the navigator, Leslie Youngs, got clear of the plane but his parachute failed to open and he fell with his comrades to his death.

The four remaining Blenheims presented an almost point-blank target to the gunners as they raced in to bomb. All were hit before reaching the target, the two at the rear staggering and quickly losing touch with the others. One, Z for Zebra, flown by Flight Lieutenant T. E. Syms, turned abruptly on its back before settling into an incandescent dive south of the target, off the island of Egholm. As it blazed towards the water an alert German soldier, camera at the ready, preserved its final plunge for posterity. Syms, a distinctive figure with flaxen hair and abnormally high cheek-bones, having already ordered his crew to jump, got out himself, alighted in shallow water, and was helped ashore by a Dane and a German. His navigator, Sergeant

Wright, also escaped, though while pirouetting down towards the fjord he found himself the target of a stream of bullets from one of the Messerschmitts – or so he imagined. Almost certainly it was a stray burst aimed at another Blenheim. Alighting near Syms, Wright was also assisted to the shore. There he got the traditional greeting from a group of German soldiers. 'For you the war is over.' There was no trace of animosity – but Syms's gunner, who was missing, was later found dead in the plane.

Bill Magrath, lying on his tummy in the nose of Blair's aircraft, was manning the backward-firing gun and banging off at everything in sight, knowing he was the last one in, with nothing but Messerschmitts behind him. He didn't expect to hit anything, but he might scare them off. Soon after dropping their bombs they lost an engine, and then the Blenheim caught fire. As the blaze scorched his eyebrows Magrath decided it was time to get out; then he saw the waters of the fjord racing up towards him and realized he'd left it too late.

Blair was aiming to ditch in shallow water north of Egholm. What he didn't know was that boulders below the surface were waiting to rip open the plane's under-belly. Next thing Magrath and his gunner, Bill Greenwood, knew they were lying in the water with lifejackets inflated. Floating a few yards away was their pilot, Don Blair, his face so disfigured they thought he was dead. Magrath himself, with a smashed hip and shoulder, a broken leg, and severe facial injuries, was drifting in and out of consciousness when, with a half-revived Blair, he and Greenwood were dragged ashore by a group of islanders who had witnessed the crash. The Danes would dearly have loved to take them into hiding but were forced by the spectacular nature of their arrival to hand them over to the Germans.

Pilot Officer Hale, the novice who had taken Wellings's place in the formation, stuck close to Wardell and got through to the airfield. His bomb-aimer, Sergeant Oliver, preparing to unload, appeared to be delaying the drop, saving his bombs for the German *Kommandatura* building, occupied at the time by the construction company refurbishing the airfield. Meanwhile gunner Sergeant Boland tried to fend off the fighters. But the plane was overwhelmed before the bombs could be dropped. It crashed almost vertically, not far short of the *Kommandatura* building, and the bombs exploded on impact, scattering fragments over a wide area. There was no chance whatsoever that Hale and his crew could survive.

The last airborne Blenheim of B Flight was the leader, S for Sugar, with Rusty Wardell in the cockpit. His plans to qualify as a doctor after the war looked likely to be stillborn. Hit by shellfire on the bombing run, he had barely got rid of his bombs before his aircraft caught fire, burning him severely on the face and hands. He gave the order to bale out and jumped simultaneously, but his crew-men, Flight Sergeant Moore and Sergeant Girvan, both perished in the seconds that followed. One was trapped in the plane, perhaps already dead, the other got out at low level but was forced to pull the ripcord prematurely and was dragged to his death as the lines fouled the tail unit. The plane crashed in a convulsion of flames and exploding ammunition. Wardell himself landed heavily but safely near Vadum.

A young Danish girl who stayed to watch while her friends sought shelter saw all five aircraft of B Flight crash, most of them on fire. These were Parfitt, Syms, Blair, Hale, and Wardell. 'You had to pinch yourself to see whether you were awake or dreaming,' said another eyewitness. 'The scene made such an impression that people around me were crying.'

The sight of a charred body so sickened one member of the German occupying forces that he wrote: 'I, as a man who is not a warmonger, wonder . . . Here lies a human being.' He noticed there was a ring on a finger, and began speculating on the reaction of relatives, pitying them in advance. But he added: 'I couldn't cry over him. I had to think of my many German comrades.'

The six leading Blenheims, although under pressure from fighters, had got well clear of the airfield while B Flight were being demolished and had all swung away seawards, intent on making good their escape. But in A flight, too, it was the second vic of three which bore the brunt of the initial fighter attack, the first victim being Pilot Officer 'Binjy' Newland, so nicknamed not for his beer-drinking capacity, though that was up to standard, but because his initials were B.J.N. Hit by flak over the target, he was striving to stay with the others when the fighters intervened. The square-jawed, open faced Newland could not evade the swarm that pounced on him, and he felt a searing pain as a bullet penetrated his left shoulder. He was aware, too, from explosions around him, that his crew, Sergeants Cyril Ankers and Kenneth Turner, had been hit and were either wounded or dead. Despite his crippled shoulder, which greatly reduced his mobility, he managed to open the hatch above his head with his good arm. He had begun a despairing call to his crew when he was violently sucked out.

Nellie Ellen and a squadron leader named Norman Jones, who was leading this second vic, managed to stick together and were now half-way to the coast. But the Messerschmitts were hot on their trail. Jones's gunner, Sergeant John 'Curly' Bristow, so called because of his crinkly fair hair, found air fighting not at all what he'd thought. Things were happening with bewildering speed. Although he believed he was accurate with his return fire the fighters seemed immune to it.

In that second a dotted line of bullets raked the fuselage, yet the area around the turret escaped. To Bristow it seemed he had been deliberately spared: for a fraction of time the enemy pilot must have lifted his thumb from the firing button. He muttered a grateful 'Thanks, pal', then called his pilot. There was no answer. Peering through the fuselage he caught a glimpse of Jones, slumped over the controls. He could see no sign of his navigator, the aircraft was beginning to burn, and he decided to go.

As he dropped through the rear hatch one of his flying boots snagged on some unremembered protrusion, leaving him suspended in mid-air. He kicked out frantically as the ground rose towards him. This was no way to die. Mercifully his boots were loose-fitting and the trapped one slipped off his foot. One last thrust and he was free. But would his parachute open in time? He pulled the ripcord and hoped.

Meanwhile Ellen's Blenheim, similarly blasted by fighters, and with no elevator control, was falling out of the sky. His intercom was dead, and he motioned to his navigator, John

Dance, down in the nose, and shouted at him to get out. Dance wouldn't have had a parachute but for Ellen, and he blessed his skipper in that moment.

Ellen could only hope that his gunner, Sergeant Gordon 'Taffy' Davies, had gone already. There was no word from the turret. He reached for the hatch above his head and pulled but it resisted all his efforts. It was jammed. The only hope was the nose hatch.

In an instant he was down there, and with no time to count up to three he pulled the ripcord as he dropped through. He was jerked to a stop almost immediately, just as his feet sank into a swamp. Shocked by an almost simultaneous thump behind him, he turned to recognize Jones's gunner, Curly Bristow, whose parachute, like Ellen's, had opened just in time. Jones and his navigator, Pilot Officer Thomas Cranidge, had been killed by the fighters, as Bristow had feared. The two Blenheims, Ellen's and Jones's, crashed in nearby fields within a few hundred yards of each other.

A farm labourer led Ellen and Bristow on borrowed bicycles to a house in an adjacent village, where they were given a meal and an escape plan was discussed. But with no Resistance movement and no escape routes yet established, they had to agree that rather than jeopardize the Danish family the Germans must be called in.

There were still three pilots airborne – Lart himself, Pilot Officer Wigley (first operation three days earlier), and the canny Sergeant Oates. All three were nearing the coast, all three were hoping to make it. One of them must surely get home to tell the tale. But the fighters persisted.

A Danish citizen in Pandrup, close to the coast, heard 'a furious roar and thunder' as three twin-engined planes flashed over, hotly pursued by fighters, which jostled for position as they sought the bombers' weak spots. 'I became an eyewitness to the most hazardous stunt flying. All the time I could hear the hoarse rattle of machine-guns.'

Showing increased sophistication as the fight continued, the German pilots attacked from below and abeam as well as from astern, forcing the Blenheims to fly through a vortex of fire.

First one and then another fell steeply, leaving a trail of smoke and exploding with awful finality on impact. The pilots were Wigley – and Lart. Wigley had done incredibly well to get so far, as had his crew, Sergeants Patchett and Morrison. It was a baptism of fire that deserved a less tragic ending; their chances had been virtually nil from the start. As for Lart, sooner or later the cold dedication and hawk-like aggression of this highly experienced pilot, not far short of middle age, could have only one ending. All six men in these aircraft perished. Of Lart's crew – Pilot Officer M. H. Gillingham, navigator, and Sergeant Beeby, gunner, together with Lart himself – only Gillingham could be identified.

That left only the Yorkshireman Oates. He knew he couldn't make base and he headed for Lossiemouth. As the fighters chased after him he felt no fear, only exhilaration, a reaction that must have been the last sensation of many. 'The bomber flew low over a village,' said another horrified Dane, 'and the combat continued at roof-top level between chimneys. Houses vibrated and villagers trembled as bullets whistled around them, but they couldn't resist staying to watch.'

Oates tasted the ultimate irony when, after shaking off the fighters and getting well out to sea, he was rejoicing with his crew when he glanced at his gauges and knew that a ditching was certain. With an aircraft more porous than a colander, it would be suicide to come down in the sea. As he turned back towards land the fighters reappeared.

The crash-landing he made under fire, on a bumpy meadow, knocked him out. Trapped in the cockpit, he was released by two Danes who had witnessed the scrap. When he recovered consciousness he found himself lying in a heap yards from the wreck with severe fractures to his back and his skull, injuries from which he would never fully recover. His navigator, Tim Biden, was also seriously hurt. Sergeant Graham, the gunner, escaped almost uninjured, and after an abortive search for a hide-out he returned to the Blenheim to burn all secret papers before the Germans arrived. Soon afterwards they joined others of their wounded and injured comrades in hospital.

*

For Headquarters Bomber Command the cost was clearly too great, whatever the missing crews might have achieved. The operations staff knew where they'd gone wrong, and next day they specifically ordered that no more formation raids were to be attempted without fighter escort.

Two days later, on 15th August, when the full strength that the Luftwaffe had intended to deploy on the 13th was actually unleashed, fifty Junkers 88s of Bomber Geschwader 30 took off from Aalborg West to raid north-east England, proving that airfield facilities were not crucially damaged by the sacrifice of the Blenheims. Yet the Luftwaffe, too, failed to provide escort for their bombers and suffered accordingly. Seven of the raiders were shot down by Hurricanes or Spitfires and three more crashed or force-landed on their return, virtually ending the threat from Air Fleet No. 5.

Three days after the action, on 16th August, the twenty men of 82 Squadron who lost their lives in the action were buried side by side in the churchyard at Vadum, north of the airfield they had sought in vain to disable. A German military padre spoke sympathetically of them and praised their courage, and a firing party and guard of honour, recruited from the crews of the anti-aircraft batteries which had caused such havoc among them, paid their respects. The ceremony was witnessed by members of the local population, who showered those in hospital with flowers, to the embarrassment of the Germans, who within a few days moved all the survivors to Germany. Meanwhile, however, there was time for visits to the hospital and floral tributes from two of the pilots who had shot them down. Two of the opposing pilots recognized each other: they had been at university together. Johnny Oates was told: 'The war will soon be over and you'll be going home.' Oates knew better. 'We haven't started yet.'

Though the raid may have achieved nothing tangible, the impression it made on the Danes was profound. Such was its emotional impact that the seed was sown for the Resistance campaign which gave so much help to the Allies in subsequent years.

Even today the Danes have not forgotten, and every year a memorial ceremony is held beside the long row of graves at

Vadum, a ceremony which in recent years some of the few remaining survivors have attended. Among these have been Bill Magrath, who was one of a handful of prisoners to escape from Germany and get back to Britain, for which he was awarded a Military Medal. Others have been Johnny Oates, despite partial paralysis, and his navigator, Tim Biden; Ronald Ellen, awarded an MBE and the US Medal of Freedom for his POW activities and subsequently promoted to wing commander, and his ever-grateful navigator Johnny Dance; also Curly Bristow (like the other gunners he was also a wireless-operator), who spent a tense and nerve-racking fifty-six months as a prisoner, building radios in secret so that his fellow prisoners could listen to the BBC news. In two different camps the hiding place was inside a piano accordion.

One who has not attended but who kept in touch for many years is 'Binjy' Newland, from his medical practice in Australia. Newland was told by the surgeons in the hospital at Aalborg that the bullet in his shoulder was so close to the radial nervous system they dare not attempt to remove it, and there it remained until his death in February 1987.

Evidence in support of Sergeant Baron's explanation that he turned back because of excessive fuel consumption was evidently accepted at his court martial; anyway he was acquitted. He was killed later, as was Wellings. What of Edward Collis de Virac Lart? What should the summing up be?

That Ted Lart was a complex character, and a leader who scorned to seek popularity, is inescapable, earning him the opprobrium which on further examination seems undeserved. He fought the air war, in one of the RAF's darkest periods, with an aggressive dedication that did not always appeal to men who liked to feel they had some chance of survival. On 13th August 1940 – which did indeed turn out to be Goering's Eagle Day as intended, although it was partly aborted – he set out to fulfil a task which he must have known was beyond the capability of the force he commanded, but which might still achieve something of value. Robb at 2 Group and Portal at Bomber Command clearly recognized his bold and dynamic leadership in those hectic weeks of mid-summer when, as already related,

1a 'George' Darley
1b 'Dickie' Dixon
1c The Dundas brothers: John (*left*) and Hughie

2a The final inverted plunge of Blenheim Z for Zebra (p. 70). Pilot and navigator had already baled out, but the gunner, Sgt. E. Turner was killed.

2b (*Inset*) Ted Lart

2c With a fractured skull and a broken back, Sgt. Johnny Oates lies helpless after being pulled clear of his crashed Blenheim by the Danes.

they recommended him for a DSO. The award was duly approved by the King on 17th June 1941, backdated to 31st July 1940.

The loss of an entire squadron on a single raid has an epic quality, yet, as war historian John Keegan has written, no national epic is ever safe from irreverence. 'The urge to find the worm in the apple', he says, 'is irrepressible.'[1] There were worms enough wriggling through into the Aalborg raid, principally from Britain's pre-war unpreparedness, but, amongst the air crews of 82 Squadron, including the solitary and much-maligned Lart, on closer inspection none can be found.

It was Sergeant Donald Blair, Magrath's pilot, who penned the most moving tribute when writing to Lart's family soon afterwards from POW camp, a voluntary act lacking any of the advantages and disadvantages of hindsight. 'It was a pleasure and a privilege,' wrote Blair, 'to fly behind such a gallant gentleman.'

The extraordinary amount of detail on the fate of individual aircraft and crews, even more comprehensive than has been utilized here, comes from a Danish detective-inspector, Mr Ole Røennest, whose task it was, together with a colleague and an expert from the Danish Army Demolition Service, to investigate the site of one of the crashed Blenheims for unexploded bombs after fragments of the wreckage – it was Syms's aircraft, Z for Zebra – had emerged out of the mud in 1981. Up to that point he knew absolutely nothing of the incident. Now he needed to know how the wreckage got where it was and whether further digging might disclose unexploded bombs. Told that after forty-one years he would never track down the full story or discover details, he responded to the challenge by diligent research into Danish, British and German records. The result was one of the most complete reconstructions of any wartime incident. Since then Mr Røoennest has met most of the survivors of the raid and today numbers them among his personal friends; in 1984 he was made an honorary member of 82 Squadron. 'The incident,' he says, 'has changed my life.'

1. *Daily Telegraph*, 1st June 1988.

THE VICTORIA CROSS

Although the VC had been awarded several times in World War I for persistent courage and skill in airborne operations, in 1940 a single act of supreme valour was taken as the requisite – hence the awards to Garland and Gray (for the attack on the Maastricht Bridges, May 1940), Learoyd (see Chapter 3), and Hannah (see Chapter 8). Had the earlier policy been reactivated – as it was much later, in 1944, in order to reward Leonard Cheshire – many more VC awards might have been made.

Ball, McCudden and Mannock, perhaps the three greatest fighter pilots of World War I, all got the VC for prolonged rather than particular bravery; but none of the great fighter pilots of World War II was so decorated. There was also the difficulty, in single-seater flying, of finding witnesses. Indeed only one fighter pilot throughout the war received the award – and he was not one of the 'aces' and was not originally recommended for it.

This exception was James Brindley Nicolson – 'Nick' Nicolson. How he came to have an apparently routine DFC upgraded to the supreme award, and the impact it made on his life, is a story within a story, almost as remarkable as the action which preceded it.

5

'Nick' Nicolson:
The Reluctant VC

FLIGHT LIEUTENANT JAMES BRINDLEY NICOLSON, the six-foot three-inch, twenty-three-year-old leader of a section of three Hurricanes of 249 Squadron, based at Boscombe Down, cursed himself for his carelessness. How could he have let the German fighters bounce him like that? In his very first air combat? He who had lectured his pilots at such length and so often on the theory – if not the practice – of air fighting? The first he knew of his undoing was when his eardrums were bludgeoned by four staccato explosions directly behind him and he knew both he and his plane had been hit.

The first shell ripped through the cockpit hood and showered him with splinters of Perspex. One of them pierced his left eyelid, and his eye smarted unbearably. As blood poured down his face he could see nothing with his left eye and precious little with his right.

The second shell punctured his spare petrol tank and set it on fire. Burning fuel was seeping in through the floor of the cockpit and flames were licking up under the control panel.

The third and fourth shells crashed low into the cockpit beneath him. One tore his right trouser leg away completely, and the whole of his uniform from the waist down was shredded. The other shell exploded at the back of his left shoe, shattering his heel and numbing his foot. He was vaguely aware that he had been wounded in many places, but he could feel almost nothing.

He rammed the nose of the Hurricane forward and dived away to the right. He had to get out of his attacker's line of fire. His left eye was still blinded but the vision was slowly returning to his right.

The cockpit was heating up rapidly. He couldn't see any flames now, but he knew that somewhere beneath him the aircraft was on fire and that at any moment it might blow up. He had better get out.

What a way to begin! *Beware of the Hun in the Sun!* He cursed himself again as he reached up to slide back the splintered hood and started undoing his straps.

Up to that moment there had been nothing very distinguished about the career of James Nicolson. It looked even more undistinguished now. Born in Hampstead and educated at Tonbridge, he had shown no special aptitudes while a schoolboy. Casual in his attitudes and unkempt in his appearance, he had consistently baffled his seniors, who found his future impossible to predict. A stab at experimental engineering lasted no more than a year, and his life did not assume shape or purpose until, in 1936, he began pilot training at the civil school at White Waltham, near Reading. Before the end of the year he had enlisted in the RAF, and in August 1937 he joined his first squadron, No. 72, at Church Fenton in Yorkshire. There his expert handling of the Gloster Gladiator marked him out as above average, he was a first-class shot, and his extroversion and tenacity earned him a reputation as a 'press-on' type and the nickname, appropriately enough, of Nick.

No one who came into contact with Nick Nicolson could easily forget him. The beanpole figure, the shock of unruly dark hair, the crumpled uniform and the crinkled cap – when he could be persuaded to wear one – revealed his brazen indifference to prevailing Service conventions of deportment. Allied to this singular appearance were qualities of geniality, gregariousness, loquacity and mimicry, and an imaginative gift as a raconteur, which made him the acknowledged hub and entertainer of any Mess group. Many of his yarns, if not pure fiction, had the most tenuous basis in fact, but they were always worth listening to. A skilful if slightly hare-brained and sometimes indisciplined pilot – he was not above a spectacular shoot-up of his girlfriend's home – he nevertheless proved when the time came to be a keen and exacting flight commander, even a disciplinarian, liable to blow his top at incompetence, and determined to drill his pilots to a high standard in time for the coming Battle.

Early in his Service career he displayed an unsuspected persistence, though in another direction altogether. He met a girl named Muriel Kendall at a dance in nearby Tadcaster. She lived with her parents not far from Church Fenton at Kirkby Wharfe. Soon he proposed to her, but she refused him. 'I'm older than you,' she said, 'and I won't marry you.' His reaction was unequivocal. 'I'll marry you or nobody.' She fought him for over a year, but eventually she realized that he meant it, and she gave in. In 1938 they were married. Now, on 16th August 1940, the third of Goering's boasted four days, she was expecting their first child.

When the Battle began 72 Squadron was still in Yorkshire, having already converted from Gladiators to Spitfires. Then in May 1940 came a posting for Nicolson as acting flight commander to 249 Squadron on Hurricanes, also in Yorkshire, with Squadron Leader John Grandy, a future Chief of the Air Staff, commanding. But raids on the north-east were frustratingly few; at that time the south was bearing the brunt. There was welcome news, however, when, on 14th August, the squadron was transferred to Boscombe Down, on Salisbury Plain, to help defend the beleaguered south-west. Although Nicolson had flown many operational sorties, he had seen no combat action – until now.

The squadron's move took place the day after Eagle Day. Thus it was that, soon after noon on 16th August, Nicolson found himself leading a section of three Hurricanes briefed to patrol the Poole-Ringwood-Salisbury line, climbing to their operational height of 18,000 feet, and heading towards Southampton.

They had reached 15,000 feet when they spotted a flight of three Messerschmitt 110s cutting across their track, four miles distant and slightly above them. The somersaulting of stomachs was succeeded by a fearful elation. This was their moment, and they flipped their gun buttons to 'fire'.

The other two Hurricane pilots, like Nicolson, had never fired their guns in anger. One was a pilot officer named Martyn King, who was only nineteen; the other, also named King, was a supernumerary squadron leader attached to the squadron to gain combat experience, senior to Nicolson but flying under his leadership.

Just as Nicolson was heading the trio into a climbing attack over Gosport, confident of the Hurricane's superiority over the twin-engined German fighters, another British squadron – of Spitfires – arrived from nowhere and intercepted the Me110s head on. The Hurricane pilots watched with admiration and envy as the Spitfire pilots chased the 110s seawards. Unknown to them, all three were shot down near the Isle of Wight.

Nicolson turned his section away to reform, resuming their climb to patrol height. But the slower 110s had had an umbrella of Me109s. They had been too late to catch the Spitfires, but they dived gleefully out of the sun at the unsuspecting Hurricanes. Bounced from astern, Nicolson was stampeded into action by those four startling detonations behind him. Why hadn't he thought of it? What had happened to the men he was supposed to be leading?

Two of the Hurricanes had been mortally hit. Eric King, the supernumerary squadron leader, had got his combat experience all right, though hardly what he was looking for. But his plane was the exception, and he made a safe landing back at Boscombe Down, only to be killed a fortnight later. Young Martyn King eventually baled out when his Hurricane burst into flames and he was parachuting safely down when a detachment of the Royal Artillery, together with a group of Local Defence Volunteers (forerunner of the Home Guard), opened fire under the orders of the RA officer, in the mistaken belief that German paratroops were landing; they had been warned somewhat melodramatically that the invaders would carry a grenade in each hand. King's parachute shrouds parted, his canopy collapsed, and he fell to his death.

Nicolson's machine, also ablaze, was careering into a diving turn as he fought to avoid his pursuers. That, anyway, was how it must have looked to the pilot of the Me109 that had fired that lethal burst. His swoop from high altitude had taken him underneath and beyond the blazing Hurricane, and now he turned with fascinated curiosity to watch the plunging torch. The fire was penetrating the cockpit. As the Hurricane fell away to the right, the velocity of its dive unchecked, it exuded flames and smoke. The pilot was trapped in an inferno, cavorting earthwards.

Reaching up to his hood release, Nicolson suddenly saw the 109 pass right across his undamaged windscreen. A moment earlier the heat in the cockpit had seemed incinerating, certain to devour him within seconds if he didn't get out. Now for a moment it was forgotten. Anger at being caught napping, and eagerness to redeem himself, were the incentives. The scrap was not quite over after all. Instinct told him to get out as soon as possible, but some other abstract quality – obstinacy, resilience, blood-lust – held him prisoner. He might still inflict damage on the enemy – at whatever cost to himself.

He withdrew his hand from the hood release and forgot about undoing his straps. He grabbed the stick again and began to pull out of the dive, while his long legs sought the rudder bar. So the German pilot wanted to stick around and watch his cremation. He'd teach that Hun some manners.

To the watchers on the ground – almost every aerial scrap had its spell-bound spectators – the amorphous mêlée of the dogfight had crystallized into a man-to-man gladiatorial clash as the Hurricane burned and spun and the Messerschmitt swooped.

Nicolson glanced at his firing button. The flames were licking up behind the rudder bars. Most of his instruments were shattered and the dashboard was dripping like treacle. But his gun-sight, like his windscreen, had escaped damage, and he had switched on his firing button when the chase began. All he had to do was to sit tight in his bucket seat amid the flames, choose his moment, and press the button.

The Messerschmitt was two hundred yards in front of him and slightly above. Its pilot was still enjoying his ghoulish view.

Nicolson lifted the nose of the Hurricane until the Messerschmitt appeared again in his sights. Then he pressed the firing button. He hit the German machine first time. He could see his tracer and incendiaries pouring into it.

The German looked up in astonishment. It seemed that the Englishman was being avenged by the falling aircraft itself. Surely there could be no one still alive in that inferno.

The German twisted and turned in a desperate effort to avoid the Hurricane's fire. First he turned left, then right, then left again. He tried three turns to the right and four to the left. Nicolson zig-zagged with him, as in an air display, keeping right on his tail, and the two planes writhed downwards together at 400 miles per hour.

Pushing the throttle wide open, Nicolson watched the airspeed indicator race off the clock. The instrument, the only one still functioning, was glowing red in the fire. His left hand, holding the throttle open, was almost in the fire itself. The skin was peeling off. His right thumb, still pressing the firing button, was blistering in the heat. Yet he felt no pain.

He was hitting the German machine repeatedly, mostly in the tail and fuselage. He seemed able to read the German's mind, to anticipate every manoeuvre, to turn in pursuit almost before the German pilot had flung the stick over. It was uncanny. But the German machine seemed indestructible, and it obstinately refused to catch fire. Meanwhile Nicolson's chance of saving himself was dwindling.

The German was still trying desperately to escape. If he could only avoid the line of fire for a second he knew that the Hurricane must plunge on past him. Then it would be his turn. But Nicolson was still flying superbly, his brain unaffected by the heat, his instinct still foreseeing each move. It had become a fight to the death.

Another burst from Nicolson's guns and the right wing of the Messerschmitt dropped sharply, as though crippled at last, and the plane careered downwards. Still for an instant Nicolson pursued it, linked to its fate by the heat of the scrap. Then he began to think about saving himself.

With his enemy gone he felt again the full shrivelling blast of the fire, goading him into action. Jumping up from his seat, he hit his head on the metal framework of the hood and cursed himself again for his carelessness. He thought he had opened the hood! He had forgotten that the Messerschmitt had filled his sights just as he was about to do so. He reached up and grabbed the handle, but it resisted his pressure. Had the framework buckled when the Perspex shattered? He tugged again at the handle and this time the hood juddered back.

He breathed deeply, the first breath he had taken, it seemed, for minutes. He jumped up again – and for a second time bounced straight back in his seat.

There were four straps holding him in. One had already smouldered and snapped. As the fire raged around him, fanned by the down-draught from the open hood, his burned fingers scrabbled with the other three. Suddenly he was free. He stood up – and parted company abruptly and painlessly with the burning Hurricane. Then he started somersaulting. After a few turns he found he was diving head first for the ground.

He didn't want to pull his parachute until he was clear of the dog-fight, which was still going on somewhere above him. But suppose the canopy had been damaged? He was desperate to try it as soon as possible, to give himself time to free it if it failed to release.

He pulled the rip-cord, and a moment later the parachute grabbed him roughly but firmly and he was floating gently down. Gently, but not peacefully. A 109 was tearing past him, perhaps intent on avenging his comrade.

He decided to pretend he was dead. It wasn't difficult to do. And anyone who had seen the scrap would believe it. He let his whole body go limp and hung like a sack from his straps, dropping his head forward and closing his eyes. He could hear the Messerschmitt circling. But the blackened, ragged scarecrow suspended so lifelessly from the rigging lines bore little resemblance to a human being. Whether the German pilot spared him deliberately or not he never knew.

Only now, as he tried to collect his thoughts, did he begin to feel pain. Worst of all were his hands. They had clenched and contracted in the heat, and strips of charred flesh were hanging from them like a lacerated glove. Blood was oozing from his left boot, he was still half blind, and the parts of his face unprotected by his mask burned like fire. Yet he had the presence of mind to prepare for his landing. After noting that he was comfortably inland, he tugged at the rigging lines to clear a high-tension cable. But now he faced a final hazard – the trigger-happy ground gunners who had already accounted for one of his comrades.

Everything had happened so quickly that he had virtually followed Martyn King down, so that, to the onlookers on the ground, the impression of some sort of paratroop landing was strong. He did not know it, but guns were being trained on him as he descended.

Scanning the ground immediately below him, Nicolson saw a boy on a bicycle and heard him whistling, in typical butcher's boy style. If sound carried so well upwards, perhaps the boy would hear him if he shouted. He saw the boy turn right at a cross-roads and heard the tinkle of the bicycle bell, and he had drawn enough breath to shout when a volley from a double-barrelled shot-gun somewhere below him peppered his buttocks and stifled his cry. Mercifully the pellets missed his canopy and shroud lines and he landed painfully but safely in the middle of a field.

He lay on the ground in a collapsed state, unable to operate his parachute quick-release because of his scorched hands. He was almost completely blind now, he had over seventy pieces of metal in his body, and his only thought was to get a message to Muriel.

People were gathering round him, first one or two, then several. The hostile greeting was changing rapidly to concern. 'Who did this?' he heard someone say, and he was sure it was the butcher's boy. 'Who shot at him?'

'I did,' said another voice. It was one of the Local Defence Volunteers.

'Who told you to?'

'My CO.'

Next he heard a scuffle and realized the boy had aimed a punch at the gunman. Fists were still flying and the volunteer was getting much the worst of it when a nurse arrived on the scene and began attending to Nicolson. Horrified by the extent of his injuries and burns, she was preparing to give him a shot of morphia when Nicolson pleaded: 'Could you get a message to my wife?' A policeman who had reached the scene simultaneously began by separating the combatants, then turned to Nicolson. 'What do you want us to say?'

'Just say . . . shot down, darling . . . very slightly hurt . . . particulars will follow . . . all my love . . . Nick.' He gave his name and the address of the cottage where they lived in Kirkby Wharfe, after which the nurse injected the morphia. He heard someone say they had seen his Messerschmitt crash into the sea, and then he passed out. The telegram was duly delivered to Muriel Nicolson, who was lunching at the time with her sister and had already burst into tears on a premonition that 'Nick' was in trouble.

The tragi-comic element persisted when the ambulance that had been sent for mistook the battered volunteer for the casualty and made off with him, leaving Nicolson to be driven to the Royal South Hants Hospital in Southampton in an old Albion lorry. Doctors gave him twenty-four hours to live, but he rallied, and for the next forty-eight hours the doctors fought to save his life. It was a fortnight before he was able to see again. But after many weeks in hospital and at plastic surgery and rehabilitation centres he made a complete recovery – apart from the damage to his hands.

It was some time before the details of Nicolson's ordeal – his heroism, self-sacrifice, stubborn stupidity, call it what you will – became known or suspected, and back at Boscombe Down the news that he had been forced to bale out and had been shot in the rump on the way down caused only hilarity. Dear old Nick, after all his good advice to others, caught napping first time out! Trust him to have a good story! 'Later, of course,' writes a colleague, 'when the extent of his terrible injuries and his heroism became known, we were much more sympathetic, and were properly impressed by his performance.'[1]

1. Wing Commander Tom Neil, DFC and Bar, AFC, AE. See also his *Gun Button to 'Fire'* (Kimber, 1987).

Similarly, in submitting the routine report called for by the regulations to follow up the Flying Battle Casualty already signalled, John Grandy did little more than record the bare circumstances, adding laconically that Nicolson 'managed to aim a short burst at one Me109 fighter before being forced to invert his aircraft and bale out owing to flames in the cockpit'.[1] He was now, continued Grandy, in the Royal South Hants Hospital suffering from burns and gunshot wounds and the next of kin had been informed. There was nothing here to suggest anything out of the ordinary, and it was not until more than two months later, on 26th October, after a report had been extracted from Nicolson, that a recommendation for an award was made. It came from Victor Beamish, station commander at North Weald, whence the squadron had moved in early September. And it was for a DFC.

What Beamish did not know was that the commanders-in-chief of the three home operational commands – Portal, Dowding, and Bowhill – had received a letter from the Air Member for Personnel, dated 29th August, couched in the following terms:–

Enclosure 16A

AIR 2/5686   29th August, 1940

The Secretary of State told me that in a recent conversation with him the King expressed surprise that the recent exploits of the Royal Air Force had not produced more recommendations for awards of the Victoria Cross.

Whilst it is appreciated that you will naturally submit recommendations in respect of any acts of gallantry performed in your Command which merit this prized decoration, both the Secretary of State and I, as Chairman of the RAF Awards Committee, know that you will not submit any which tend to lower the very high standard of

---

1. Nicolson himself seems – not surprisingly – to have been uncertain whether his adversary was a 109 or a 110. Francis K. Mason, in *Battle Over Britain*, credits Nicolson with a 109 destroyed.

bravery which is rightly required. This is apparent from the description of the deeds which have earned the three awards of the Victoria Cross which have so far been made to the Royal Air Force during the course of the war.

It is, however, at the request of the Secretary of State that I write to inform you of the interest which His Majesty is taking in this matter.

(Sgd) E. L. Gossage.[1]

Air Chief Marshal Sir Hugh C. T. Dowding,
    G.C.V.O., K.C.B., C.M.G.
and to Sir F. Bowhill and C. Portal

Dowding had passed this intelligence on to his group commanders, and two days after Beamish's submission, on 28th October, Keith Park added this note to the Beamish citation under 'Remarks of Air Officer Commanding':–

> Flight Lieutenant Nicolson showed exceptional courage and disregard for the safety of his own life by continuing to engage the enemy after he had been wounded and his aircraft was burning.
> For this oustanding act of gallantry and magnificent display of fighting spirit, I recommend this officer for the immediate award of the VICTORIA CROSS.

Dowding concurred, and on 3rd November, under 'Remarks of Air Officer Commanding-in-Chief,' he added, in a handwritten note:

> I consider this to be an outstanding case of gallantry and endorse the Recommendation for the award of the Victoria Cross.

In passing the recommendation to the Permanent Under-Secretary, to the Chief of the Air Staff, and to the Secretary of

1. Later Air Marshal Sir Leslie Gossage, KCB, CVO, DSO, MC. As already recorded, he had been succeeded earlier that year as AOC-in-C 11 Group by Keith Park.

State, Air Commodore R. D. Oxland, Director of Personal Services, explained how the original recommendation for a DFC had been upgraded by Dowding and Park, and he also revealed another singular circumstance – that the usual review by the RAF Awards Committee had not taken place owing to the sickness of the Chairman, Leslie Gossage, the Air Member for Personnel. He went on:

> . . . I have given the recommendation careful considera-
> tion and it appears to me to be less strong than those which
> earned the VC for F/Off Garland and Sergeant Gray, F/Lt
> Learoyd and Sergeant Hannah . . . The following factors
> need, however, to be taken into account (i) on the 29th
> August A.M.P. addressed the letter [he gave the refer-
> ence] to operational commands, suggesting in effect that
> more VCs should be recommended and (ii) no member of
> Fighter Command has yet received this decoration. In the
> circumstances, an award to F/Lt Nicolson might, perhaps,
> be approved.

Both P.U.S. and C.A.S. marked the Oxland minute 'concur', and next day, 7th November, the Secretary of State was 'glad to submit this recommendation'.

Eighteen days later, on 25th November 1940, Nicolson was decorated with the Victoria Cross at Buckingham Palace. In expressing his thanks to the King he never guessed how de-cisive a role his Sovereign had played in stimulating the award. What he did feel, though, and came to believe with mounting conviction, was that he had somehow been 'selected' for the award, almost indeed that his name had come out of a hat. Those who put him up for the award had not perhaps con-sidered the effect it might have on a young man of otherwise modest achievement who was bound to look round and see a surfeit of pilots who had done so much more. Even his very survival he now saw as unworthy.

So diffident was he of parading the mauve ribbon that he was reprimanded for not wearing it, and when travelling in uniform he wore his greatcoat even in summer, though few perhaps would have recognized the ribbon. But then, they might have

a

3a Roderick 'Babe' Learoyd

3b 'Nick' Nicolson with wife Muriel and infant son James Gavin outside their cottage at Kirkby Wharfe.

b

4a Pat (*left*)
and (b) Tony
Woods-Scawen, with
(c) 'Bunny' Lawrence
(inset), and
(d) Peter Townsend
and Caesar Hull.

asked what it was. 'It is not too much to say,' said Muriel
Nicolson recently, 'that the award *haunted* him.'

There was only one possible remedy, and that was to get back
to flying. His left hand would never properly unclench, but as
he himself said, 'it may not be pretty, but it can still handle a
throttle.' While still not medically fit for full flying duties he
agitated persistently for a training appointment, emphasizing
wherever he went the burden he carried. 'Now they've given
me the VC, I've got to go back and earn it.'

After spells of instructional and experimental flying he was
posted in March 1942 to a staff job in India. 'There may be a
chance to get back to operational flying,' he told Muriel, 'I've
got to go.' He got his wish in August 1943 after much lobbying
when he was transferred to Burma to command No. 27 Squadron, flying fighter-bombers (Beaufighters) in the jungle campaign. How he appeared to a distinguished colleague during
this period has been lovingly recorded in the writings of a man
whose experience of wartime air crew and their strengths and
weaknesses is unparalleled. This was Dr Roland Winfield, who
in the course of his researches in aviation medicine flew 120
night-time bomber sorties over Germany and Occupied
Europe, attaching himself to all manner of crews and being
awarded the AFC in 1942 and the DFC in 1944. 'I admired
Nicolson', he wrote, 'because he had moulded his squadron
into the finest instrument of war that I came across in India.'
He had done this by example, choosing the most hazardous
operations for himself and flying more sorties than anyone else.

Yet still the VC award troubled him. 'What would *you* do', he
asked Winfield, 'if you'd been given a decoration you couldn't
refuse but were not sure you'd earned?' Answering his own
question, he continued, 'the only thing to do is to shape your
life so that what's left of it is an honest attempt to show yourself
and the rest of the RAF that at least you've tried to earn it.'

Flying several times with Nicolson, and knowing something
of the background, Winfield concluded that Nicolson had without a doubt earned his VC, and moreover that by his dedicated
leadership of 27 Squadron he had earned a Bar to it. 'Like
many, if not all, of the great squadron commanders that I had

the high honour to work for on operations, every particle of his personality was devoted to the single and simple object of destroying the enemy.'[1]

Even after leading 27 Squadron for nearly a year, at the end of which he was awarded the DFC, Nicolson found frequent opportunities, as wing commander in charge of training at a headquarters in Bengal, to visit squadrons and study the results of training methods by flying on actual operations and seeing things at first hand. Reports that he was decorated yet again for this work, this time with the Air Force Cross, have proved impossible to substantiate, though it is said that some decorations awarded in Burma were never gazetted owing to loss of despatches.

Photographs taken of him on ceremonial occasions in this period, showing hair neatly barbered and brushed and tropical uniform pressed and fresh from the *dhobi*, suggest that the tousled, unkempt flight lieutenant of four years earlier had matured as he became more senior. But he was still as enthusiastic and voluble as ever, impatient to put plans into action, and with the same short fuse as of old. Unlike most of his contemporaries, and strangely for a man who could not bear grudges and had no time for feuds, he hated the enemy, whether German or Japanese, in a personal way.

Talking his way into taking part in yet another bombing sortie as an 'observer', Nicolson joined the crew of a Liberator of No. 355 Squadron on 2nd May 1945. Although not obliged in any way to fly on these sorties, he remained anxious to keep in operational touch. They had reached a point 130 miles south of Calcutta when an engine burst into flames and they were forced down in the Bay of Bengal. Sixteen hours later a Catalina flying boat located the scene and picked up the survivors. There were only two, and Nicolson was not one of them. The telegram reporting him missing reached his wife at Kirkby Wharfe on the last day of the European War.

For forty years Muriel Nicolson continued to live in the cottage at Kirkby Wharfe where she had first settled with Nick.

---

1. *The Sky Belongs To Them*, Dr Roland Winfield, DFC, AFC (Kimber, 1976).

She never remarried, and she devoted her life to the service of others, bringing up her son James Gavin on a war widow's pension, which meant forgoing luxuries and managing without things that most would regard as necessities. She nursed both her parents in turn through long terminal illnesses, and then nursed a sister dying of cancer.

The final blow, which would have destroyed most women, came five years ago, poignantly on her late husband's birthday, when her son James, who with the help of friends had been educated at Rugby, had been a Kitchener Scholar at Oxford, and had subsequently established a thriving business in Tadcaster, was killed in a motor accident at the age of forty-five. He had married, but the union hadn't prospered and there were no grandchildren. Muriel still lives in Kirkby Wharfe, not in the original cottage but in the house that her son vacated so tragically.

EPISODIC AND EXCLUSIVE

After a dogfight, involving a changing and often unverifiable number of combatants, scenic composition was hard to achieve. Every pilot had his own perspective and saw little more than a sequence of snapshots. Any attempted montage was bound to be incomplete, since those who fell could not contribute to a reanimated, panoramic view. Thus reconstructions of air combats tend to be episodic and personal, seen through the eyes of one man.

Just as no one combat is typical, so no one pilot who lived through that summer is generic. They were individual, displaying every known human characteristic. But Dowding's ruling (to which there were of course exceptions) that no squadron commander should be more than twenty-six emphasizes how young they were. What consistently emerges from their letters and the recollections of loved ones is the dichotomy between their adult fixity of purpose and their callow, adolescent, often juvenile attitudes and behaviour. One of their number, already referred to in Chapter 2, Hugh 'Cocky' Dundas, who celebrated his twentieth birthday during the Battle, and who at twenty-four became the youngest group captain in the Air Force, has written of his amazement, when reading his 1940 diary half a century later, at 'the extent to which the flavour of the writing demonstrates my immaturity at that time'.[1] He goes on: 'I was also amazed that I should have been so unashamedly introspective.' The experience caused him embarrassment rather than pride. Yet there are countless other documents preserved from the period which provide an authentic record of the lack of sophistication of the majority of the 'Few'.

1. Sir Hugh Dundas, *Flying Start: A Fighter Pilot's War Years* (Stanley Paul, 1988).

6

Brothers-in-War:
Patrick and Tony
Woods-Scawen

THE STRIDENT WAIL of an aeroplane as it plunged to destruction climaxed in a crescendo of sound as it impacted with earth. The time was a quarter to three on a Sunday afternoon, 1st September 1940.

Those who were first on the scene of the crash – a recreation ground at Kenley, Surrey – recognized from the twisted scraps of metal strewn round the crater that it was 'one of ours'. It was, in fact, a Hurricane. They were relieved to find that the cockpit was empty. Mercifully, the pilot had baled out.

Less than twenty-four hours later, at twelve minutes past one on Monday 2nd September, two boys out for a cycle ride on Romney Marsh scanned the sky for signs of an aircraft in trouble. A dogfight was going on some distance inland, and what they hoped to do was to get to the scene of a crash and grab souvenirs – it would be a German plane, they had no doubt of that – before the Army or the Home Guard could warn them off.

'Look! There's one going down now!'

The crippled plane was already below a thousand feet. As they watched its unsteady progress, traced by a scribble of smoke, it dived steeply. But it was not a German plane after all: their aircraft recognition, honed to perfection in the preceding weeks, told them it was a Hurricane. Just before it disappeared behind a screen of trees towards Ivychurch they glimpsed a parachute. They were too far away, though, to have any hope of being first on the scene.

The two incidents occurred at different times and on different days. The pilots came from different squadrons and different bases, fifty miles apart. The crash sites were separated by half as much again. True, both pilots had been flying Hurricane fighters, and both had evidently baled out; but there the resemblance ended. There was nothing, on the face of it, to connect the two incidents. Yet the link could not have been stronger. The pilots were brothers, in love with the same girl.

'Why don't you two boys join the RAF and learn to fly?'

The question came from the boys' uncle, their father's brother, who was home on leave from India. To him it seemed a natural progression. The boys' childhood interest in mechanical things had stimulated a passion for speed as they grew up. First it had been motor-bikes, then sports cars. Both boys, in those job-scarce 1930s, had had to be content, on leaving school, with mundane jobs, Patrick as a storekeeper, Tony as a clerk. But they were *not* content, as their uncle knew. What he didn't know was that both, living as they did within sight and sound of the Royal Aircraft Establishment at Farnborough in Hampshire, were attracted to a flying career.

The year was 1937, and Patrick and Tony Woods-Scawen were twenty-one and nineteen respectively. The family was a Madras one, from the days of the Raj, but the two boys were born in Karachi, where their father, Philip Woods-Scawen, had been an accountant in an overseas bank. (The hyphenated name acknowledged an adopted addition to the family many years back.)

Philip Woods-Scawen had been forced to bring his family back to England in 1924 because of his wife's ill-health. Casting around for someone to take care of the boys until his wife recovered, Philip, a devout Roman Catholic, had sent them as boarders to the Salesian College in Farnborough. The Salesian Order, a teaching order, was familiar to him because of its strength in Madras. But when his wife died he had to find a more permanent solution.

Writing to his sister, who was teaching at a convent in Madras, he asked her if she would consider coming to England and making a home for the boys, by then aged ten and eight. A spinster, in her late thirties, from a strictly religious background, and, like her brother, prematurely white-haired, Nell Woods-Scawen seemed at first glance an unlikely surrogate mother. But she abandoned her teaching career to answer the challenge, and the boys soon found the soft centre beneath the formidable exterior. For them she became a sort of real-life Margaret Rutherford, and they adored her as much as she adored them. The red-bricked semi-detached house which 'Pop' Woods-Scawen rented at 55 York Road, round the corner from the Salesian College – which the boys now attended as day-boys – became open house. Aunt Nellie loved every minute of it, and on Sundays the aroma of her curries proved almost embarrassingly magnetic. No less magnetic was the brown bread and home-made marmalade that was always available during the week.

Although she had no favourites, Aunt Nellie's soft spot for Tony, as the younger and weaker vessel, was notorious. 'Will one of you boys fill the coal scuttle, Pat?' was a family joke.

The daily invasion of 55 York Road was almost exclusively male. But not quite. By the time they had reached their middle teens the boys had gathered in tow a vivacious and affectionate ash blonde who lived nearby, had the same sense of fun and adventure, and who loved them both. Three years younger than Tony and five years younger than Patrick, she joined in most of their exploits and escapades and was equally loved in return.

Her name was Una Lawrence, but she was known as Bunny or Bun-Bun, nicknames she had acquired as a child. When the boys graduated to motor-bikes, and they set off with their friends to the coast for a swim, she was the girl on the pillion, generally the only girl in the party. She herself saw to that. She wasn't having anyone else muscle in on the Woods-Scawen boys.

Their juvenile pranks were not much different from those of normally high-spirited youngsters. A girl who slipped for a time through Bunny's net, Doreen Green (née Palmer), remembers Tony being dared to extinguish a gas street-lamp and climbing the lamp standard to do it with everyone cheering. If anything, the younger boy was the more tearaway, the older the more serious minded; but the distinction was narrow.

Both boys were of less than average height and inclined to be scrawny, with Patrick, a keen rugger player, the more robust. He duly joined the Air Force on a short-service commission (probationary) in October 1937 at the age of twenty-one and was sent for elementary flying training to Prestwick in Ayrshire; Bunny saw him off at King's Cross. Having left the Salesian College in the previous year after passing School Certificate, he had no trouble with the entrance exams.

For Tony it was not so easy. He had lost a year's schooling through suspected TB, and although the patch on his lung had cleared, the improvement in his French following a spell in a Swiss sanatorium was offset by a deterioration in most other subjects. A love of music, a pleasing baritone, and a flair for the guitar could not compensate, and he left the Salesian College without getting School Certificate. Worse still, his vision, presumably as a result of his illness, was permanently impaired, and for reading he had to wear glasses. His chances of getting into the RAF seemed remote. But what Patrick did Tony usually emulated, and he was not the first candidate to learn the eye-test card by heart. Six months after his brother, and soon after his twentieth birthday, on 7th March 1938, he too joined the RAF on a short-service commission.

Meanwhile Patrick had soloed on a Tiger Moth at Prestwick and described the experience blow-by-blow in a letter to Bunny. The same letter revealed something of the easy-going atmosphere in the RAF of those days. 'I went up for an hour solo, and I climbed to 4,000 feet, then did some medium turns and dives, as I'd been told to, then I got fed up and flew over the Isle of Arran . . . I saw some seals on a rock and dived down and chased them off, and nearly collided with a fishing boat. Next I flew inland and couldn't find the aerodrome.' Low in fuel, he was on the point of landing in a field to ask the way when a colleague on a similar exercise appeared out of the blue and led him back to Prestwick.

Discipline was no tighter off-duty, where a lusty group of trainees, vaguely aware of what fate had in store for them, indulged themselves in carousal and horseplay which some would call hooliganism. There were frequent confrontations with the local police, which threatened to become more serious when the Course moved to No. 11 Flying Training School at Wittering, on the Great North Road, where motoring when not strictly sober was no more than routine. They left their mark as far afield as Nottingham, where they clashed with university students, while in the Peterborough area they earned themselves the soubriquet of the 'Wittering Wreckers'.

A fracas at Peterborough Fair, recounted by Patrick to Bunny, clearly got out of hand, though Pat showed no remorse in his letter. 'Yesterday we had a hangover so we dispersed it with another booze-up . . . Then we went to the Fair. We got thrown off the Dodgems because several of us collided with an attendant . . .' On the roundabouts the attendant tried to make them ill by spinning them at high speed. 'We were OK at the end, having bellies toughened by flying, but the women who were with us couldn't move, so we paid for them to stay on for another go and left. We didn't know them and they were horrible anyway . . . they had drunk a lot of our liquor. Next we shot about 1,000 rounds on the miniature rifle range. We shot all the bottles, all the clay pipes, every target, and finally shot out the lights. This was rather tactless and several people appeared to be getting quite heated so we sped back to our cars before we were imprisoned. This same Fair is starting in Stamford tomorrow so we are all going to wear false moustaches.'

The brother/sister relationship with Bunny was confirmed in these letters at first by such salutations as 'Dear old Bun'. 'Don't think I'm falling in love with you or anything like that,' wrote Patrick in April 1938. That would have been against the rules. But after a fortnight of home leave Bunny suddenly became 'Darlingest', 'Lovely Bun', 'Sweetest', 'Delicious Bunny', and so on. 'Gosh I wish I had an excuse for writing what I feel, but I've told you so many times you know it all by heart.' They had reached an understanding that she would marry him when he was promoted to squadron leader, which to a young pilot officer, and certainly to Bunny, seemed a comfortably long way off.

'Did you manage to break the news to Tony OK?' he wanted to know. 'If so, was he mad?' He knew well enough that Tony – 'my unruly brother', as he called him – was a rival, and he was relieved to hear that Tony too had begun his flying training, removing him from the Farnborough scene. 'I haven't heard from him,' he told Bunny, 'I'm sure he'll be OK though, he always had a heap of guts.'

He had been urging Bunny to have her photograph taken, but she had resisted, to his chagrin. What was the use of having an understanding with a girl as attractive as Bunny and not being able to swank about it? 'Delicious,' he wrote, 'do get your photo taken because all the blokes have got their women's photos stuck on their mantelpieces. Why don't you like your photo being taken? You've got these chaps' women whacked and that isn't flattery.' Eventually Bunny relented – but she sent a copy of the result to Tony as well.

A transfer of Patrick's Flying Training School from Wittering to Shawbury in Shropshire brought him another spell of leave. 'Oh Gosh I did enjoy that fortnight Bunny Rose,' he wrote afterwards, 'you were damned sweet, the only trouble is I can't get you out of my mind.' Nevertheless he managed to be one of only three pilots (out of twenty-nine) on his course to get an above average assessment. He spoke glowingly – if immaturely – of his instructor. '. . . that chap is my idea of the ideal man – he's a wonderful bloke honestly Bun – tough as hell – drinks like hell – real good-looking – and my does he cuss! Best of all he can fly.'

Pat and his fellow trainees proved no more popular in Shropshire than they had further south. 'The males in Shrewsbury resent the attentions we are getting from the Shrewsbury females . . . and not a night passes without a scrap.' But the wild apprenticeship days were almost over, and from Shawbury

Pat was posted to No. 85 Squadron at Debden, near Saffron Walden, on the Essex/Cambridgeshire border, where the squadron was being reformed. 'I have flown a Hurricane,' he told Bunny,' 'so have reached the eighth heaven. The seventh, sixth and fifth are you. But my God, what an aeroplane!' He had been home to Farnborough between postings, and had driven up to Debden to report on a Sunday. Again he provided evidence of a *laissez-faire* attitude on the roads. 'The car went damn well,' he wrote, 'the only trouble was I lost my way and night overtook me, to my serious disadvantage as the headlight fell off and I had to follow lorries and push-bikes for the last twenty miles.'

The last peacetime summer was ending, and soon after war was declared the squadron was posted to France as one of four squadrons of the RAF Component with the British Expeditionary Force. The others were 87 (also Hurricanes) and two Auxiliary squadrons, 607 and 615 (Gladiators). Now it was Tony, posted at the end of his training to No. 43 Squadron at Tangmere in Sussex, also on Hurricanes, who was home on leave at Farnborough. 'My kid brother gets all the luck,' wrote Patrick. But Tony had evidently blotted his copybook with Bunny. 'So the old romance rocked a bit, did it?' wrote Patrick smugly. 'Good show! Still, my kid always did trick you a trifle, didn't he?'

He went on to quote something in jest which was to have poignant vindication. 'The boys here have got a saying: "For you I have ze grande pash – but for your leetle brother, Oh La La!"'

He left Bunny in no doubt of the dangers – and temptations – which surrounded him. 'One of the sergeant pilots got written off the other day – he spun into the deck. Rotten luck because he was a cracking type.' And of the temptations: 'We had a colossal session last night in the local large town, gosh the girls are pickative . . . and my! is it hard on the morals!' Bunny forecast he would come home a lecherous type, but he protested that he was still the same innocent boy whom she knew.

Celibacy in these circumstances was not without credit. One squadron commander was known to wait outside Madame's in his staff car late at night to make sure of getting his ruttish young pilots back for flying next morning.

There remained uneasiness about Tony, stationed only fifty miles from Farnborough, getting home frequently, and gaining marks for escorting Bunny to hospital when she developed an ear infection; Patrick protested that it was something he'd love to have done had he been there. But brotherly love survived their rivalry. Tony sent Patrick a pair of the latest flying boots – 'invaluable', said Pat – and a tin of cigarettes. 'I thought that was rather keen of him,' conceded Pat. 'Keen' was one of their 'in' words. 'Keen popsies', for instance (Tony's phrase), meant nothing more immodest than 'attractive'.

For Patrick, Christmas 1939 was one long celebration. He had been promoted to flying officer (but was still a long way from squadron leader). Then, at a dinner given by the French, he had to make a speech. '. . . luckily I was well hoggers by then and it came quite easily. Do you know my lovely Bunny that we've had so much champers lately that I for one have quite lost my liking for it. I only drink beer now.'

French hospitality was unbounded that Christmas and Pat became an enthusiastic Francophile. 'When we get married, you sweet thing, we must pay a visit to this wonderful place – the people are crackajack – every one of them – and the town itself is the most beautiful I've seen . . . We were lucky enough to see the place covered with snow – at Christmas too – it has all the Christmas cards beaten easily.'[1] Such was Patrick's appreciation of the make-believe atmosphere of the phoney war period in France.

In mid-January he got ten days home leave, during which he drove Bunny down to Tangmere for a reunion with Tony. The wrench of the subsequent return to France was greatly alleviated by the allotment of a replacement Hurricane, 'one of the newest with metal wings, trick variable pitch propeller etc., oh what a poem! And it handles as lightly as a butterfly at considerably more speed than the old ones. I've quite fitted into the old routine again.' But – 'I enjoyed that trip to Tangmere more than

1. The Squadron was based at an airfield near Lille.

you'd probably imagine.' She had been indisputably *his* girl that day. 'Do you realize that it was the only time we went out by ourselves?'

Tony and the problem of propinquity still bothered him. 'How is my evil brother? Don't forget that you're going to marry me when I'm a squadron leader, my sweet. You'd better watch my meteoric progress carefully.' With the rapid expansion of Fighter Command that was in prospect, the pace of promotion might accelerate.

He was home again in April; and on 1st May, nine days before the German blitzkrieg began, he wrote: 'It was a wizard leave, wasn't it? You're a different girl, my lovely Bunny, you're more lovely, and you make me laugh more.' Tony by now was posing no problems – he had been banished with his squadron to the frozen north, first to Acklington, near Newcastle, then to Wick in Caithness, to work alongside a new sector station and to help protect the Home Fleet in Scapa Flow. But Pat knew that Bunny kept in touch with him. 'I'm glad you've written to my kid,' he said, 'because he must be pretty browned off where he is.'

Then on 10th May the action started, and Patrick would have precious little time to write letters. It is time to follow Tony's experience, as revealed in his letters to Bunny, in the two years since he had begun his training.

Tony's probation period was marred by repeated failures to pass the written exams, and at one point he seemed likely to fail altogether. 'Poor lil Anthony thinks he's going to get the Bowler Hat,' he confessed to Bunny. 'Navigation again. Because I ploughed badly the first time, they keep damn well pestering me with more Test Papers and tomorrow is going to begin with just one more final one. If I don't get 80% I get slung out.' Somehow he scraped through, and meanwhile, with his flying training in mind, he had a pair of goggles specially made with corrective lenses, and with the aid of these he went solo and passed all his flying tests, showing a natural flair. Graduating to Flying Training School, first at Woodley, near Reading, and then at Netheravon, on Salisbury Plain, he 'ploughed' meteorology – 'but the CGI (Chief Ground Instructor) said I will get my wings pronto because of my flying report.' Later he wrote: 'I've had my usual freakish good luck and have wangled a pretty good report, how I don't know.' This was not false modesty; air and ground instructors, vulnerable to Tony's boyish appeal, took a protective attitude towards him and made concessions which they might not have made for others.

Off duty there were exploits roughly equivalent to those of brother Patrick. 'Mackphie[1] and I went to Cheltenham yesterday and eventually drifted into the sweetest ball-room I've ever seen with a terrific swing band. Had the most riotous time – bar open till 2 a.m. On the way home Mack fell asleep at the wheel – or unconscious, I don't know which – and we mowed a bank down leaving two mudguards behind and ended up facing the opposite direction and still on four wheels, to our perpetual amazement.' And pride in sharing his own Hawker Fury with another trainee, Brian J. Wicks (destined to win the DFC in the Battle and to survive it but to be killed later), was not matched by flying discipline. They polished up their Hawker Fury and made it 'the prettiest on the Station'; but given a dual control Audax to take up for an hour they flouted orders and 'shot up' Wicks's home, where father, mother and sister 'poured out of the house onto the lawn and danced about waving things. Brian got thoroughly roused and nearly went through the roof about ten times, terrific fun . . .' No doubt it was, but many valuable lives were wasted on these homestead and girl-friend shoot-ups through a mixture of exuberance and misjudgement.

Recording his spare-time activities, Tony listed dancing, swimming, drinking, and chasing the 'wimming', as he called them. But always he was 'Yours, as always.' He loved his flying but was certainly not the military type. When he arrived at Netheravon for advanced training, he wrote: 'Am now a proper officer . . . They gave me a ruddy great rifle and bayonet today, horrible weapon, should hate to have to use it.'

---

1. This was probably Pilot Officer C. H. MacFie, who won the DFC during the Battle with No. 616 Squadron.

On 43 Squadron at Tangmere, where he learnt to fly Hurricanes, Tony took some time to settle down. The pilots of this crack squadron, seeing a new man in the Mess wearing glasses, were horrified: the RAF must be scraping the barrel. But as in his training days, Tony attracted sympathy. Two of the senior pilots, Caesar Hull and Frank Carey, took pity on this lean and patently vulnerable youth who had been thrust so mercilessly amongst them and decided to put him through his paces, no doubt encouraged by flight commander Peter Townsend. 'For some strange reason,' Tony told Bunny, 'they have been giving me the benefit of all their terrific flying skill by taking me up for wizard dogfights and drilling me in aerobatics. I can now roll at 2–300 feet without being too scared, thanks to them, but I still get plenty frit on occasion.' This was priceless experience, and the two senior pilots, for their part, were pleasantly surprised at the tyro's natural ability.

A long letter in mid-July 1939 was divided into three parts. First came news of his dog Lindy Poo, ill with distemper and severely mauled by another dog. 'I am horribly afraid she will lose the sight of one lamp, an aftermath of that bloody distemper. I have spent eight smackers on her in vet fees so the little woman should pull through.' This, at twelve shillings and sixpence a day, amounted to two weeks' money. Carelessness of his own skin was not accompanied by callousness to his pet.

Second was a flying mishap. 'I was widdling around the Isle of Wight when – to my horror – I heard the elastic break and mentally cursed my fitter for winding it up too tightly. Seeing a field . . . and noting at the same time with vast satisfaction a pub nearby, I executed a forced landing which frightened the life out of me.' But it showed him he could get a dead-engined Hurricane down.

Third was a car accident, which he reported in full. 'On the night of July 10th 1939 at approx. 10.10 pm I was motoring erratically in a North Westerly direction conversing amiably with the ten other occupants of my two-seater car, at the same time negotiating a 359-degree bend in the lane, when I struck another vehicle head-on, to my vast amusement. This however changed . . . at what I saw behind me. There, strewn as far as the eye could see, were bodies, bodies, bodies ("Boots", Kipling), contorting, cartwheeling or simply summersaulting [sic] into various ditches and hedgerows. Before the last person had touched the ground a will-of-the-wisp policeman appeared . . . and proceeded to charge me with ninety-two varied and different motoring offences despite which we soon became great friends. In actual fact the police have satisfied themselves that (i) there were eight others besides myself on the Bitza (which is now incidentally very much a Bitza); (ii) that I was on the wrong side of the road; (iii) that the other car was stationary, which I think will do for a start. One girl – the only casualty – is still in Hospital with a fractured backside, very painful I should think. I shall probably be fined anything up to £50.' We are left to imagine the scene in the magistrate's court, where Tony 'talked his way out' (via a typical letter) of any penalty whatsoever.

'How am I?' he echoed, repeating Bunny's query. 'I am fine, except that I get drunk much too thoroughly and much too often but thank you for asking.' A pencilled post-script to this seven-page bulletin read: 'Don't forget your promise about a long letter to your languishing lover.'

Just as instructors nurtured him, seniors befriended him, and magistrates indulged him, older women wanted to mother him, young women wanted to have him, some in between wanted to do both. Returning to Tangmere from the detachment to Wick he told Bunny: 'I have been a very bad boy but only half-heartedly as regards "Wimming". The fun I referred to [they had spoken on the telephone] was getting drunk a lot . . . really hoggers . . . an idiotic waste of dough.' He had been baby-snatched – or was in danger of it – by a well-known actress, 'who last time I met her bade me lie with her. She is old enough (35) to pick a better mate, thought I. Through the heavy fog of a semi-drunken stupor I cleverly evaded the maid, but she phoned me repeatedly with fresh demands on my person. As you have gathered, she is not very beautiful and only looks it on the stage.' Nevertheless he was flattered by her interest. He did not tell Bunny that he had earned a reputation on the squadron as a lady-killer.

His basic puritanism again asserted itself when he went to a night club 'haunted by "queer" people, I was honestly shocked ... disgusting mob.' He would not be showing his 'angelic countenance' there again.

He always addressed Bunny in the same terms of endearment as his brother did, and although he knew well enough of Patrick's prior claim he was 'buoyed up with splendid hope which looms eternal in my cadaverous breast. I'm afraid you are still the menace to my mental security you have always been. I still think more of you than any other; but this must be rather boring to one so firmly entrenched in someone else's heart. Write and tell me so in a very definite manner and I shall cease to write half-witted amorism and confine myself to my normal brand of tiresome chatter.' In another letter he told Bunny that he didn't think he had much chance with her, and that he knew she loved another. But Bunny was still playing the field.

The shooting war for Patrick started at ten past four on the morning of 10th May 1940. The pilots of 85 Squadron were only on the ground long enough to re-arm and re-fuel as wave after wave of bombers roared overhead, and it went on like that from dawn till dusk. Pat's best day in this period was May 19th, when he claimed four aircraft shot down and was finally shot down himself over Lille, escaping by parachute. But the German advance could not be stemmed, and next day the squadron was evacuated to England to reform.

The change brought a new squadron commander, transferred from 43 Squadron: none other than Peter Townsend, who thus got to know the elder Woods-Scawen equally well. His opinion of Tony, formed at Tangmere and on detachment at Wick and Acklington, was that he was 'as brave as a lion and as blind as a bat'; Tony was known by the nickname of 'Wombat' on 43 Squadron, apparently because of a certain rabbit-like mien. Patrick had been dubbed 'Weasel' on 85 Squadron because of his sharp features and small size. 'Little Patrick', Townsend called him, 'who smiled with his eyes'.

For his work during those chaotic ten days in France Pat was awarded the Distinguished Flying Cross. He ordered himself a new uniform for the investiture, and Bunny, promising to go with him to the Palace, sewed on the medal ribbon. It was an outing that Aunt Nellie, too, looked forward to with a thrill of pride, and she bought herself a new costume for the occasion, a rare extravagance for her.

Over Dunkirk a week later it was Tony's turn. Ordered to protect shipping evacuating troops at Dunkirk, 43 Squadron found themselves facing odds, on their first patrol, of six to one. Tony was not the only pilot who felt that half the Luftwaffe were after him; his squadron commander, George Lott, reached the same conclusion. Tony could do nothing but concentrate on evasive action as one German fighter after another bored in. In those critical minutes the thoughtful friendship of Caesar Hull and Frank Carey saved his life. Eventually he fastened on to one of the Messerschmitt 109s which had been tormenting him and got in two long bursts, knocking bits off the German's port wing. Then another 109 soared up beneath him and scored hits on his radiator, smearing his windscreen and deluging his cockpit with glycol. With the plane's structure weakened, the hydraulic system punctured, and the flaps useless, he returned to Tangmere to make a perilous but successful landing. Shaken but exhilarated, he emerged from the cockpit covered in oil from head to foot, his face as black as pitch. The ground maintenance boys, amazed at the sight of the stricken Hurricane, and shocked by the apparition that emerged from the cockpit, recovered sufficiently to ask eagerly what it had been like. Tony's reply summed up his whole attitude to air fighting. *'Dee-licious!'*

On 7th June he asked Bunny: 'Are you engaged or married or anything equally horrible yet? I won't be so enthusiastic about it if you go and do something silly like that.' But he added: 'You were never faithful to me anyway.' As for the war: 'We have been having prodigious Hun-fun, but little else.' He was not ashamed to reveal his fears. 'Will tell you all about it when, and if, I see you again.' For pathos he concluded, in brackets, 'Sob.'

Patrick too was conscious of the precariousness of a fighter pilot's life. Hearing that the policy of a famous London military outfitter was not to press next-of-kin to meet the bills of casualties, he ordered himself an expensive herring-bone suit which he couldn't afford. If he survived he would be pleased enough to pay up.

Evidence of Tony's staying power, which was to be a vital quality in the battle ahead, came when 43 Squadron were detailed to cover the withdrawal of the remnants of a British division by patrolling the Amiens-Abbeville line. Tony was flying No. 2 to George Lott, and they were crossing the French coast, still a long way from their patrol line, when they sighted German fighters. Tony went into line astern behind his leader and they dived after their quarry. The next thing Tony knew was that something had hit his machine hard from behind. Any hope of a forced landing was ruled out by the suffocating heat in the cockpit – 'too hot for comfort', as he afterwards described it – and he was forced to bale out. He landed behind the German lines and hid in a ditch before trekking twenty-five miles across country, in continual danger of discovery, and hampered by the folds of his parachute, which he refused to abandon and had gathered under his arm. Eventually he fell in with a retreating motorized transport unit which took him to Rouen. Here he found himself on his own again. The bridge over the river had been blown up, but he coerced a ferryman at pistol point into taking him across, just ahead of an advancing German column. Bombed and within sight and sound of gunfire in the next few days, and sometimes sheltering in cellars, he finally escaped to England from Cherbourg after being missing for a week. Bunny, anxiously awaiting news, and incapable of analysing her feelings, 'knew' instinctively that he wasn't dead.

He turned up in the Mess at Tangmere in a tin hat and an Army major's jacket, with his parachute still clasped in billowing folds under his arm. Of the eleven pilots who had taken part in the patrol, nine had been shot down, but six were safe and already accounted for. Tony was the seventh and last. 'You've been a long time,' was the welcome he got from George Lott.

'Why have you brought that ragged old thing back with you?'
'Because,' said Tony, 'I know this one works.'

So depleted were 43 Squadron they had to pause to reform, and the Woods-Scawens' private war was continued by Patrick; but it was not until 29th July that Pat was able to claim another victim. Flying convoy patrols from Martlesham in Suffolk, he intercepted a Dornier bomber and chased it to the Belgian coast. The pilot took no evasive action when under fire, and suddenly the Dornier slowed up and skidded seawards, one wing down and beginning to disintegrate. Then Pat ran out of ammunition, and with German fighters threatening to cut off his retreat he dived for home.

On 6th August Goering told his Luftlotte commanders that the invasion of Britain would be launched in the first fortnight of September, and that Eagle Day would be announced soon. Bad weather caused a delay, but attacks on coastal shipping were stepped up from 8th August. For Tony, as for many others, this was the day when the Battle really began.

At 15.40 that afternoon the re-formed squadron – twelve Hurricanes – was sent off to protect a westbound convoy off the Isle of Wight, code-named *Peewit*. It consisted of twenty merchant ships with nine naval escort vessels and was attempting to pass through the Dover Straits undetected. But from daybreak on it came under repeated attack, and four ships had already been sunk (609 had been one of the squadrons involved earlier in the day, see Chapter 2). Ventnor radar had warned of a further strike, and Tony was leading Yellow Section – the second section of three. A formidable array of German fighters, single- and twin-engined, about seventy in all, was sighted as the Hurricanes reached St Catherine's Point, flying in long line astern and stretching from the French coast to the island. At top level, about 20,000 feet, were the Messerschmitt 109s; 5,000 feet below them were the 110s. Somewhere under this huge umbrella, undetected as yet, were eighty-two Stuka (Junkers 87) dive-bombers, mounting the biggest strike of the day. First the 110s would set fire to the balloons, then the Stukas would dive-bomb the ships while the 109s gave what protection they could.

Tony immediately led his section towards the high-level fighters in an attempt to outclimb them, but the 110s pre-empted him by diving on his section from above and astern. Tony's response was to turn through 180 degrees and lead his section into a head-on counter-attack. Three 110s in line astern singled him out and he accepted the challenge, choosing the third and last and giving it a long burst from his eight machine-guns, holding his aim almost to collision point. The closing speed was terrific, and soon he had left the 110s far behind. Glancing back he saw white smoke pouring from the one he'd attacked; but then he spotted the convoy, which was already being dive-bombed by the Stukas south of the island. He had no chance to check on his 110.

The Stukas, having sunk three more ships and damaged others, were now heading south, making for home. Overtaking them, he plunged straight through the formation, firing his guns as he went, hoping that because of the danger of hitting each other they would be forced to stay their fire. Many of the gunners accepted the risk, and he flew through a curtain of fire.

The first Stuka he attacked emitted clouds of smoke before breaking away to the left. The next emitted rather less smoke but dived steeply through the formation, narrowly missing one of his colleagues.

Tony was now more than half-way through the formation, with his ammunition almost spent. But he saved his last and longest burst for the Stuka ahead of the previous one, aiming from astern. The turbulence within the formation roughened the airflow and distorted his aim, but by the end of the burst he was right on target. Then, as he sped through to the front of the formation and beyond, he was pounced on by a fighter that had been lying in wait.

As he took violent evasive action he glimpsed his last Stuka far below him, hugging the water and spewing black smoke. With no ammunition left he shook off the fighter in cloud before heading inland back to Tangmere.

In its efforts to protect the convoy the RAF lost twelve pilots killed, buttressing the protest made earlier by George Darley of 609. But twenty German aircraft were shot down and many more were damaged, while the radar and control organization came through the test well.

Awe-struck at the sight of Tony's battered machine – it was a write-off – his ground crew approached him in silence, fearing that his wounds must be multiple. The cockpit had been spattered, and they exclaimed with relief when he emerged in one piece. His squadron colleagues had not been so lucky. Two of them had been shot down, and both were dead. A third – his mentor Frank Carey – had been wounded, and a fourth had crash-landed. Tony had not escaped completely, but his wounds were superficial, though the diagnosis of the station medical officer that he had 'multiple foreign bodies in both legs' he took as an insult. Foreign bodies indeed! He had acquired them legitimately. But they soon worked their way to the surface. Escaping for a few hours to Farnborough, he got Bunny to help him pick out the pieces.

With no time for letters, contact with Bunny was mostly restricted to the occasional phone call. Patrick, still at Martlesham, made dates to meet her in London, where they usually went to a night club. Tony, so much nearer at Tangmere, would persuade her, when he couldn't leave camp, to come down on the bus. He would smuggle her into his two-seater, pile macs on top of her, and drive her out to a secret rendezvous at dispersal. Later she would catch the bus home. It was on one of these excursions that her dilemma was clarified, if not exactly resolved. She could not choose between the two brothers, and it was cruelty to expect her to do so. But Tony was irresistible. With him, the physical attraction was stronger.

He was pressing her now to marry him. 'I'll marry you in a fortnight,' she told him, half in jest. She had promised to marry Patrick when he was a squadron leader. Now she was marrying Tony in a fortnight. But even a fortnight, in that packed summer, seemed like an age.

Tony, catching her mood, took her half-seriously. A friend had offered to lend him a dream cottage near Tangmere. It would make an idyllic spot for a honeymoon.

In his next letter he reminded her of her promise. 'Don't forget you're going to marry me in a fortnight!' The exclamation mark eased her conscience a little, but not enough. Was she now bound to Tony? His letter assumed it. 'Thanks for that one night of love sweetheart which will stay in my memory for aeons to come, Yours, Anthony.' But uncertainty remained, and he ended his letter with a bracketed post-script. '(To marry or not to marry, that is the question?)'

Soon – on 11th August – he was back in the air again, and so was Frank Carey, his wounds notwithstanding. They flew four uneventful sorties in which no contact was made, searching for targets in vain. But in the third of five sorties next day, Tony was successful again. With Carey, now commissioned, leading – and Tony, thus leap-frogged, welcoming him as the natural leader – Tony ordered his section to chase three Heinkel bombers leaving the coast at 15,000 feet off Portsmouth. As usual he held his fire until he was within two hundred yards and closed right in to fifty; but he had learned to be cunning as well, approaching so that the Heinkel he selected would shield him from the other two. To counteract this the German pilots promptly staggered their heights, and although one of the Heinkels was left burning on the water thirty miles from the French coast, Tony's Hurricane was hit in the engine and oil tank and he had a struggle to get home. Once again the ground crew whistled through their teeth at his escape.

Such was the pressure now that he was airborne again before breakfast next day – Eagle Day – in a highly eventful sortie in which he led his section into the attack against two separate formations above cloud. He got astern of one bomber and gave it a long burst without visible result, then broke away to attack the other formation. A volley at a stray Heinkel was rewarded by the sight of a stopped propeller and a stream of black smoke. Seeing another Hurricane take up the attack, he followed the main formation round and fired at another bomber which immediately emitted jet black smoke from the port engine followed by vivid red flame. The bomber dived steeply and disappeared into cloud. Next he attacked three stragglers, but they returned his fire accurately and his own engine was hit. It was his turn to trail flames and smoke. He was considering a bale-out, but the fire didn't seem to take hold. Remembering his preference to stay with his plane if he could, he hung on for another few minutes, eventually crash-landing twelve miles from Midhurst. He had scarcely got clear when the wreckage erupted.

Telephoning for a lift back to Tangmere, he was airborne again by lunchtime, guarding the rear of the squadron in a dogfight.

That night, hearing that two of the men he had shot down were being held prisoner at Chichester Police Station, he demonstrated that the bond between warring airmen still existed by personally delivering to them two tins of cigarettes. In return the Germans gave him a toy pistol which, unlike the guns they had aimed at each other a few hours earlier, fired only blanks.

The frenetic pace at which the Battle was being fought drew the last ounce of endeavour out of the small group of defending pilots involved. How long could they last? Tony might not be one of the aces, but he had had his successes, and day after day he took such a pasting and came back for more that he was regarded with special affection and had become one of the squadron's biggest morale-builders. Equally, at dispersal between sorties, his dreamy, melodious strumming of the new guitar he had bought was soothing to raw nerves, not least his own.

On 15th August he was acting as rearguard again with his section when, 'seeing that the enemy fighters weren't going to play', he attacked a box of four Heinkels and sent the outside man crashing down into the sea, with a witness from his section to vouch for it. He then approached from the other flank and damaged a Heinkel on that side, silencing the gunners. The bomber was streaming smoke and losing height but Tony had no more ammunition and was far out to sea, so he ordered his section home. His Hurricane, riddled with holes as usual, had to be towed away for repair. His overworked ground crew worshipped him for it.

Such was the influence exerted by Tangmere-based aircraft that on 16th August, soon after midday, the Luftwaffe mounted a determined and damaging dive-bombing attack on the airfield. (Half an hour later, the rear formation of this raid switched the attack to the naval airfield at Gosport: it was in action against this formation that 'Nick' Nicolson won the VC – see Chapter 5.) Fortunately for 43 Squadron they were already airborne in time to greet the raid on Tangmere. Carey saw the raiders first, and the new squadron commander, John 'Tubby' Badger, who had recently succeeded George Lott (wounded and having lost the sight of one eye), ordered a head-on attack. Tony broke up a sizeable formation of Stukas off Selsey Bill by shooting two down into the sea; but with his own radiator hit by return fire he turned for home. At once he was set on by four 109s, and with his engine faltering he let his plane fall out of the sky. With the Isle of Wight filling his windscreen he somehow pulled out, but he was forced to crash-land, wheels-up, in a field near Parkhurst. How he got the plane down, in an incredibly small space, seemed a miracle to those who ran to his aid, but in the crash he was thrown forward on his straps, and he knocked out three of his front teeth.

Still half-dazed, he got a lift to the ferry and crossed to Southampton, but decided it was too late to get back to Tangmere that night. Putting up at a Southampton hotel, he was not short of company to celebrate his escape and help drown his sorrows. Next morning, bleary-eyed and lisping, he telephoned the squadron adjutant. 'If you want me to go on fighting,' he told him, 'you'd better send someone down here to fetch me – and to pay my bill!'

Of the nine Stukas that had been shot down on the 16th seven were credited to 43 Squadron. Meanwhile the adjutant had no choice but to pick up and pay up, and Tony arrived back bruised and disfigured to a prodigal's welcome. Caesar Hull, one of the men who had taught him combat flying, had also lost some front teeth in a crash, and when he heard of Tony's misfortune he sent along his spare plate. Tony, taking the hint, was back in action within 48 hours. He told Bunny he wanted a billiards set as replacements – one red, one white, and one spot.

In another day of desperate fighting on 18th August, Biggin Hill, Kenley and Croydon airfields were heavily bombed. Meanwhile 43 Squadron were again prominent in dispelling a massed Stuka attack, shooting down four confirmed and damaging three others. Among their own casualties was Frank Carey, wounded and out of the Battle, this time for good (but by no means out of the war). Once again Tony came back with his plane damaged; but these two clashes, on 16th and 18th August, in both of which Tony was fiercely engaged, spelt the end of the Stuka threat in the Battle of Britain, a significant victory.

Such was the story of eleven kaleidoscopic days in Tony's life as a fighter pilot. They culminated, deservedly enough, in a citation for a DFC. He had taken part in all engagements carried out by his squadron since the war started – an amazing record. He had definitely destroyed six enemy aircraft and probably destroyed many more. 'In spite of the fact that this pilot has been shot down six times,' concluded the citation, 'he has continued to fight with unabated courage and enthusiasm and has shown outstanding qualities as a resourceful and determined leader.'

Unassuming and even self-effacing about his flying skill – he knew that many of his colleagues were technically superior – Tony was nevertheless delighted. Not only had he caught up with his brother, but even more importantly, he would now qualify for that extra under-the-counter gallon of petrol from pump attendants that the purple-and-white medal ribbon virtually guaranteed. Such were the incidental rewards.

Bunny went to Tangmere especially to sew the ribbon on. With Tony at his most persuasive, she finally gave in. Yes, she would marry him. The cottage at Tangmere remained available.

Two nights later she had a date with Patrick in town. Somehow she would have to tell him. In a quiet corner of their favourite night spot, she thought she could do so; but the words wouldn't come. Suddenly Pat noticed she was crying. 'What's the matter, Bun-Bun?'

She told him what she had decided. 'But if I marry Tony, I can't marry you.'

'That's all right, Bunny,' said Patrick. 'It can't be helped.' Wryly, he was remembering the squadron's old catch-phrase back in France. 'For your leetle brother, Oh La La!'

She knew she had delivered a devastating blow, and she

sensed what his composure was masking. She had known for a long time that she would marry one of them, and she had always thought it would be Pat. But all summer she had feared for them both, dreading to lose either. If Tony were killed she would marry Pat; but she could hardly tell him that.

Pat, the practical one, soon came down to earth. 'You'll starve on Tony's money. Now that I'm a flying officer, I'll make you an allotment out of my pay.' The gesture was so generous it started Bunny weeping again. For Patrick, Tony was still 'my kid'.

At Tangmere, sporting his new medal ribbon, Tony told his ground crew that the award was just as much theirs, for keeping him flying, as it was his, and he apologized for the trouble he had given them. To the ground maintenance 'chiefie', Ted Parker, he confided: 'To tell you the truth, Flight, I don't really see too well these days, my eyesight is giving me trouble. I never see the Hun that hits me. But for God's sake don't breathe a word to a soul or they'll take me off Ops.'

All he needed, almost certainly, was a rest. He was suffering a temporary physical deterioration through fatigue, which was impairing his senses, and keen eyesight was the most vital of them all. Dowding, at Fighter Command, and Park, at 11 Group, fully appreciated the problem, and they were switching front-line squadrons to quieter sectors whenever they could. But for the moment they could not manage without 43.

Visiting Tangmere, Bunny noticed the strain Tony was under. The high spirits of a few days earlier had been replaced by an insatiable desire for sleep, and his embraces were those of an exhausted man.

Both sides had fought themselves to a standstill, and a brief lull, extended by a spell of bad weather, now intervened. So far from being eliminated in four days, the RAF was still giving as good as it got, sometimes better. The Luftwaffe had lost 194 planes between 15th and 18th August. Goering summoned his commanders to express his displeasure, and to plan the final destruction of Fighter Command.

The respite coincided with the arrival at Croydon of Peter

Townsend's 85 Squadron, replacing a flagging squadron with-drawn to the north. The move thrust Patrick even further into the vortex of the battle than Tony, if that were possible.

It was during this hiatus that Winston Churchill found time to phrase and declaim his immortal panegyric, 'Never in the field of human conflict was so much owed by so many to so few.' There had been a remarkable transformation from the boos and hisses of two months earlier. But the crucial phase was still to come.

85 Squadron's arrival at Croydon was greeted by a night raid in which three Hurricanes were either destroyed or damaged. But at 07.58 next morning, 24th August, the squadron, led by Townsend, and dodging the craters, took off on patrol. The battle had been rejoined. And that night, for the first time since 1918, bombs fell on the City of London and on the densely-populated East End boroughs of Bethnal Green, East Ham, Stepney and Finsbury, causing civilian casualties.

Three, four and five times daily in that last week in August, Peter Townsend led 85 Squadron against the massed forma-tions of the German assault, with 'Hammy' Hamilton's Red Section on his right, 'Sammy' Allard's Yellow Section on his left, and Pat Woods-Scawen's Green Section under his tail. In support of the incomparable Townsend the section leaders comprised a formidable trio, with Allard, recently promoted from sergeant to flying officer, among the top-scoring pilots of the battle. On the 26th Pat was leading his section when he sighted eighteen Dornier bombers flying in threes in stepped-up formation, with an escort of a dozen Me109s. Townsend gave the order for a frontal attack, and the whole squadron swept in head-on.

Pat got in a two-second burst at the bombers, then broke away below. Climbing back into position, he delivered another frontal attack on the main formation, from which three of the Dorniers staggered away. This time he was travelling too fast to adjust his aim, so he used his excess speed to make a climbing attack on the fighters, which were descending in a shallow dive to defend the Dorniers. He put a three-second burst into the belly of one of the fighters, climbing all the time, and saw fragments of its airframe scatter like confetti, after which it appeared to whip-stall. By this time his own speed had fallen right off, and as his Hurricane stalled he dived away from another German pilot seeking revenge.

Finding himself in the rear of the bomber formation, he joined up with two of his colleagues and attacked one of the Dorniers from astern. A puff of smoke burped from the Dornier's starboard engine and the bomber dropped away through the clouds. Seeing that others were chasing it down, he climbed back for a final attack on the main formation, which was turning for home. The machine he singled out emitted clouds of smoke but ploughed steadily on. Out of ammunition, he dropped down to ground level and followed the remaining Dorniers as they fled seawards, giving the ground controller their location and course.

Tony had been in action too, on a day when the RAF lost thirty-two fighters, seventeen of them Hurricanes.

Early drizzle next day was succeeded by blue skies and warm sunshine, but the Luftwaffe did not appear again in strength until the 28th. Then 85 Squadron found themselves in the vanguard of an afternoon scrap against fighters, just the kind of clash it was Dowding's policy to avoid. Fighters by themselves could do little harm. But 85 had been warned of the approach of a bomber formation. They were patrolling at 18,000 feet when they sighted twenty Me109s south-east of Dungeness, just above the cloud layer. Although there were no bombers in sight, Townsend judged that he had the advantage, and he led his pilots in a surprise attack out of the sun. The Germans failed to spot them until the penultimate moment, and Patrick, leading his section, got in two long bursts at his selected target, first from the quarter and then from astern. Petrol from the wing tanks poured from his quarry and it dived ever more steeply until it reached the vertical, trailing black smoke. Pat followed it for several thousand feet until he was sure it was out of control. The German fighter splashed into the sea off Dymchurch – and the action was watched by none other than Churchill himself, who was inspecting south-east defences.

After two tremendous tussles on the 29th Pat made no

claims. Townsend got a 109, but it was a bad day for the squadron, three machines being shot down, with the pilot of one of them, flight commander Hammy Hamilton, failing to bale out in time. Earlier in the day he had saved the life of a colleague, shooting down a 109 (confirmed) when it was poised for a victory, killing the pilot.

On 30th August the Luftwaffe flew 1,345 sorties during the day, their biggest effort since the 15th. Fighter Command responded with over a thousand. Patrick was one of many pilots that day who flew five interception sorties, but his toughest scrap came in his first. The Germans were now putting up a greater proportion of fighters to protect their bombers, and by eleven o'clock some forty Heinkels and thirty Dorniers were converging over Kent attended by sixty 109s and thirty 110s. The Heinkels were spotted at 16,000 feet by 85 Squadron over Bethenden and were chased inland, where the squadron duly overtook them. Having got well in front, they executed a shattering head-on attack and the bombers dispersed in chaos. In the dogfight that followed Pat sent a twin-engined fighter down with its starboard engine on fire, and it crashed near Dover, killing the crew.

Five minutes after Pat got his 110, Tony was leading Red Section of 43 Squadron with orders to patrol over base; it was believed that the bombers were heading for Tangmere. Realizing that the main formation was too far away to attack, and seeing that a straggler from another Hurricane squadron was being hard pressed by four 109s, Tony led a counter-attack. Only by using full boost and diving for several thousand feet was he able to catch up, and he was exceeding 350 miles per hour on the clock when he got within range.

At 250 yards he began a burst which he held for a count of three. Half-way through it the fighter started to leak smoke from the wing-roots, yet somehow it accelerated away. Suddenly it turned on its back and dived at high speed, still streaming smoke. Tony was convinced that no pilot could pull out of such a vertical plunge, and he looked for other targets. His 109 – he was sure it was his – was seen from the coast to crash at terrific velocity into the sea.

One pilot from 43 Squadron was killed in this action, and later in the day they lost their commanding officer, Tubby Badger, shot down and so badly burnt he died later.

The Battle was quickening to a pace that no air force could reasonably sustain. Yet somehow both nations continued to sustain it. The RAF had reached a stage where they could replace lost aircraft, thanks to the work of the factories, but not pilots. Many overdue for a rest had to fight on.

There was no let-up on the 31st as two waves of Dorniers and Heinkels with strong fighter escort came over at lunchtime to bomb Croydon and Biggin Hill. At Croydon, bombs started to fall on the east side of the airfield just as Townsend got his twelve Hurricanes airborne. They caught up with the bombers at 9,000 feet over Tunbridge Wells and Patrick, leading Blue Section, got ahead of them and attacked them head-on.

After a short burst he was forced to break away to avoid collision, and he had no chance to assess the result, but he closed on one of the accompanying 109s and gave it a long burst, then watched it pull up before spinning away. He got in a quarter attack on another 109, the pilot of which half-rolled and attempted to climb out of trouble, but Pat waited for him, caught him in the climb, and got in a telling burst from astern. The fighter streamed a pendant of flame before diving steeply, leaving a funnel of smoke.

Despite the certainty of damage, none of these planes could be confirmed as shot down. The powers of recovery, of both man and machine, were astonishing. Confirmation of one bale-out that day, however, came from Peter Townsend: his own. Shot down during the lunchtime mêlée, and hit in the foot by a cannon shell, he had aimed to force-land, but finding himself over wooded country near Hawkhurst with a dead engine he was forced to bale out. That evening, in Croydon General Hospital, the cap of the shell was extracted from his foot and his big toe was amputated. Simultaneously his parachute was put on display by Hawkhurst Police to raise money for the Spitfire Fund.

With its leader out of the Battle and two flight commanders

dead, Patrick found himself leading the squadron. In practice he continued to head B Flight, leaving Allard to lead A Flight.

Following that lunchtime scrap, Pat flew four more sorties before the last day of August ended. At 17.30, accompanied by nine other Hurricanes, he intercepted a mixed enemy force south of the Thames Estuary which was composed of thirty bombers and about a hundred fighters. He opened up on a 109 from dead astern and it caught fire and went down, belching black smoke. The pilot, although wounded, escaped. Between them, in this teatime raid, the squadron claimed three 109s destroyed and six probables. Even then the day was not over.

Ordered that evening to patrol off the Kent coast near Hawkinge, Pat saw the raiders pass to the north as he circled out to sea, and then, wheeling in from the flank, he caught them off their guard. This time he sprayed a 109 from abeam and watched it go down with wing tanks afire.

Whereas Tony, in the heat of a scrap, with guns blazing, was apt to ignore every Hun except the one he was after, Pat, the more mature and skilful flyer, had disclosed, in his earlier reports, an equal desire for combat but a moderating caution. This could be partly explained by the two years' difference in their ages. But by this last day of August, all hint of caution had disappeared from Pat's leadership. Although this made him ever more vulnerable, only maximum aggression could repel the air siege. There was no room for prudence now.

Seven times in four days 85 Squadron had been in action, losing nine aircraft. 'For this squadron,' writes one historian, in a masterpiece of understatement, 'the battle had reached its climax.'

The same was true for 43 Squadron. This battle-weary squadron had lost two successive commanders; but it was given a much-needed boost by the return, as August ended, of a much-loved leader to take command, the legendary Caesar Hull.

The last two days of August had seen the fiercest 48 hours' fighting of the whole battle. But the redeployment of squadrons that Dowding devised on 1st September, in a desperate effort to close his ranks, brought no relief to 43 or 85. As it happened, 43 were not over-stretched on Sunday 1st September. But for 85, vectored into the thick of it, the day was a disaster.

During the morning things went well enough as the squadron destroyed two 109s without loss. But when eleven Hurricanes took off from Croydon at 13.50 to intercept a raid estimated at 150 to 200 planes heading for Biggin Hill, the warning came late, and the pilots of 85 Squadron found themselves 5,000 feet below the intruders. As they climbed to reach the bombers they were jumped by the German fighter pilots, who knew how to make the most of a height advantage.

Trapped as they were, Patrick and his squadron had only one option: to sell their lives dearly. With Pat leading, they broke through to the bombers and accounted for four. But when the final tally was taken, six out of the eleven Hurricane pilots were missing.

Sammy Allard had force-landed at Lympne only to see his plane bombed and destroyed as mechanics worked to repair his engine. One mechanic was killed and another seriously wounded, but Allard escaped unhurt (only to be killed later). A sergeant pilot named G. B. Booth, shot down near Purley, baled out with a damaged parachute which failed to open fully; six months later he died from his injuries. Flying Officer A. V. Gowers, DFC, baling out over Oxted, suffered severe burns and was wounded but survived (he too was killed later). Another pilot, landing wheels-up, escaped injury. But when night fell, two squadron pilots were still unaccounted for. One was a Sergeant J. H. M. Ellis. The other was Patrick Woods-Scawen.

When they failed to show up, and no reports of their whereabouts came through, they were reported missing, believed killed.

The mystery of the two absent pilots was still unsolved next day, by which time the news of their disappearance had reached next of kin. Of Sergeant Ellis, no trace had been found of pilot or plane. But Pat's plane had been identified, partly buried in the recreation ground at Kenley, its cockpit empty.

So Pat, for the moment, was missing. Could he be dead? To Pop and Nell Woods-Scawen, and to Bunny, it simply wasn't believable. Earlier that summer Tony had been reported missing, and they had agonized over his disappearance for a week, but Bunny especially had refused to believe he was dead, and her faith had been justified. She just had to be right about Pat. Yet the portents remained dire.

For Bunny the news, if the worst was confirmed, was doubly poignant. She need not have told Pat of her decision, need never have inflicted that pain. Yet he must have baled out. Somewhere perhaps he lay wounded and immobile, hidden in woodland. Surely tomorrow they would find him, and get him to hospital.

Meanwhile the war of attrition had reached its peak and on paper the RAF was losing it. Yet the Germans were paying too high a price. If Fighter Command could go on exacting that price for a few more days, the German tactics might change.

When Tony was scrambled from Tangmere next day, 2nd September, he was unaware that his brother was missing. For him, as for every other Fighter Command pilot, there was still a job to be done. As the massacred 85 Squadron was withdrawn from Croydon, the remaining squadrons braced themselves for the next sequence of raids. These swelled in strength until by noon a massive concentration of 'bandits', estimated at about 250, was plotted approaching Dover. Reinforcements were called for by controllers, and soon more than seventy Hurricanes and Spitfires were racing eastwards. Among those vectored forward were twelve Hurricanes of 43 Squadron from Tangmere, led by Caesar Hull.

Tony, as usual, was leading Yellow Section. The dogfight started between 18,000 and 20,000 feet and continued with mounting ferocity as the bombers headed inland towards Maidstone. At least two 109s were shot down by 43 Squadron, but when the pilots eventually returned to Tangmere, three were missing. Two of them had baled out and were safe. The third was Tony.

Tony's No. 2, Sergeant G. Jefferies, reporting back at Tangmere, described how, after a scrap with seven of the enemy, he had chased a 109 down and seen it explode on impact. Tony had been leading at the time, but Jefferies had seen nothing of him thereafter. However, the two boys cycling near Ivychurch on Romney Marsh had seen him. 'I didn't actually see Woods-Scawen's Hurricane attacked,' remembered one of them, Len Green, many years later, 'but when I looked he had just come out of the plane and they seemed to fall together for a few seconds. The plane seemed to be alight and the pilot's parachute didn't seem to open fully and was flapping at about 2,000 feet or less. It all happened so quickly – it was over in a few seconds.'

Nearer the scene, an Anglican parson saw the pilot bale out, in his view dangerously low – certainly not at anything like the 2,000 feet estimated later by Green. But, whatever the height, it proved to be too low to save the pilot's life.

Tony was dead when the parson reached him. His body was taken into the nearby church.

For the Woods-Scawens, and for Bunny, the double tragedy was totally benumbing. They simply could not grasp that these two vibrant, high-spirited boys would never again come bursting into the semi-detached at 55 York Road, with their spontaneous affection and laughter. And yet, was there not still hope for Pat? But as the days passed, hope faded.

On 5th September, at Folkestone, Pop and Nell Woods-Scawen, with Bunny Lawrence, attended Tony's funeral, bleak and inescapable confirmation of his death. Next day, in the unkempt, overgrown garden of an empty house in Kenley Lane, the discovery of Pat's body – 'little Patrick, who smiled with his eyes' – made their anguish complete.

Mercifully, Pat had been killed on impact. He had not died a lingering death, as Bunny had feared, unable to attract help. As with Tony, his parachute had seemingly failed to open, leaving an element of mystery, and of heightened tragedy, about both deaths.

Only a few days earlier, Tony had told Frank Carey that he believed he could almost always get a Hurricane down. That confidence might explain why he left his bale-out so late. Rumours of pilots being shot at on their parachutes, by ground fire as well as – legitimately enough, perhaps – by the enemy, had disturbed him.

Patrick, flying over a built-up area on the outskirts of

Croydon, may have feared that his plane would plunge into houses. Both crashed near Battle of Britain airfields, which they may have been trying to reach.

In terms of recorded 'victories' they were not perhaps 'aces'. Tony scored six confirmed in the Battle, Patrick four. But this takes no account of the numbers they damaged and drove off or of the example they set. Even for the so-called aces, the numbers eventually confirmed appear modest. Among the top scorers, 'Ginger' Lacey was credited with 15, plus one shared, Bob Stanford Tuck ten, plus one shared. Post-war reference to German records pared many claims down.

Of Tony, George Lott, his one-time commanding officer, wrote: 'Tony was one of the most amazing of fighter pilots. He was not a particularly good pilot, nor was he a particularly good shot; but – by ardour and all the stars! – he was a fighter. Always in the heart of a scrap, never taking the slightest notice of any Hun but the one he was after – this probably explains not only the number of Germans he shot down, but the number of times he was shot down himself!'

What of those he led into battle? One raw newcomer, Cliff Gray, who flew more often than not in Yellow Section of 43 (and himself won a DFC), said that Tony had only one idea, to bore in regardless of any Hun in sight. This, in those desperate days of action and lightning reaction, was the kind of leadership that counted.

As for Patrick, his merits were fully appreciated on 85 Squadron, where he was truly loved. Had he survived, rapid promotion to the rank of squadron leader would have been his.

The investiture which Pat was due to attend inevitably went ahead without him. When, in the following June, Pop Woods-Scawen went to Buckingham Palace with Bunny to collect both boys' medals, Aunt Nellie was still too grief-stricken to go. For the rest of her life she wore black, and it was many years before, plucking up courage, she allowed the boxes that contained Pat's new uniform and her own carefully chosen costume to see daylight. They were still wrapped in the tissue paper in which they had been delivered.

Bunny was so vital a person that she was bound to pick up the pieces and re-shape her life, but for many months the numbness remained. It was not until a third Woods-Scawen, Gerald, a first cousin of Pat and Tony, who had joined the RAF as a pilot on the day Pat was killed and had escorted her to the investiture in June 1941, was reported missing on a fighter sweep over France four months later that desolation struck her, and for a long time she was inconsolable. Nothing was known of Gerald's fate for more than a year, when news was received from the Netherlands Red Cross that his body had been washed ashore at Noordwijk, in the province of South Holland, on 20th October 1941, and that he had been buried in Noordwijk Municipal Cemetery.

Patrick was buried in the churchyard of St Mary's Parish Church, Caterham on the Hill. The remains of Tony's aircraft were traced to Old Romney and excavated in September 1977 by members of the Brenzett Aeronautical Museum, Kent, their museum having being founded in 1972 'as a sincere tribute to all airmen who flew, fought and died over Southern England during the Second World War'. Len Green was a founder member.

Bunny writes: 'I joined the WRAF (naturally) and became an MT driver, but would probably never have passed my map-reading test had the examiner not turned out to be the very policeman who had called to tell Pop Woods-Scawen about one of the boys' "prangs".' Still only nineteen when Pat and Tony were killed, she married at twenty-three and talks today of 'six smashing children and fourteen grandchildren. But I have such memories of two boys that will never die.' She still has the toy pistol the Germans gave Tony.

Tributes are still being paid to Patrick and Tony by their surviving contemporaries. That would have brought great solace to Pop and Nell Woods-Scawen, who believed that their boys were forgotten. Pop died in 1955 and Nell in 1960, never guessing that the boys would still be remembered fifty years on.

A CHANCE TO TAKE STOCK – AND A FATEFUL FORTNIGHT

Goering's initial charge on Eagle Day, 13th August, misfired through bad weather and poor communications, but before the day was out the Luftwaffe had flown 1,485 sorties and were claiming seventy Hurricanes and Spitfires destroyed. In fact only thirteen fighters were lost in combat (one more was destroyed on the ground) with six pilots saved. RAF claims in seven hundred sorties were far more accurate – sixty-four against forty-six later confirmed by German records.

The four days in which Fighter Command was to be overwhelmed did not prove in the event to be consecutive. And after the massive raids which were mounted on 13th, 15th, 16th and 18th August, inferior weather gave both sides a chance to take stock. For Goering, the exaggerated claims of his pilots gave a spurious comfort; but he had lost 236 aircraft in the four days. He could afford this provided RAF losses were similar; but he realized he had made a mistake in not concentrating his destructive effort on the enemy fighter force. He showed less wisdom in abandoning attacks on radar installations, which he mistakenly believed to be unproductive, and in deploying more of his fighters in defence of his bombers, denying far too many of his pilots their favourite free-chase role.

Fighter Command's losses, in fact, were not dissimilar: 213 Hurricanes and Spitfires in the ten days from 8th to 18th August, with replacements barely keeping pace; and 154 pilots killed, missing or wounded, with an influx from the training units of 63. At this rate Fighter Command would soon bleed to death. Yet Dowding and Park, despite further pressure to change their tactics and commit more of their forces, stuck to their original plan, in which conservation and restraint were the key. Dowding retained the same line of battle, preserving the four geographical groups and rotating only tired and depleted squadrons. Park still aimed, by attacking, harrying, diverting and destroying the bombers, while eschewing contact with the fighters as far as was possible, to keep his force virtually intact.

The lull in the fighting, which extended to five days, enabled fighter production to catch up with and overtake losses; there was a marginal improvement in pilot strength; and the Civilian Repair Organization, inspired and cajoled by Beaverbrook, worked day and night to put damaged planes back into action.

When the Luftwaffe resumed the offensive on 24th August, Air Fleets 2 and 3 were combined under Kesselring, and Park's sector airfields were singled out for vigorous attack. By the final week of August, six out of the seven had sustained critical damage, and the massed German formations, with their strengthened close escorts, were proving almost impenetrable. On that first day, only two out of twelve of Park's squadrons vectored to the attack found a way through, more bombers than ever before reached their targets without being intercepted, and Park had to commit an ever greater proportion of his force. Goering's new tactics thus began well, the RAF losing twenty-two fighters initially against Goering's twenty-six of all types, a ruinous ratio for Park. Yet day by day the German fighters, absorbed in their protective role, destroyed fewer of their British counterparts, hindering Goering's prime objective of the progressive dilution of Fighter Command. Even so, between 24th August and 6th September, 262 Hurricanes and Spitfires were lost and many more seriously damaged.

Even more disturbing for Dowding and Park was the loss of pilots, one quarter of Fighter Command's strength being eliminated in this period. Replacement squadrons themselves needed relieving before the squadrons they were replacing had had time to re-form. The transfer of available pilots from Bomber and Coastal Commands was accelerated, but they needed specialized training before posting to squadrons. Finally Dowding gave his assent – long with-held because of anticipated language and discipline difficulties – to the addition of Polish and Czech squadrons to the order of battle, and they quickly proved themselves staunch comrades and fearsome adversaries. These timely reinforcements narrowed but did not totally plug the gap.

Throughout the period, detachments of enemy bombers broadened the assault into a day and night, round the clock offensive, striking at aircraft factories and RAF installations as well as dockyards and ports. It was on one of these raids, on the night of 24th/25th August, that several crews lost their bearings and jettisoned their bombs on the City of London and neighbouring boroughs. Hitler had specifically ruled that London was off limits until he ordered otherwise, and the errant crews were disciplined. But to the British this seemed an unlikely tale, and Churchill immediately ordered reprisal raids on Berlin.

Meanwhile Kesselring now had six hundred fighters concentrated against Park's sectors, and as the sky teemed with Messerschmitt 109s the odds against Park's squadrons became inordinate. On 30th August he was obliged to scramble his entire force, the first time this had been necessary, and his pilots were regularly flying four and five sorties a day, occasionally even more, falling asleep after they landed, at the meal table or even in their cockpits. Biggin Hill became almost untenable after attacks on successive days, and all Park's sector stations, in his own words, were 'pretty groggy'. All-round flying skills deteriorated with fatigue, morale faltered, and even some of the stalwarts, the men who had fought through France and Dunkirk and throughout the Battle and had seemed indestructible, fell. Distressing as it was to see eager young newcomers, raw and inadequately trained, falling at the very first hurdle, as happened tragically often, there was something even more poignant and irreconcilable about the exit of legendary characters around whom the squadrons were built.

By early September, British aircraft losses corresponded ever more closely with those of the enemy, thereby straining all the efforts to keep pace; the pilot situation was deteriorating still further; and Fighter Command was facing defeat. On the German side, however, impatience was growing as the planned date for the invasion drew near. Park's trick of rejecting combat unless a vital target was threatened frustrated Goering on the one hand and encouraged him to believe in the RAF's growing impotence on the other. Yet when cornered the RAF could still put up a fight. There was one target, surely, which would bring the rump of Fighter Command into desperate contention: London. In the process, the last remnant of the pool of Hurricanes and Spitfires and their stubborn pilots would be exhausted.

Using Bomber Command's raids on Berlin as the pretext, Hitler gave the order, on 2nd September, for attack on the populations and defences of Britain's cities, and especially on London. Two days later, in a speech at the Berlin *Sportspalast*, he developed his theme for all to hear. One by one, Britain's towns and cities were to be wiped off the map. Finally, on the 7th, the full weight of the assault was switched to London. Fighter Command's sternest test had arrived.

For Dowding and Park the switch was more than a relief; it was a deliverance. The breathing-space they craved had been granted, by the enemy themselves, and they geared up their forces to repel Goering's last throw.

7

Some Village Hampden:
James Coward

THE VOICES in the kitchen of the farmhouse – a man's and a woman's – were strangely muted, their movements almost feline. King's Farm was a huge mansion of a house, rambling but well-proportioned, partly seventeenth century, partly mid-Victorian, but at that time of the morning, an hour before dawn, sound carried, and there were others in the house to consider.

The man, six feet one-and-a-half inches tall, slim and of classical profile, with aquiline nose, had undoubted presence. For him, generally bubbling over with enthusiasm and humour, the murmuring was a constraint. For the girl, of a gentle, stoical disposition, talking quietly came naturally. To move gracefully, too, was characteristic, heavily pregnant though she was.

All that escaped from the kitchen was the aroma of breakfast. After a plate of porridge the man tucked in to eggs and bacon, fried bread, toast, and coffee. It might be many hours before his next proper meal.

Getting up to see her husband off to work was no hardship for Cynthia Coward. She and James were very much in love. And if, on one of these early mornings, she felt like having a moan, she suppressed it. When her husband came home at night, or left in the morning, it could so easily be for the last time.

She was incredibly lucky to have him with her, here in the family home. Just in case these short hours of darkness were the last they would share, she took special care not to do anything that might spoil them.

Her sister Joan, two years older, was not so fortunate. She too was married to an RAF fighter pilot, once stationed, like James, at the nearby airfield of Duxford, but he had been promoted and posted away. It was Joan's baby, five weeks old, that they must be careful not to wake.

The Bayon girls, Joan and Cynthia, the latter always known as Cyn or Cinnie, had lived in the picturesque Cambridgeshire village of Little Shelford since childhood. Their father, Dr H. P. Bayon, had moved there in 1926 to be near his work in cancer research at the Molteno Institute in Cambridge. The villagers, quick to take to the two girls, and to mark the contrasts between them, had watched them grow up.

To the villagers, Joan was always the tom-boy, Cyn the 'little lady'. Yet Joan was the intuitive one, and perhaps the more artistic. Cyn, it was said, had the brains. Both loved animals, but here again there was a difference. Joan favoured dogs, Cynthia cats. Fortunately their spouses concurred.

The village ran lengthwise, hugging the high street, as the country road through it was flatteringly called. Thatched, whitewashed dwellings and terraced cottages graced either side. There was a 'general' store and a post office, and a baker next door to King's Farm. A butcher from neighbouring Great Shelford delivered daily, and everyone grew their own vegetables.

The secluded life of Little Shelford, little changed for a hundred years, was enlivened by the presence, in startling juxtaposition, of the peacetime RAF station four miles distant at Duxford. It brought great excitement to the girls as they passed through their teens. It also brought husbands. Both chose young pilots with obvious futures. And both chose opposites. Joan, at twenty-one, married the reticent, whimsical Bill Smith, Cynthia at nineteen the ebullient James Coward. As she was under twenty-one he needed her father's permission, but his pilot officer's pay left little enough to support a wife on after mess bills etc., and the rejection he got was brusque. 'Certainly not – and close the door quietly when you go out.' 'Happily,' he says, 'my future mother-in-law was in the Hall when I came out of the study and when I told her of her husband's refusal she said: "Never mind about that – what date shall we fix for the wedding?"'

The two young couples lived for some months in the spacious comfort of King's Farm, with its ten bedrooms, its magnificent living-rooms, and its wide, elegant staircase leading down to the hall. Rents were cheap, so were staff, and Dr Bayon, whose income was modest, and who cycled to and from Cambridge daily, could afford to employ a cook, a maid, two 'daily women', and a gardener. With its coach-house and stables, its well-tended lawns, two tennis courts, the roses in flower, and the herbaceous borders a riot of colour, King's Farm, in the summer of 1940, preserved an atmosphere of gracious living where time seemed to stand still.

During that summer, both James and Bill were posted away. Then James, after a tonsilectomy, was posted back to 19 Squadron at Duxford. Accommodation was short and the authorities allowed him to live out. It seemed too good to be true.

Bill and Joan remained separated. But as soon as they could they swapped dogs, Joan's bull-terrier having proved much more adaptable when moved from station to station than Bill's spaniel, which was duly welcomed back to King's Farm in exchange. For Joan the dog was a link with Bill, however tenuous. Meanwhile Joan's less home-loving bull-terrier established himself quickly, joining his adoptive master daily at dispersal and learning to recognize his plane when it took off and when it landed, presumably by some decibel of engine sound beyond human detection. If he felt it was his job to keep track of Bill, he could not have acted more intelligently.

As for Cynthia's cats, they prowled and slept much as before, draping themselves round James's neck when he was home.

On the morning of Saturday 31st August James was warned to be at the satellite airfield at Fowlmere, a grass field visible from the Royston road, by first light. His baby Austin, striated in camouflage paint like all other vehicles allowed on the station, would take him there in ten minutes.

Coward normally exuded confidence, and it was a confidence, born of long training and tremendous faith in the Spitfire, that was genuine. But this morning a nagging doubt was gnawing at his subconscious. His squadron had been the first to get Spitfires, and recently they had been the first to get cannon to replace their Browning machine-guns. The results had been disappointing: the cannon-guns rarely fired for more than a second or two before they stopped. This was more than a mere frustration. It left the pilots shockingly vulnerable in the middle of combat. Coward and his fellow pilots called for the return of their eight machine-guns, but armament experts back at group headquarters insisted that if the cannon weren't operating properly it was because the squadron armourers did not know their job. Meanwhile the men at the sharp end, while not shirking battle, approached it with diminishing confidence.

For Coward, a whispered good-bye to Cynthia in the darkness of the porch, and an encouraging smile, had become routine. But this morning he said something he had never said before, quite out of character.

'Pray for me today, Cinnie.'

Conditions at Fowlmere were primitive, with no permanent buildings of any kind, just four Nissen huts and a hangar, on the edge of a grass field set on an almost imperceptible plateau. The atmosphere amongst the pilots, whether commissioned or non-commissioned, was bantering and boyish, with much leg-pulling. Few had any clear vision of the meaning of the Battle, but everyone wanted to be in it. There was a hut for officer pilots and a hut for sergeant pilots, and the messes, too, were separate, but long hours at dispersal, at readiness or on standy-by, soon broke down any barriers between the two.

Coward drove through the flat countryside to Fowlmere just as dawn was seeping through under the skyline. He arrived to find everyone still in bed. The squadron had not yet been brought to stand-by, and he could have risked another hour or so's sleep.

Sleep was an obsession with the pilots at Fowlmere. Detached from the main station, they had unusual freedom. No

a

5a James Coward with Cynthia after their wartime wedding, with her cat Su Ling on his shoulder (note the masked headlight of the Austin 7); and 5b brother-in-law Bill Smith and his mangled Hurricane, with Joan's perceptive bull-terrier on guard.

b

a

6a John Hannah with his Canadian pilot Arthur Connor after their awards were announced.

6b Mrs Janet Hannah at RAF Scampton with her three daughters after presenting her husband's VC to 83 Squadron, 6th May, 1967. The medal is on the table, bottom right.

b

one thought of getting up before they had to. Their distance from the hub of events in the south-east gave them confidence that they would get ample warning in the event of a 'scramble'.

In fact, radar stations on the Kent coast were reporting enemy activity from an early hour, and it was still well before eight o'clock when this activity crystallized into four waves of raiders, one approaching Dover and three bisecting the Thames Estuary. Squadrons from 11 Group vectored to intercept were already suffering losses as the pilots of 19 Squadron slept.

One of the bomber formations, with a strong fighter escort, was actually making for Duxford. This was the sector station where Douglas Bader, commanding 242 Squadron, was shortly to get the go-ahead from Leigh-Mallory to form the 12 Group 'Big Wing'. But these tactics, although already tried out, were not yet established. Meanwhile the Duxford sector controller, realizing that one enemy formation had by-passed the London area and was heading for Debden and Duxford, requested urgent action from 11 Group. At the same time he scrambled 19 Squadron, but they would be far too late to greet this formation. Fortunately an 11 Group squadron already airborne was well placed to intercept, and they did so with such vigour that the leading section of the bombers jettisoned their load and turned back.

A second section, however, also heading for Duxford, some-how got by unchallenged. As nine pilots of 19 Squadron – due to losses and crashes in the previous few days there were only nine aircraft available – pulled on their flying jackets over their pyjamas and raced out to their Spitfires, the bombers were already approaching the fighter airfield at Debden, which was on their track for Duxford, fifteen miles to the south-south-east. The time was 08.15. Hurriedly gaining height over Dux-ford, the pilots of 19 Squadron sighted the raiders to the south.

'Tally-ho – there they are!'

The shout came from Coward. With Little Shelford almost directly beneath him, and some of his colleagues still wiping the sleep from their eyes, no one had keener vision or a stronger incentive than he did for turning the raiders back.

There were twenty Dornier bombers and an escort of some

forty or fifty twin-engined Messerschmitt 110 fighters approaching, about seventy aircraft in all. The 19 Squadron plan was for two sections of three Spitfires each – Blue Section, led by New Zealander Wilf Clouston, and Green Section, led by Coward – to attack the bombers while Yellow Section, led by another New Zealander, Frankie Brinsden, went for the fighters in an effort to drive them off. There was another family link here: twelve months earlier, Brinsden had been Bill Smith's best man.

The German tactics were to keep close together and to step up their formations in such a fashion that their return fire against attack from the rear could be devastating. Head-on attacks in a Spitfire, besides achieving a frightening closing speed, left little time for accurate sighting. And whereas bursts of machine-gun fire could be sprayed almost indiscriminately in the hope of scoring a hit, accurate sighting was something that 19 Squadron's new cannon-firing Spitfires needed above all else.

The available burst of cannon fire was brief at the best of times – about six seconds. From bitter experience they knew it would probably be very much less.

Some of the bomber crews, aware that interception awaited them, were preparing to drop their bombs on the airfield at Debden. Others were pressing on – for Duxford, or perhaps for Fowlmere.

As the nine Spitfires, led by Clouston, climbed into the attack, Coward had King's Farm, and especially Cynthia and the child she was carrying, vividly in mind. With Bill Smith fighting similar battles elsewhere, he felt personally responsible for Joan and her baby as well.

At Little Shelford, 20,000 feet below, the scrap seemed to be developing right overhead. Reuben Litchfield, a forty-year-old farmer who rented White's Farm, on the opposite side of the high street to King's Farm, had long since milked his cows. Now, having finished his breakfast, he went out into the yard with unhurried gait to load his threshing machine on a horse-drawn cart, preparatory to lending it to a fellow farmer. As he did so, the attenuated roar of aircraft engines, buzzing like bees high overhead, interspersed with the pop-pop-pop of distant cannon and machine-gun fire, reached his ears. He looked up briefly and saw the now-familiar condensation trails, a white-crayonned doodling on the blue blotting-pad of the sky. They seemed quite unrelated to war. At that moment his mother, notoriously deaf, appeared in the doorway of the whitewashed cottage. 'What's that noise?'

'Go back inside – it's an air raid.'

Attacking from the flank and from slightly below, Clouston came up under the leading clutch of Dorniers in copy-book style, his section neatly echeloned to starboard. Between them they accounted for one of the Dorniers. But as vibration caused the cannon in one Spitfire after another to jam, the initial thrust deteriorated into a shambles.

With his cockpit hood closed, which was how he liked to fly, Coward could hear nothing of the fighting and firing ahead. He was discovering that for all its avowed individualism, the notion of man-to-man aerial combat was exaggerated. It was a strictly impersonal war.

Picking out the second clutch of Dorniers, and swinging in behind Clouston, Coward took a quick glance at his Nos 2 and 3, saw they were formating nicely, and attacked from astern. In the same moment the escort of 110s, with the advantage of height, timed their counter-attack.

Coward's No. 2, David Cox, was having an uncomfortable flight: the top half of his body was warm under the flying jacket while his pyjama-clad legs were half-frozen. But he saw the 110s coming and was just in time to break off his attack and turn towards them. He turned too violently and blacked out.

Coward was committed. Aiming carefully, he was about to jab the firing button when something struck him in the leg with roughly the force of a kick in a rugger scrum – painful, but quickly forgotten. Some clot, he thought, must have left a spanner or some such tool lodged under the dashboard, from where it had vibrated loose during flight and dropped on his leg.

Absorbed in the attack, he opened fire in almost the same instant, and immediately his guns jammed. In his fury he scarcely bothered to look down at his leg. Yet a numbness in the left ankle, or somewhere above it, eventually caused him to do so. He saw a bare foot on the rudder bar, and a jumble of ligaments. It took him a double-take to realize they were his own.

He was hurtling straight for the Dornier he had attacked, too late to avoid a collision. He ducked as the cockpit hood smashed into the underside of the Dornier, shattering the Perspex dome and ripping the whole structure clean off.

He was only half-aware what had happened, but obviously he had been wounded. He tried to slide away, found the Spitfire careering into a shallow dive, and eased back the stick. Nothing happened. As the Spitfire sank in a vertiginous spiral, with the air flow buffeting and disorientating him, he realized his controls had been severed.

Petrol was gushing into the cockpit, soaking his clothing and seeping through to his skin, causing extreme discomfort in the crutch and under the arms. The smallest spark would turn him into a human torch. The only thing to do was to get out.

He undid his safety straps — and the blast of air acted like a vacuum and sucked him straight out. But as he went his parachute pack snagged on an obstruction, glueing him to the top of the fuselage. Like a fly flipped over on its back he kicked impotently to regain equilibrium, then ceased abruptly as he felt his lower leg flapping against his thigh. Then without understanding how or why he was suddenly free of whatever had held him, and he found himself somersaulting through the sky.

With blood streaming from his half-severed leg he knew he must make a delayed drop, pulling the ripcord of his parachute below 2,000 feet, reaching the ground, and medical help, as quickly as possible. A slow descent and he would bleed to death before he got down. But he could not manage to stabilize his fall, and as he cavorted through the sky his foot, precariously attached to his leg by the ligaments and a splinter of bone, twisted agonisingly. The pain became excruciating; in a moment he would pass out. He would have to pull the ripcord.

As soon as the canopy opened and his descent steadied he

could see the blood pumping out of his leg. The trail swirled below him, bright red in the sky.

From the immense height at which he had baled out, not much less than 20,000 feet, he could only guess how long it would be before he touched ground. Ten minutes? Fifteen? Twenty? It scarcely mattered. He would be dead before then.

In the right-hand top pocket of his uniform jacket was a first-aid pack, and he reached for it. Across the pocket, pulling tightly now that the canopy was billowing, was the strap of his parachute harness. He had lost his gloves as he lay struggling to free himself, and already, in the cold, rarefied air, his fingers were numb. He scrabbled at the pocket in vain.

Before baling out he had unplugged the lead of his flying helmet from its socket, and the helmet was still clamped on his head, securely strapped under his chin. He had coiled part of the lead to shorten it, reducing the risk of getting it tangled up in the cockpit. If he could stretch that lead out fully, and wind it tightly round his leg above the knee, it would make an effective tourniquet.

Even when he tugged the lead to its full length it was not long enough for his purpose. He would have to take off the helmet. Loss of blood, which had already dulled his senses, had left him with a bemused contentment, and he had to concentrate hard to undo the strap under his chin, flexing his fingers to restore the sense of touch.

Winding the lead round his thigh, he put on a half-hitch knot and kept on tightening it, holding the leg up to his chin by the two ends of the flex. Soon the bleeding stopped.

Nellie Litchfield, Reuben's sister, out on the milk round, saw a parachute, still at a great height, drifting across the village. That would be one of those Germans, shot down by the RAF boys at Duxford. She did wonder for a moment if it might be one of the RAF boys; but she would hear all about it soon enough.

Despite its sequestered location, Little Shelford was always first with the gossip. Many of the villagers had found employment at the airfield, in the messes or as batmen and batwomen. Word went around with telegraphic speed.

At King's Farm, Joan was unwell, and Cynthia was bathing her baby. She saw and heard nothing of the scrap overhead. Meanwhile the wind had changed and her husband, having drifted near enough to Duxford to watch Spitfires landing there to re-fuel, realized he was being wafted in the opposite direction.

For a time he was again disorientated, and then he made out the variegated slates of the roof of the Red Lion Hotel at Whittlesford, and glimpsed the half-timbered façade. It was a favourite hostelry for the squadron. Nestling beside it was the railway station, the bridge over the track, and the adjacent signal box, looking for all the world like a toy railway.

He was coming down on the far side of the Newmarket-Royston road, with dramatic suddenness as it seemed to him. The ground soared to meet him, and he jarred the stump of his leg as he fell. Gathering his parachute canopy around him, he fashioned a pillow to protect his leg from the dirt.

He heard a panting noise, and looking round he saw a farmhand, a lad of about fifteen, running towards him excitedly, brandishing a pitchfork. The fool must think he was a Hun. He was in no mood to tolerate a prodding with a pitchfork. Forgetting the natural authority which stamped all he did, he employed every four-letter word he could lay his tongue to, determined to impress the lad with his Anglo-Saxon origins. 'Don't be an idiot,' he concluded, 'fetch me a doctor.'

Coward was incredibly lucky. An army doctor, on his way to breakfast from a nearby anti-aircraft battery, hailed by the farmhand, hurried across the field to tend to his leg. 'I've got just about everything I want in my bag except morphia,' said the doctor. When morphia proved unprocurable, Coward consented, by no means unwillingly, to make do with brandy.

He was not suffering from shock, or so it seemed, just the same deep lassitude and contentment which had threatened to overcome him many thousands of feet up, the effect, as he had fortunately realized, of the loss of blood.

It was the local baker, on his rounds, who learned via the bush telegraph that 19 Squadron had had a bad morning. They had lost three planes. Pilot Officer Ray Aeberhardt, aged nineteen and the youngest man on the squadron, trying to get his badly damaged Spitfire down, had flipped over on his back through unequal flap operation, and the plane had crashed and burst into flames. Aeberhardt had had no chance to get out. Two pilots had baled out, but only one, Frankie Brinsden, was known to be safe. The other, James Coward, was apparently missing.

Dramatic as the news was for the people of Little Shelford, the baker, living next door, was loath to impart it to the girls at King's Farm. Yet that, surely, was the first place he must go. He was banging on the door of the tradesmen's entrance when the family doctor, on a similar errand, but with more up-to-date news, was knocking at the front.

Cynthia Coward had finished washing and drying her sister's baby and had wrapped him in a towel. Hearing the knocking, she started down the stairs, still holding the baby. She had got rather more than half-way down the wide staircase, almost to the landing where the banisters turned towards the hall, when she heard someone calling to her from the back of the house. At the same time she almost collided with the doctor as he mounted the stairs. Thus it was that she heard the later news first.

The astonished doctor, trying to work out how his still-pregnant patient had acquired this new baby, stammered for a moment uncertainly. 'He's all right. He's been shot down but he's all right. They've taken him to Addenbrooke's Hospital.'

James Coward lost his left leg, just below the knee, but it never occurred to him that he wouldn't get back to flying. He had been serving in the same sector as Bader – and that fellow could fly with no legs at all. All he said, when he came round from the anaesthetic and saw Cynthia, was: 'Hello Cinnie. I shan't play rugger again.'

It was ironic that the squadron chosen to introduce cannon should suffer losses in consequence. But the point was made, and four days later, after another rash of stoppages, Spitfires mounted with machine-guns arrived and the cannon-firing Spitfires were withdrawn.

Many Battle of Britain pilots had more than one narrow

escape; almost daily they seemed to be cheating death. But most of them could recall one outstanding incident when survival seemed almost miraculous. This one was James Coward's. For Bill Smith the miracle came five weeks later, when the tailplane and rudder of his Hurricane were mangled and almost severed in a dogfight. Forced to fly at low level to avoid the German fighters he had been scrapping with, and knowing he would have no chance to survive a bale-out if his Hurricane became unflyable, he somehow nursed it 65 miles back to his home base at Northolt. His faithful bull-terrier – Joan's faithful bull-terrier – seemed that day to come bounding to meet him even more eagerly than usual.

The two sisters from Little Shelford were among the lucky ones. The men they had married so blithely in 1939 both survived the war. Both, too, kept up their flying, serving in the RAF with distinction until the time came for retirement.

THE BARGE-BUSTERS

During the second week of August the RAF's Photographic Reconnaissance Unit, the brain-child of an unorthodox but inventive and persuasive Australian named Sidney Cotton – he managed to manipulate Dowding into parting with two of his precious Spitfires for fast unarmed high-level reconnaissance – began to bring back negatives on which the photographic interpreters noted small accumulations of barges in Channel ports. These ports, in Belgium, Denmark and France, were conveniently situated to be departure points for a cross-Channel invasion. Photographed daily, the accretions swelled perceptibly in early September. At Ostend the count virtually quadrupled in two days, from 18 on 31st August to 70 on 2nd September. Another two days and the count reached 115; two more and it had passed 200. Similar multiplications, at Flushing, at Dunkirk, and at Calais, were noted by the interpreters; and on the evening of 6th September the Government ordered Invasion Alert No. 2, the second most urgent warning, a code meaning 'attack probable within three days'.

Invasion Alert No. 1, the highest priority – 'Invasion imminent, and probable within twelve hours' – followed almost immediately. It was stimulated first by the Luftwaffe's switch, on 7th September, from the attack on fighter sector stations to the bombing of London, and secondly by the further assembly of barges, now packed together so invitingly that their departure must surely be imminent, before bombing could reduce their numbers. Either that or the Germans were contemptuous of our bombing so far.

Soon the tally of barges exceeded a thousand, with hundreds more waiting their turn up river and canal. By 13th September the light bombers of 2 Group – the Blenheims – were joined by the so-called 'heavies' – the Wellingtons, the

Whitleys, and the Hampdens – until the whole of Bomber Command was absorbed in a concerted attack on invasion targets.

Spectacular damage was certainly done, barges at Ostend, according to one account, being up-ended, with fragments turning over and over in mid-air. 'Photographs taken next morning showed two stone jetties blown away to the water's edge; all barges vanished from the inner basins; and devastation over a mile radius.' These and other anti-invasion operations contributed to a second postponement of Hitler's original schedule – from 21st to 24th September.

It was on one of these raids that the third VC of the Battle was won.

8

The Shop Assistant from Paisley: John Hannah, VC

THE YOUNG SCOTS LAD selling men's footwear in the Glasgow shoe-shop, in the summer of 1939, was of a shy if cheerful disposition. One might have thought that he didn't have much to say for himself. But he was of independent mind, and he didn't intend to remain for long in his present trade. He had applied to join the Royal Air Force on a six-year engagement. And he meant to fly. He was not yet eighteen.

Son of a crane foreman on the Clyde, John Hannah was fair-skinned, blue-eyed, intelligent, and literate. But he had left school at sixteen, and he lacked the academic achievement that might have qualified him for training as a pilot or navigator. Five feet, five inches tall, and of slight build, he was more fitted for the role of wireless operator/air gunner, and it was in that capacity, on 15th August 1939, much against his parents' wishes (he had to get a doctor and a parson to sign his papers), that he joined up.

A year later, in August 1940, he had become a member of one of Bomber Command's front-line squadrons, waging a desperate battle against the forces Hitler was massing for the invasion of Britain. By mid-September he was a veteran of ten operational sorties against the enemy. And he was still not nineteen.

As the battle approached its climax, the spectacular role fell to the Hurricanes and Spitfires of Fighter Command. But Bomber Command was still charged with vital tasks.

'We're going over tonight after their invasion barges,' the group captain was saying. 'Our target is the port of Antwerp.

And we don't want any of this 8,000 feet stuff. 2,000 feet, you've got to get down to – lower still if you can.

'These are the basins where the barges are concentrated,' continued the group captain, indicating the target area on a series of maps and photographs. 'We've got to get those barges. Without them the Nazis can't invade us. There'll be a harvest moon tonight, and the barges will show up, so make every bomb count.'

Hannah's pilot, a twenty-six-year-old Canadian named Connor, born and educated in Toronto, had enlisted in the RAF in 1938 and was now a pilot officer. Of average height, and well built, with a fair pencil-line moustache, he had the good looks and carriage of a guardsman. A fortnight earlier he had graduated from second pilot to captain of aircraft. Hannah had quickly discovered that there were pilots who aggravated his own natural fears, and others who calmed them. He would have gone anywhere with Arthur Connor.

Dougie Hayhurst, the navigator, had joined the Air Force a few months before Hannah and was the most experienced man in the crew. A month earlier he had celebrated his twenty-first birthday. Recalled from leave for this series of operations, he was a young man of open visage and patent honesty who, when his bombs went astray, was not afraid to say so, and to write 'unsuccessful' in his log book. This was his thirty-ninth sortie.

'Buffy' James, the other gunner, was a robust extrovert, and something of a rough diamond. Short and thick-set, he looked a good man to have around in a tight corner. For weeks he had been flying as a leading aircraftman, drawing sergeant's tapes from the squadron office before flying, in case he was taken prisoner (he would have got better treatment), and returning them next day. He had been made up to sergeant that morning.

Every time Buffy James left his billet to go flying, his mates would rifle all the attractive items in his locker. When he turned up again next day they would feign disgust – 'Oh God, he's back again!' – and hand it all back. The squadron had been short of gunners, and one day he had volunteered. He could never think afterwards what had made him do it. He had had a good job in the parachute section. He was twenty-three.

Hannah's squadron, No. 83, was flying Handley Page Hampdens from Scampton, in Lincolnshire. One of the pilots was a young flying officer named Guy Gibson. He was on the detail that night.

After briefing, the crews wandered back to their Messes. This was the hour when dates made earlier were cancelled, and when those with a premonition wrote their last letters, to home and girlfriend. It was a strange sort of limbo, and Hayhurst, for one, found himself looking speculatively round the Sergeants' Mess, wondering who the unlucky ones might be. Almost always, there was somebody missing at breakfast.

Hannah, like most of the air crews, had left a permanent letter in his locker for his parents. Just in case.

Buffy James, still in the airmen's billets, called out as the truck drew up to take him to dispersal: 'Sorry, blokes – I shan't be back.' What made him say it he had no idea. He'd had no sort of presentiment. No sooner had he said it than he forgot about it.

The hot news on the radio, as the crews left the Messes, was that Fighter Command had had its greatest day: 165 German aircraft had been shot down. That was the figure – vastly exaggerated – that was computed that evening. The date was 15th September.

The crews went off to dispersal buzzing with excitement. The fighter boys had done their stuff. Now it was up to them.

Some of the crews, Connor's among them, felt a sense of elation. The weather was good, and although the invasion ports were well defended, they entailed no deep penetration. It would be a short trip, four or five hours at the most, and they'd be back for eggs and bacon by two or three o'clock rather than five or six. Tucked up in bed early, they'd be down to the Crown Hotel in Lincoln next day.

Connor was airborne at 22.28, the last aircraft to take off from Scampton. Of 173 bombers operating that night, 24 Hampdens were going to Antwerp, 15 of them from 83 Squadron. Connor would be one of the last on target. The lessons of concentration in time and space had not yet been learnt.

Hayhurst gave Connor a course to steer for Skegness Pier,

and from there they set course in a straight line south-east for the approaches to Antwerp, climbing to 5,000 feet. Once over the sea, Hannah and James tested their guns.

The Hampden fuselage was narrow, and Connor, from the pilot's cockpit, had a steep-angle view either side; but it was also of considerable depth, so much so that Hayhurst, in the navigator's position in the Perspex nose, was a long way below the pilot. When he wanted to go aft to the astro-dome, immediately behind Connor, he had to crawl under the pilot's seat. The astro-dome section also housed fire extinguishers and a portable loo.

Aft of the astro-dome was an aluminium fire-door, behind which was the radio cabin. Then came the two gun positions. Going into action, Hannah would climb up from his folding seat at the radio into the upper turret. The floor of the radio cabin was then stepped down two feet, the vertical section of the step being cushioned to provide a back-rest for James, who sat throughout in this lowest point of the aircraft, in what was contrarily known as the balcony gun position, or more colloquially as the 'tin'.

These two gun positions were roughly amidships and marked the limit of the cabin accommodation. Further aft the fuselage tapered off thinly before the twin tail unit finally crossed the T.

It was an uneventful sea crossing, and not much was said on the intercom. But when midnight came, Hayhurst reminded the crew that they would be in the Crown at Lincoln 'later today'. James's rich, fruity laugh reverberated in their earphones.

They made their landfall south of the island of Flushing and began the passage of the Westerschelde, a 50-mile stretch of water at the end of which lay Antwerp and their target. Connor began losing height steadily.

As they approached the target area they could see searchlights probing the sky, and a familiar excitement took hold of them, spiced as always with fear. There seemed to be no other aircraft about, and no flak. They must be the last plane in.

The ruled lines of the canals and the neat rectangles of the basins adjoining the Schelde were etched in indigo in the moonlight. The ranks of barges, packed like pencil-boxes beam to beam, were unmistakeable. 'My God,' said James. 'Look at that lot! They're coming over all right!'

Connor's clipped Canadian tones intervened. 'Bomb doors open.' Then he called Hannah and James. 'As we come in, let them have it.' Anything to put the ground gunners off their aim. The flak had started drifting up at them but it was inaccurate. Connor throttled back, still losing height, and began his bombing run.

Face down at the bomb-sight, microphone clamped to his mouth to pass instructions, Hayhurst realized that because of a slight tail wind they would barely get down to 2,000 feet before the drop. Then a shell burst under the starboard wing and threw them over to port.

For any ordinary target Hayhurst would have given Connor a small adjustment and carried on. But he remembered the words of the group captain at briefing to make every bomb count. 'We'll have to go round again,' he told Connor. Connor turned steeply to port and swung round in a wide arc for a second approach.

Down in the nose, Hayhurst was alternately standing up to get a general view and then lying face down to line up the target. But the German gunners were getting the range, and once, as Hayhurst stood up, a shell passed directly between his legs and out through the roof. Had he been lying face down it would have killed him. The clatter of jagged steel and bullets on the stressed metal skin of the fuselage blended with the rhythmic rat-a-tat of machine-gun fire from Hannah and James and the roar of the two 980 horse-power Pegasus engines to produce a cacophony of sound. Yet Hayhurst's voice still came through loud and clear in Connor's earphones.

'*Steady.*'

In this vortex of flak and machine-gun fire Connor was finding it impossible to keep the Hampden straight and level, and the target was swinging from side to side in Hayhurst's bomb-sight. The entire defences of Antwerp docks seemed to be concentrated on them in a continuous barrage that repeatedly scored hits on wings and fuselage, and once the Hampden was thrown almost to the vertical. Somehow Connor regained control.

'*Left left. That's it. Steady. Steady.*

As the toy boats moved forward in the wires of the bomb-sight, the Hampden came into point-blank range of the defences massed round the docks. Hannah and James, whose guns could only fire abeam and aft, could not reply to this barrage from ahead and below, though they blasted away at every gun position they saw.

'*Steady . . . steady . . . Bombs gone!*'

Hannah and James felt the unpleasant sensation of stall that always accompanied the release of the bomb-load. For a long moment it felt as though the Hampden had stopped altogether.

'Keep on going down,' called Hayhurst. He judged that they would escape the barrage more quickly at low level. Then, peering below, he saw his bombs burst fair and square on the target. 'That wasn't bad,' he reported.

In that moment, as Connor was closing the bomb doors, there was an explosion louder than anything that had gone before, followed by another of equal volume. Everything loose in the fuselage was hurled to one side, many small conflagrations broke out on board, and the floor of the radio cabin burst into flames.

An incendiary shell had scored a direct hit in the half-closed bomb compartment, setting fire to the strengthening wooden slats on the inside of the bomb doors. Other hits had blown gaping holes in the fuselage shell, and the rush of air streaming through these gaps was fanning the flames in the radio cabin.

Scorched by the heat from the furnace beneath him, Hannah jumped down from his turret and began beating at the flames with his gloved hands, meanwhile calling to Connor. 'The aircraft's on fire!'

The flickering brightness of the flames, shining through the Perspex window in the upper part of the fire-door, was reflected in Connor's windscreen. 'Is it very bad?' he asked.

'Bad. But not *too* bad.'

Hannah's anxiety not to alarm his pilot unduly led him into understatement. But Connor was scarcely deceived.

7a Eddy Egan
7b Ray Holmes

a

b

c

8a Four stalwarts of 501 Squadron at Kenley: 'Mac' Mackenzie, Gus Holden, Bob Dafforn, and 'Ginger' Lacey, standing behind sketches by Cuthbert Orde.

8b Air Marshal Sir Harold Maguire

8c Spitfire SL574 after belly-landing on the cricket-field near Bromley. After repairs to the pitch, the game goes on.

'Prepare to abandon ship. We're on fire.'

Although Hannah was in the midst of the flames, the blow-lamp effect of the airstream was driving the main jet aft, where James, in the lower turret, was directly in its path. He was being roasted where he sat.

Over enemy territory he always kept his parachute pack handy on top of the guns. But when the Hampden rolled to the vertical, the pack had been dislodged. Now he couldn't find it.

His anti-dazzle visor was already on fire, and in knocking it away he displaced his oxygen mask. He was practically breathing the flames, and he jammed it back on again. But he still couldn't find his parachute.

He glanced at his altimeter. 1,800 feet. Would he stand a chance without a parachute if he jumped into water? Impelled by the flames, he began kicking at the escape hatch under his feet. Suddenly it gave way. He was caught unawares, but as he fell through he grabbed the sides of the aperture and somehow pulled himself back in. In doing so, miraculously, he put his hand on his parachute pack.

The pack had fallen clear of the flames and he clipped it on. Then, literally burned out of his seat, he dropped through the hatch.

As he passed clear of the burning Hampden he saw monster-sized flak-bursts all round him. In his confusion he mistook them for barrage balloons. Not quite realizing that he had severed all connection with his crew he shouted a warning. 'For Christ's sake watch those balloons!' Simultaneously he pulled the ripcord.

Fully clothed in flying suit and helmet, Hannah felt himself well protected, and he continued to beat at the flames, first with his hands and then with his wireless log book, stamping on them at the same time wherever he could. But the fire in the bomb-bay was gaining. Electrical leads were sparking and igniting, and the aluminium sheet metal on the floor of the cabin was melting away, exposing the grids formed by the cross-bearers. The molten metal, blown backwards by the draught, was plating the rear bulkhead in ugly blotches and smears.

Unknown to Hannah, the wing fuel tanks on both sides had been holed; but he sensed that the fires near these tanks were the greatest danger, and he attacked them vigorously. Then he saw that the homing pigeons, which they always carried in case they came down in the sea, were threatened, and he pulled the cage clear.

He could not damp these fires down by himself. He had to get a fire extinguisher, and they were on the far side of the fire-door. Taking off his helmet, which was still plugged in and would restrict his movements, he grasped the handle of the door and pulled. It resisted all his efforts.

The fire had buckled the door-frame, and the door was jammed. Yet somehow he had to get through. 'We've got to live,' he told himself. 'We're not going to die.'

There was, for Hannah, one clear alternative – to plug his head-set back in, make a final call to Connor, grab his parachute, and follow James through the hatch. But all he thought of was extinguishing the fire.

As the heated metal expanded, the door tightened still further. Gripping the handle with both hands, Hannah pulled at it in tug-of-war style, and suddenly it gave way, precipitating him backwards into the fire.

Recovering quickly, he entered the forward compartment. Small fires had broken out there as well, but they were nothing compared with the conflagration in the Hampden's under-belly. He wrenched both main fire extinguishers from their clips and returned through the door.

The fire in the cabin had worsened, partly because he had doubled the draught by opening the door. He would have to close it again. If he was trapped he could always get out through the hatch. But as the fire intensified, he feared that the plane might blow up. He played the jet of one of the extinguishers on the core of the flames, then made for his parachute, which was still clipped in its stowage. He wanted to have it handy. Then he saw it was already on fire. There was no escape route for him now.

Afraid that his hair would be set alight, he replaced his helmet. But his exertions had made him breathless and he tore off his oxygen mask. At once he was choked by the fumes and smoke and was forced to replace that as well.

The heat and stench in the cabin were suffocating, and he feared he would lose consciousness. Somehow he had to get some fresh air. Dragging off his helmet again, he opened the tap of one of the spare oxygen bottles and breathed deeply straight from the tube.

'How's the fire going, Hannah?'

Once clear of the target area, Connor had given up taking evasive action, and now he was back over the Westerschelde, heading for home. But he had heard nothing from Hannah and James for some minutes. When he got no answer he called Hayhurst.

'Things have gone very quiet in the back, Dougie. Go and see what's happening.'

Hayhurst disconnected his helmet and began the claustrophobic crawl under the pilot's seat that would take him through to the astro-dome. When he emerged behind the armour-plating that protected Connor he found several small fires in that section. After stamping on the smaller ones, and cuffing the bigger ones, he grabbed at a small fire extinguisher only to release his grip at once – it was red hot. Turning to the communicating door, he grasped the handle gingerly and pushed. Like Hannah before him, he found it was jammed.

Peering through the eye-level window, he stared at a scene of unbelievable carnage. There were gaping holes in the sides and floor of the cabin through which he could see the ground, the aft hatch had gone and the rear gunner with it, and the whole radio compartment was gutted. But most appalling of all was the glimpse he got of Hannah. His flying-boots were just visible, and Hayhurst got the impression that he was standing in the flames. His body was out of sight, apparently slumped against the side of the fuselage, and Hayhurst could draw only one conclusion. Hannah must have died where he stood.

After a last despairing jerk at the door he went forward and stood behind Connor, tapping him on the shoulder and shout-

ing in his ear. 'James has gone. Hannah's dead. I'm going now.'
The sooner he went himself, the sooner Connor could follow.

He did not hear Connor's reply; but the gesture Connor gave
as he waved him on his way was abundantly clear. Repeating
the laborious process of crawling under Connor's seat, he
regained his position in the nose, lifted the hatch, noted that his
altimeter read 1,500 feet, and dived head first through the hole.

For a few moments, almost certainly, Hannah had been overcome by the smouldering, sweltering heat. But he was roused
from his stupor by a volley of uneven, staccato explosions. The
ammunition in the spare magazines had heated to the point of
detonation, and, in the cockpit, Connor could hear it cannon-
ing off the armour-plating at his back.

Hannah felt little benefit from the oxygen. Fighting back a
wave of panic, and still gasping for breath, he climbed back
briefly into his turret, swung the guns fore and aft, pulled back
the cupola, and for the first time for a good many minutes took
a deep inhalation of air.

Revived and strengthened, he returned to the fire and attacked it with renewed energy. When the fire extinguishers
gave out he beat at the flames again with his log book. Dripping
with sweat under his flying suit, he was forced to take off his
mask again, though he knew his face was scorched and his
eyebrows were singed.

As he smothered the flames his right foot slipped through a
gap in the cross-bearers, trapping his ankle. With a tremendous
effort he dragged his foot out. He had to get rid of the exploding
magazines, which were erupting all round him, but he daren't
step down into the tin, where the floor had collapsed. Forced to
climb up a second time to his turret for air, he realized that here
was the answer. Seizing the magazines in his gloved hands, and
pulling away the blackened woodwork of the bomb-doors, he
carried load after load up into the turret and tipped it over the
side.

As soon as Hannah had mastered one outbreak of fire,
another replaced it. The draught was still fanning the embers,

and ammunition went on exploding, but to Connor, watching the reflection in his windscreen, there was no doubt that the flames had died down. At one point he had actually felt – or imagined he felt – the heat on the back of his neck.

A final assault with his log book and Hannah found he was beating at dying embers. One charred relic that he recognized ruefully was his parachute pack, the canopy incinerated, leaving only a tangled mass of blackened rigging lines.

Despite his efforts to save them, the two homing pigeons were dead.

Connor had heard nothing from his crew for several minutes and he thought they must all have baled out. Now, as he called them tentatively on the intercom, he hardly expected an answer. But Hannah had put his helmet back on, and miraculously, as it seemed to Connor, his mild Scottish tones came up loud and clear.

'The fire's out, sir.'

'Good work. Is James all right?'

'He baled out, sir. His turret was right in the fire.'

Getting no answer from Hayhurst, Connor asked Hannah to go forward to check the navigator's position. Wrenching the door open again, Hannah crawled under Connor and worked his way down into the nose, wondering what he might find. He was relieved to see the open hatch and no sign that Hayhurst had been hurt.

He plugged his helmet into the nose socket. 'There's no one here, sir. We're on our own.'

'Bring the maps back, then.'

Hannah scrambled back to the main cockpit, and Connor turned to take the maps and check his course for home. As he turned, his eyes met an appalling sight.

Hannah's face was sooted and scarred, his eyes were narrowed and swollen, and his eyebrows and eyelashes had disappeared. The skin on his hands was parched and tautened, and although his leather flying suit appeared to have protected his body, it was so heavily carbonized as to be unrecognizable. How serious Hannah's burns were, and whether he would survive them, Connor could not tell, but he was greatly encouraged when the little Scots gunner gave him his usual cheerful grin.

While Connor flew the half-gutted Hampden back across the North Sea, Hannah stood behind him and helped him to navigate. They landed at Scampton at 03.05.

When they told their story, it was obvious that they had achieved something out of the ordinary. But what spoke infinitely louder than words was the state of the Hampden. There were holes in the aft compartment large enough for a man to crawl through, and the radio cabin looked like a burnt-out junk yard, perforated and skeletal.

Next day the group commander, Bert 'Bomber' Harris, viewed the wreckage at Scampton with the station commander, Group Captain Hugh Walmsley. 'This almost deserves the VC,' suggested Walmsley. Harris merely grunted, and his personal assistant, Michael Tomlinson (brother of David, the actor), formed the distinct impression that Harris was not in favour. However on the way back to his headquarters at Grantham Harris could not get the sight of that gutted fuselage out of his mind, and after a long silence he ruminated aloud. 'This will be an opportunity', Tomlinson heard him say, 'to decorate a non-pilot, as we have been urged to do.' Recruitment for the less glamorous aircrew roles needed stimulating. Pilots tended to get the honours and the publicity, and deservedly so, but even when Garland's navigator Sergeant Gray was coupled with him for the VC award after the attack on the Maastricht bridges in May 1940, Leading Aircraftman Roy Reynolds, the gunner, who died with them, was left out, causing lasting contention.

Back at Grantham, Harris drafted one of the most persuasive VC citations ever written. After describing the inferno in which Hannah had operated, he continued:

While flying clothing is to some extent fireproofed, the time quickly arises when, if it is exposed to such conditions, it will burst into flame. Had that occurred, Sergeant Hannah, as he must well have known, would have been burnt to death even had he then succeeded in getting out with his parachute. In the outcome the parachute was burnt with the rest of the equipment in the radio cabin. Here again Hannah no doubt realized that by delaying his own escape, he was depriving himself of his last chance of getting away from the aircraft if he failed to subdue the fire.

Through his action Sergeant Hannah very probably saved the life of his pilot. He certainly saved the aircraft, and he saved the pilot and himself from becoming prisoners of war.

I can only add that no one who has seen the condition of the aircraft can be otherwise than amazed at the extraordinary presence of mind and extreme courage which Sergeant Hannah displayed in remaining in it.

Three weeks earlier, as has already been related in Chapter 5, King George VI himself expressed his surprise that the exploits of the RAF that summer had not produced more recommendations for the VC, and both Nicolson's and Hannah's awards may owe something to the royal nudge. The Chief of the Air Staff later ruled that the VC should more often be given to men who displayed exceptional valour in getting themselves *into* great danger rather than in getting out of the kind of desperate situation latent in all air operations; but even then the phrase 'more often' provided a qualification.

Was Hannah lucky, then, to get the VC, as some have averred? Only in the sense that many VCs are earned and few are awarded. But it was certainly a help to have, on the one hand, the King's prompting, and on the other the inclination to decorate a non-pilot. Connor's coolness and skill in getting the Hampden home was another factor: had he not succeeded, the evidence might have been destroyed (as must have happened to many unknown heroes), and Hannah's actions lost beyond recall.

Had these actions, however courageous, been dictated solely or principally by self-preservation, Hannah could not have been recommended. It was true that at one point he had resolved that as a crew they must live. But it was abundantly plain from all he had done that he had thought least of all of himself. On 10th October 1940, three days after leaving hospital – where the King had visited him and told him of the award – and with the scars of his facial burns still clearly visible, he received his VC at Buckingham Palace.

At the same investiture, Arthur Connor was awarded the Distinguished Flying Cross. 'Most of the credit,' said Hannah, 'ought to go to him. People don't realize that while I was doing my best with the fire, he was sitting up aloft as cool as a cucumber, taking no notice of the flames.'

Connor was to live only another twenty-four days after the investiture. Returning on the night of 3rd/4th November from his thirteenth bombing sortie, again with a badly damaged aircraft, he failed this time to make land, coming down in the North Sea not far from the east coast. His body was discovered next day in an otherwise empty dinghy, with no survivors this time to tell the story. He is buried in the village of Brattleby, near Scampton, where he was living with his young English wife.

In 1978 a wartime member of 83 Squadron named R. G. Low visited Connor's grave and found the gravestone green with moss. 'I shall go and clean it,' wrote Low, 'because he was a very brave man.' Connor is the only wartime casualty buried at Brattleby, which might account for the years of neglect.

Hayhurst and James spent four years eight months as prisoners, but they survived the war, as did Hannah. Thanks to the surgeons, fears that he might be permanently disfigured proved groundless, and within a few weeks he was able to take on instructor duties at Cottesmore, near Oakham, where he met the girl who, in June 1941, was to become his wife. But the shy boy from Paisley never got back to full health and fitness. Even before the investiture he was receiving treatment for a chest weakness, and two serious crashes while he was on instructor duties set him back still further. In December 1942 he was invalided out of the Service with a 100% disability pension of £3. 7 *s*. 3 *d*. a week, plus the small annuity of £50 that goes with a VC.

For a man with a wife and child who was restricted to light work this was not a princely sum, and after making many personal appearances for service charities he accepted an offer of £25 to appear for a week in an Ipswich theatre, tell a few anecdotes, and talk modestly about his award. 'I just happened to be handy with a fire extinguisher' was his summary of his own part in the incident. But this led to 'Music Hall VC Needs Money' headlines and unfortunate misunderstandings, and he refused all further bookings. Hannah himself always strongly rejected any inference that he had been treated shabbily by an ungrateful government, or that he should have been treated as a special case.

For a time he went into a business partnership, running a cycle shop in Leicester; but on 7th June, 1947, leaving a wife and three daughters aged five, four and three, he died in a sanatorium of tuberculosis. He was still only twenty-five.

NERVES, NIGHTMARES AND
NEWCOMERS

Even during the Battle of France there were pilots who sweated every time they got into an aeroplane. Yet there were others who regarded their whole precarious existence as fun. After the workaday routine of civilian life from which many had escaped, the Services offered fresh mental and physical challenges and a level of job satisfaction to which they were unaccustomed. The fact that one was liable to get killed only enhanced the motivation.

Nerves were worst during states of readiness before scrambling. Once in the air the effort of flying and fighting left no time for reflection. Yet flying brought new depths of awareness, and a tension visible afterwards in the voluble and violently enacted pantomimes of gesticulation that relieved it.

The narrower the escape the greater the exhilaration and the bigger the joke. Even losses, once the shock was absorbed, could be the subject of levity. Sometimes they had to be.

The first glimpse of those black crosses could chill the stoutest heart, and long after landing a stranger to dogfights might be shaking with fright. But after three or four sorties – if they were survived – familiarity bred confidence, and a career of some length might be possible. Yet the average airborne life in the Battle was brief.

New pilots who escaped early death but failed to acclimatize were posted elsewhere, recognised as a menace to their colleagues. Veterans who lost their nerve and fell victim to nightmares, irritability and the 'twitch' were treated in the same manner.

Off-duty, pilots lived well, at least until fatigue overtook them. £4.7s.6d. a week (£4.37p) for a sergeant pilot was riches. Although temporarily unpopular after Dunkirk, young pilots in uniform could let their hair down outside camp boundaries and expect indulgence. At Kenley, on 501 Squadron, evening sorties to the Greyhound pub in Croydon were well attended, pilots piling into cars left behind by men who'd been killed. Lacking licence or insurance, and often sprayed with dope to camouflage them, they became squadron cars, pilots for the use of. 'A police car stopped us once,' recalled 'Ginger' Lacey, 'we were all very drunk, but they simply asked for our identity cards and then said "Drive on".' The police knew well enough what emergencies they might be called out for next day.

New pilots looked for kindred spirits, and if they drank at all they drank locally among themselves, graduating to the squadron 'thrashes' in due course. Many were denied the chance to achieve that degree of acceptance. Lacey has related how one young pilot officer (he himself was still a sergeant) arrived at Gravesend (before the Squadron moved to Kenley) on the morning of 2nd September 'in a beautiful red Bentley', watched by his new colleagues with a mixture of envy and compassion. How long would he last? To his question 'Where is my room?' he was told: 'No time for that, there's an aeroplane waiting for you. Report to dispersal.' His name was Pilot Officer Arthur Thomas Rose-Price, he was a brother of Dennis Price, the actor, and he was twenty-one. He was no novice as a flyer, but he had no experience of fighters. He had already served on a bomber squadron and as an instructor before volunteering for fighters when the pilot shortage became acute. From 17th August to 1st September he learnt to fly Hurricanes at a training unit, after which he drove to Gravesend. Stopping only to rummage for his flying kit, he found himself, soon after midday, facing a daunting baptism when the airfield was bombed in the course of a raid and he formed a part of a defending force outnumbered by four to one. The raid was successfully broken up, but not without loss; 501 Squadron escaped unscathed, but among the casualties was Tony Woods-Scawen. Then at tea-time another raid of equal strength, 250 fighters and bombers, was intercepted over Kent, and although German losses were heavy, 501 were not so lucky this time. Of four pilots who baled out, three got down safely although two were wounded, but the exception was Rose-Price, killed over Dungeness on his first day in the Battle, with no combat report to tell of what happened. His kit was still in the back of the Bentley.

Flight commanders tried to keep an eye on these innocents and advised them to 'stick close to me', but once a combat was joined they could watch out for no one but themselves. Nevertheless these youngsters, led as they were to the slaughter, did not follow like lambs. They made a significant contribution, sold their lives dearly, and in a gratifying number of cases survived.

9

Eddy Egan and the Climactic Four Days

'I'M NOT GOING TO HAVE YOU,' the squadron commander was saying. 'It's murder.'

He was talking to a fresh-faced, boyish-looking sergeant pilot who had just been sent to him as a replacement. The third week in August had come and gone and Goering was no nearer to victory. But in the fortnight that followed, Fighter Command lost 103 pilots killed and another 128 seriously wounded. Many more, having fought themselves to a standstill, were succumbing to battle fatigue. Yet, to the squadron commander, to expose the novice in front of him to the violent chaos of air combat seemed criminal.

On the far side of the Channel, the final air assault by the Luftwaffe, the assault that was confidently expected to clear the skies of the last of the RAF fighters and make the seaborne invasion little more than a formality, was about to begin. In fact, there was no shortage of aircraft to prevent it. The desperate need was for pilots. To plug the gaps, a new breed of ardent but inexperienced young men, traduced only a few months back by friend and foe alike as spineless and decadent, were being thrown into the fray.

Some, like the squadron commander quoted above (it was Mike Crossley at Biggin Hill), put it differently. The odds against them were stupendous. Half-trained and half-acclimatized, yet eager for combat, they were seen by hardened fighter pilots, men who had won their spurs at Dunkirk, as under sentence of death.

Barely out of school in many cases, and looking forward only a few months earlier to a seemingly limitless future, they refused to resign themselves to the obvious truth: that the threshold of life was likely to coincide with its exit. Pride in their maturity and achievement, manifested above all in the RAF wings on their tunics, and shared with mounting anxiety by their parents, was all too often to be only briefly enjoyed.

So transient was the involvement of some of these youngsters that even to their contemporaries their names and faces quickly dissolved beyond recall. Yet without them the Battle would have been lost.

Typical of these raw but dedicated youngsters was nineteen-year-old sergeant pilot Eddy Egan. Posted to Kenley, four miles south of Croydon, on 25th August 1940, he had already done a few patrols with a Blenheim night-fighter squadron; but he had never flown a single-engined fighter in his life. It was not just a question of learning how to handle a modern high-performance aircraft, infinitely faster and more powerful than anything he had flown before. He would have to coax and coerce it into combat, against machines of equal and sometimes superior performance, manoeuvred by skilful and aggressive adversaries. Yet Egan welcomed the move. Nothing could have suited him better. Something of a loner, he preferred the idea of single-seater fighters to the responsibility, in the Blenheim, of having the lives of others in his hands.

A short conversion course on to Hurricanes at Kenley, where he adapted well, followed by a crash course in aerobatics, formation flying, air firing and simulated dogfights at Prestwick in Scotland, improved Egan's confidence but did little to lessen his vulnerability. The RAF did the best they could for these young tyros in the time available: but for many, their first real taste of combat would be their last.

For Eddy Egan, then, and for others like him, arriving late to the Battle, the fight would hold little glory and less glamour. Although as dedicated to their task as any, the fame of the Douglas Baders, the Stanford Tucks, the Sailor Malans, was not to be theirs. Yet their contribution was to be no less crucial. Thrown in at the deep end at the climax of the campaign, they held the fate of their country, perhaps of very much more, in their hands.

Eddy Egan did not correspond to the cartoon-strip image of the fighter pilot — the silk-scarved public schoolboy, clearing the daylight skies with nonchalant arrogance before relaxing with his pint and his popsie in the local pub at nightfall. His was the story, becoming more typical as the casualties mounted, of the young engineering apprentice who left school at fourteen, who paid for flying lessons with his meagre pocket money, and who finally graduated to the RAF volunteer reserve as a sergeant pilot.

Born at Farningham, Kent, the county above which he was destined to fight, he was a shy, reserved lad, of medium height and slight build, whose interests outside flying were few. At school he had shown boyish pugnacity as a boxer, but a love of music, chiefly expressed in a modest proficiency with violin and guitar, had prompted more careful use of his hands. They were sensitive hands, as he was soon to show.

Ever since he could remember he had wanted to fly, and he had chosen a mechanical apprenticeship with the London Passenger Transport Board solely because they ran a flying club at Broxbourne for employees. At seventeen he went solo, and soon afterwards, in November 1938, he joined the volunteer reserve and from there, in 1939, was called up for war service.

If the outcome of the greatest of all air battles had to lie in the hands of nineteen-year-olds, Britain could not hope for better than Eddy Egan.

Returning to Kenley by train from Scotland with two other pilots, Pilot Officer E. B. Rogers and Sergeant Cyril Saward, to reinforce 501 Squadron, Egan was interviewed by his new CO, Squadron Leader Harry Hogan, on 11th September. Six months earlier, at Lossiemouth, Hogan, as chief flying instructor, had passed Egan out for his RAF wings. A glance in Egan's log book and the name and face registered, which did wonders for Egan's morale. Hogan kept the three newcomers together to form Blue Section of B flight, with Rogers leading. Meanwhile the squadron's top-scoring ace, 'Ginger' Lacey, took pity on all the newcomers, who he could see had little idea what they were in for, and decided they needed to be shocked out of any over-confidence or complacency. '*These chaps are trying to kill you,*' he warned. '*You've got to get them first – or get out of the way.*'

When one newcomer quoted the old adage about trusting in God and keeping one's powder dry, Lacey demurred. 'I don't know much about trusting in God. The Germans pray to the same God as we do. Put your trust in the training the RAF's given you. And in your luck. That's something you're going to need plenty of.'

Only twenty-three himself, Lacey felt a lifetime older than these raw youngsters who were so keen to play their part. And he feared for them. He already knew what it was to have a complete change of room-mates twice in one week. Since sergeant pilots lived four to a room, this was a chilling turnover. But while they lasted they were well catered for, in a large requisitioned private house just outside the main gates, their wants ministered to by a petite WAAF corporal named Jean Campbell.

For two days, 12th and 13th September, while Hitler and Goering fretted, heavy cloud prevented major engagements. And on the morning of Saturday the 14th Hitler postponed his invasion decision until the 17th. That for him was the ultimate day. His navy wanted ten days' notice, and the 27th was the last day on which the tides would be favourable. But like Goering he remained hopeful. 'Four or five days of good weather,' he said, 'and a result will be achieved.' Time was so short, though, that when the weather showed signs of clearing on that Satur-day afternoon, attacks on London, which the Luftwaffe had started a week earlier, were resumed.

At 13.50, on the eve of what was to become known as Battle of Britain day, Sergeant Egan took off from Kenley on his first patrol. He was keyed up, anxious, fearful of bungling his chance and letting himself and others down; but once he was airborne, and the formation was on its way, he felt exhilarated.

For Eddy Egan, that first sortie quickly deteriorated into an anti-climax. The squadron was recalled to base, and he had been airborne for only fifteen minutes. But after twenty-five minutes on the ground the squadron was scrambled again, and at 15.25 nine Hurricanes took off in three sections of three. One of the sections was Blue Section, with Rogers leading, Egan No. 2, and Saward No. 3.

It proved a traumatic baptism for Egan, and in a letter to his mother which he began next morning he described what happened.

We were patrolling at about 16,000 feet when the Jerries suddenly attacked us from behind and out of the sun, but one of our chaps spotted them coming and yelled a warning over the radio and we all ducked.

I went down in a steep aileron turn to shake anything off that might be on my tail, and I was about to pull out and climb up again when petrol began streaming into the cockpit, so I kept going down, intending to make a landing in a field. Then I discovered that one of my wheels was half down and jammed fast and I could not get it up or down.

I was floating round deciding what to do when the stream of petrol stopped, and a good job too, as the fumes were making me dizzy.

At first I thought the plane had been hit, but it turned out in the end that both petrol and wheel trouble were caused by the steep diving, in which I think I touched 500 mph. I headed back to the 'drome and flew low over the dispersal point to show them what was wrong, but I needn't have bothered because another Hurricane pilot who had seen me on the way back landed and warned the ambulance and fire engine.

I brought the plane in to land with one wheel up and one half down and pancaked on to the deck, bending the propeller. The CO complimented me on the landing, though, so everything is OK.

He had been airborne for an hour and twenty minutes and the time was 16.45.

If his hand was shaking slightly when they handed him a cup of tea and a sandwich at dispersal, no one seemed to notice. And he had no time to brood. At six o'clock that evening he was airborne again, still flying Blue 2 but in a different machine. This time the enemy was not sighted. The Luftwaffe was husbanding its resources for the morrow.

Dawn on Sunday 15th September in southern England was not unseasonal. It began with a dew-laden ground-mist that clung tenaciously to the North Downs. But by ten o'clock the sun was shining on the high plateau of Kenley airfield with unusual penetration for early autumn, and the light, reflected by banks of broken cloud, was of startling clarity, giving a sense of heightened perception. In the far corners of the plateau the parked Hurricanes, hump-backed and squat, stood deceptively still.

No one knew it as yet, but this was to be the day of destiny. An impatient Hitler had given Goering four days to complete the annihilation of Fighter Command. Goering had convinced Hitler that the Luftwaffe could do it.

At 10.50 on that Sunday morning, mass formations of bombers building up over France were detected by British coastal radar stations, and at precisely eleven o'clock the two squadrons of Hurricanes based at Kenley, Nos 253 and 501, were called to readiness.

Down the hill from the airfield, at Whyteleafe Parish Church, the congregation, swelled by the sobering events of recent weeks, but still dressed for summer, were assembling for Matins. But there were no church bells to summon them. The bells would only peal as a warning: a warning that the anticipated invasion had begun. But that would only happen if the young men at the top of the hill, already donning their bulky yellow life-jackets, failed in their task.

With his instinct for drama, Winston Churchill had chosen this day to pay a visit to Keith Park at his group operations room at Uxbridge. 'I don't know,' said Park, 'whether anything will happen today. At present it's all quiet.' They did not have long to wait.

When news of the build-up over France reached him, Park guessed what the enemy tactics would be. A strong force of bombers as bait, heading for central London, with an escorting shield of fighters packed around and above them, waiting to pounce on any attempt at interception. Eight days earlier more than four hundred Londoners had been killed in the biggest raid yet. Although combat between fighter and fighter for its own sake was still discouraged, the basic threat to the capital could not be ignored.

The first wave of bombers consisted of a hundred sleek, twin-engined, twin-tailed Dorniers. By 11.35 they were crossing the English coast. Fifteen minutes earlier the two Hurricane squadrons had taken off from Kenley. Vectored east towards Ramsgate, they would clash with the Dorniers about half-way.

Eddy Egan was again flying as Blue 2 with Saward on Rogers's left, completing one of four sections of three aircraft from 501 Squadron. Shortly before midday Harry Hogan, who was leading the Kenley Hurricanes, sighted the great phalanx of Dornier bombers approaching over Maidstone. They were a thousand feet above his own formation.

'Bandits. Twelve o'clock. Angels 16. '

As five squadrons of the Duxford Wing under Douglas Bader wheeled in from the flank to attack the close escort, it fell to the Kenley Hurricanes, with two other Hurricane squadrons, to attack the bombers head-on.

Churchill, watching the chessboard presentation on the operations table at Uxbridge, noted that all Park's squadrons were airborne.

'What reserves have we got?' he asked.

'There are none.'

On this culminating day, every available Fighter Command squadron, brought up to strength by a hundred Egans, had been committed to the Battle.

Opening up so as to clash over a wide spread, bringing as many guns to bear as possible, the Hurricanes tore into the advancing Dorniers. The ideal would be for the whole formation to open fire simultaneously. Then, as elements of the bomber formation broke up, each pilot would select his own target.

'Stand by to open up. Stand by. Now!'

For Eddy Egan this was the greatest moment of his life, his first real taste of combat, the moment when all he had learned in a few hectic days would be put to the test, the moment that, if he lived, he would never forget. The combat that followed is fully documented: but none of the reports are more vivid than Egan's own account, added to the letter he had begun that morning, which he still did not have time to complete. Coupled with what he wrote in his combat report, it reveals a young man of scrupulous honesty – honest above all with himself.

Two or three hours ago I had to stop writing this letter as we had to rush off to intercept some Jerry bombers making for London. I shoved the letter in my pocket and so it came along with me.

We met the bombers at about 15,000 feet on their way in. They were coming head-on so most of us put our noses straight up in the air as we were below them, and sent up a barrage of bullets for them to fly through. Bits flew off one or two, but then we had to break away as the Jerry fighters were coming down and had us at a disadvantage.

I dived down to about 9,000 feet and joined up with some other Hurricanes which had also dived down. Sergeant Saward was amongst them so we went along together behind the rest. Suddenly someone shouted 'Look out!', so we split up and dived away once again.

I went down about 3,000 feet and had just levelled out when I spotted an Me109 with bright yellow wings and nose below me on the port side, overtaking me and diving for a bank of cloud. I dived after him, and just as I got on his tail he banked left towards another cloud. But as the Hurricane can turn faster I got in a quarter attack with a four-second burst. He then increased his rate of turn and made for yet another cloud, but I increased mine and got in another five-second burst before he reached it.

He dived into the cloud and I followed, but then I lost sight of him. So far nothing seemed to have happened to him.

As I came out of the cloud on the far side I looked round

184

for him but could not see him anywhere. Then about five to six hundred yards in front of me and slightly below I saw what looked like an Me109 going down in flames with a parachute floating down a little above it. I followed the plane down and saw it crash in a field.

Saward too watched the plane falling in flames and saw the parachute go down, so the victory would be confirmed. But was it the plane that Egan had attacked before it went into cloud or was it another? Egan himself recognized the doubt. 'I don't know if he was mine or if he had been shot down by someone higher up. Anyway I have made out a combat report and will just have to wait and see if anybody else claims it.' No one did, and on the combat report he was credited with destroying his first 109.

When he got back to Kenley he learned that Hogan and a Belgian pilot named Van Den Hove were missing. Hogan, it emerged, had baled out safely and would be returning to the squadron that night, but Van Den Hove was dead.

Although the number of German aircraft shot down that day was greatly exaggerated at the time, they were the heaviest losses sustained by the Luftwaffe in a single day for a month. On that Sunday, sixty German aircraft were shot down over Britain for the loss of only ten Allied pilots killed, although many others were shot down or wounded. But the precise figures were of little significance. What mattered was whether the remaining pilots of Fighter Command, with their teenage reinforcements, were still in good spirit, and whether the losses were too much for the Luftwaffe to bear.

Shrugging off the humiliation of 15th September, Goering still clung to the belief that Fighter Command was on the verge of collapse. He had two more days, 16th and 17th September, to prove it.

High winds and heavy rain restricted the Luftwaffe to isolated sorties on the 16th, but 501 Squadron was at readiness from dawn. 'We went up early this morning,' wrote Egan, continuing his letter to his mother, 'and blow me if it wasn't cold at 20,000 feet.' At one o'clock the squadron was stood down. 'We will be able to have a lie-in until 8.30 am tomorrow,' he forecast in his letter, which he now had time to complete. 'It may not sound very late, but for the last two or three mornings we have been warming up our engines at 5.30.'

In the midst of these adventures he did not forget that, with the night bombing of Britain's cities continuing, his family in south London might be in even greater danger. 'I hope the old bombs haven't been coming too close; but I have watched the flashes at night and it hasn't looked too healthy around that direction.' That night, on his way down the hill for an hour's relaxation at the Whyteleafe Tavern with another nineteen-year-old sergeant pilot, Tony Pickering, he posted the letter.

Pickering, too, had served an engineering apprenticeship and meanwhile joined the VR, and the two found much in common. As short of experience of the bright lights as they were of aerial combat, they confined themselves, on these rare moments of freedom, to a single drink, or at the most two. These two nineteen-year-olds, called upon to play their part in one of the decisive battles of history, were shy boys who, although pairing off readily enough with the WAAFs in the pub in the evening, or in the air-raid shelter at night, never got further in these encounters than holding hands.

Next day, Tuesday the 17th, Goering changed his tactics. His plan was for a single major attack, mounted by successive waves of Me109s, using a handful of bombers as bait to draw up the Hurricanes and Spitfires. The British knew what was afoot and again avoided combat where they could, but they could not ignore the bombers. Spitfires from Biggin Hill and Hornchurch were ordered to attack the top fighter cover while the Hurricanes went for the bombers at medium altitude. But it didn't quite work out as planned.

At 15.10 that afternoon, twelve Hurricanes of 501 Squadron, accompanied by eight of 253, left Kenley with orders to patrol over Tenterden at 17,000 feet. Hogan was leading, and the formation included Ginger Lacey, Tony Pickering and Eddy Egan. There was broken cloud from six to eight thousand feet, but above that the sky was clear. In orbiting Tenterden the squadron involuntarily drifted in high winds over Ashford.

There, at 15.35, while circling at 18,000 feet, they were jumped by 109s.

'Break!'

Hogan shed about 3,000 feet as the formation disintegrated around him. All four section leaders, Hogan, Lacey, Rogers, and a young pilot officer named Hairs, lost touch with their wing men. Hogan chased two 109s and damaged one of them. Hairs, looking apprehensively up, down, left, right, and behind, saw an aeroplane coming in to join him and thought: 'That's my No. 3 – he's coming in too fast and he'll overshoot.' Then he recognized the gaping hole in the propeller boss and knew it was not a Hurricane but a 109. There was a flash as a cannon shell flew from the gaping hole. It went through his starboard wing and sent his Hurricane into a spin.

Tony Pickering kept up his dive down to 5,000 feet, where he found himself below cloud somewhere in the Maidstone area. Soon he was joined by another Hurricane, Z for Zebra, which he immediately recognized as Egan's. He had seen Egan in the thick of the mêlée but he had evidently come through unscathed. Egan gave Pickering the thumbs up, and the two men grinned at each other, then flew alongside, looking for the rest of the squadron.

'501 from Red Leader. Reform over Maidstone. Angels 13.'

Lacey heard Hogan's call and headed for Maidstone. On the way he spotted fifteen Messerschmitts 5,000 feet below him. Diving straight at them, he misjudged his speed and finished up in front of their guns. They promptly shot him down.

Pickering and Egan were still keeping loosely together when they heard Hogan's call. Climbing to the north-west, they had just emerged through the cloud-tops when, behind him to the left and some 3,000 feet above, Pickering saw what he took to be three Spitfires, identifying them from their rounded wing-tips. The 109s, in his brief experience, had squared-off wing-tips. Then with a shock he saw the now familiar black crosses under the wings. Either he had been mistaken or this was a later mark of Messerschmitt.

Before he could shout a warning the leader of the German section opened his throttle and dived at the two Hurricanes, selecting Egan as his target and locking in behind him. Pickering could see the flashes from the German's guns. Peeling away, he climbed steeply to meet the attack. But out of the corner of his eye he saw the cloud below him turn crimson as Egan spun down.

The German pilots simply pulled back on their elevators and soared away from Pickering, content with what they had done. There was nothing left for Pickering to do but recover his composure and see if he could help his friend Egan.

Far below, through a gap in the cloud, he could see a plane spiralling down. It could only be Egan. There was no sign of a parachute, and the machine was leaving a trail of smoke. He feared that Egan was still in it and that he had probably been killed instantly by that first point-blank burst.

He himself had escaped by the merest chance. Had the German section leader gone for him instead of Egan, he would be down there now.

The Hurricane had stopped spinning and was diving vertically. It was falling into a wood. Pickering lost it against the dark background, and he didn't actually see it go in. But he saw the puff of the explosion.

Minutes earlier Egan's mother, Grace Egan, sitting in a south London cinema with her daughter, had pointed to the clock over the front exit and said: 'We shan't see Eddy again.'

Of the other members of the squadron, all made their way back to Kenley except Lacey. He baled out safely, for the second time in a week, and got a lift back to Kenley in an ambulance late that night, where he found Jean Campbell waiting up for him. But for Egan she waited in vain.

When Pickering landed he reported having seen Egan crash in a wood somewhere south of Maidstone. The Observer Corps also reported seeing this and several other planes go down, but with dozens of aircraft, German and British, falling out of the sky almost daily, searches were sometimes perfunctory.

When a single-engined fighter plunged vertically to earth it often disappeared altogether. All that might then be recorded was: 'Wreckage lies buried. Nothing visible. Pilot dead.' In Egan's case the position of the crash, deep in a hundred-acre wood 'somewhere south of Maidstone', was never pinpointed. After fourteen days he was struck off the strength and his death was presumed.

When he flew his first sorties on September 14th, the German pilots were reporting less effective opposition, and it had seemed to Hitler and Goering that one last effort would wipe Fighter Command from the skies. By the 17th, the day Egan was killed, they knew better. 'The enemy air force is still by no means defeated,' wrote the compiler of the War Diary at German War Headquarters. 'On the contrary, it shows increasing activity . . .

'The Fuehrer therefore decides to postpone "Sealion" indefinitely.'

There had been no choice for Fighter Command but to throw in the nineteen-year-olds, and what they lacked in experience they made up for in audacity and flair. For four climactic days Eddy Egan helped to stem the tide of Nazi conquest and hurl it back from whence it came. Typical of the unnamed heroes of the battle, he contributed more than his share to victory. Indeed, like many others, he contributed his all. But his four-day vigil in the skies of southern England, in the company he had wished for, was to prove decisive. The Battle of Britain had been won.

Six months later, Tony Pickering was asked if he could re-pinpoint Egan's crash. He got his maps out and made a fresh report, but he heard nothing more.

For thirty-three years, Egan's family resigned themselves to the fact that he had no known grave. His name was recorded on the Runnymede memorial, and in the Memorial Chapel in Westminster Abbey, and that was distinction enough. Then in 1973 his mother, by this time in her mid-seventies, hearing criticism of the activities of wartime aircraft recovery groups, on the grounds that their work was ghoulish and that the dead were better left undisturbed, spoke up. 'I'm a mother,' she told her local paper, 'and I would like my boy found.'

Among those stimulated by this forthright opinion was a

twenty-six-year-old south London aviation archaeologist named Tony Graves, and in the months that followed he gathered together an intricate mosaic of evidence that would have done credit to Scotland Yard. On 11th September 1976 he took a mechanical digger into the recently grubbed-out Daniel's Wood, midway between Smarden and Bethersden, on the edge of the Kentish Weald, and there, as by this time he was confidently expecting, he turned up the remains of Eddy Egan and his plane, raising it from the spot where it had lain for thirty-six years.

Vindication of his meticulously researched evidence came on 25th February 1977 when Dr Mary Patricia McHugh, at the conclusion of an inquest at the coroner's court at Croydon, confirmed that the remains discovered were those of Edward James Egan, killed on active service. The circumstantial evidence on which this conclusion was based, however, although carrying absolute conviction in the coroner's court, did not satisfy the rigid standards applied by the Ministry of Defence, and this proved a stumbling block when it came to granting Sergeant Egan the military funeral that his surviving next-of-kin were anxious he should have.

For the Ministry, the process of elimination – place and time of the crash confirmed by eye-witnesses and agreeing with RAF and ARP records; plane certainly a Hurricane; no other Hurricane pilot missing on that day still unaccounted for – was not enough. They demanded incontrovertible proof of identity, and no identity tags or engine or airframe numbers were found.

After much heart-searching the family decided that, rather than forgo the right to a military funeral, they would accept an anonymous burial. When, on Wednesday 8th March 1978, Sergeant Edward James Egan – the family, at least, were satisfied that the remains were his – was buried in the RAF plot of the Military Cemetery at Brookwood, near Woking, with full military honours, the inscription on the grave, poignantly and, for some, distressingly, was that of 'an unknown airman'.

In a way, perhaps, this was not a completely unhappy outcome. For more than thirty years the name of Eddy Egan, to all but a few relatives and friends, had indeed been unknown, and he could now be said to represent the countless other anonymous airmen who surrendered their identities and their lives to win the Battle of Britain. But Tony Graves, for one, was not satisfied. Excavating again in what was left of Daniel's Wood, he dug deeper this time, finally uncovering serial number plates that provided the absolute confirmation the Ministry of Defence had demanded.

For the Egan family, whose anguish over many months and years may be imagined, the correction on the gravestone at Brookwood brought a long-awaited and long-deserved serenity.

THE KILLER INSTINCT

At an early stage, pre-war RAF fighter tactics, which called for tight formation flying, were found to be cumbersome in the heat of combat, and more open formations became the norm. But the air battle was never static, first one side and then the other revising their tactics and forcing the opposition to adjust. Park's original instructions were for the Spitfires to tackle the high-flying Messerschmitts while the Hurricanes were left free to deal with the bombers, but he amended this when Goering doubled and trebled his escorts and made penetration of the fighter screens more difficult, both types then being directed against the bombers. This instruction was revised again in early September when it was found that the closely-grouped machine-guns of the Hurricane were more effective against the bombers than the staggered guns of the Spitfire.

Park was forced in this phase to employ bigger concentrations of fighters when major attacks were threatened, but he never embraced the 'big wing' theory. Strategical arguments and tactical changes meant little to a pilot involved in a scrap, where, if he survived the initial clash, his focus frequently narrowed into a gladiatorial one against one. Then it was the killer instinct that counted. Some pilots had it in greater measure than others, and indeed there are veterans who will say that there were only two types of pilot in the Battle, those who had this instinct and the 'passengers', the men who might perform bravely enough when combat was forced upon them but who wouldn't obsessively seek it.

The instinct was not the preserve of any one type, nor did it depend on experience or the lack of it, or even on a particular skill. Thus some of the most thrilling deeds were accomplished by comparative beginners.

The Day They Bombed Buckingham Palace

'DEAR MUM,' *wrote the evacuee child, 'we had an air raid yesterday and the village is wiped out. I am the only evacuee still living. Will you let me come home?'*

This imaginative appeal, the work of a homesick child, was symptomatic of the nostalgia that had already brought many thousands of evacuated Londoners back to the capital in the early months of 1940. But that had been during the 'phoney' war, before Dunkirk, and before the Nazis singled out London as the main target for their bombers. The evacuee child was writing in September, at the height of the Battle of Britain. London under siege had an irresistible magnetism, and the great exodus of a year earlier was not repeated.

Not all those attracted to London like moths to a flame were Londoners. 'The hottest tip', cabled London correspondent H. R. Knickerbocker to his New York newspaper, 'is that the German invasion of England is coming tomorrow, Friday.' Friday the thirteenth. He added that there was no place on earth where he would rather be.

Also drawn towards London were the men of the fighter squadrons, the pilots whose task it was to defend it. One such was a young Merseysider named Ray Holmes, Sergeant R. T. Holmes. With his Hurricane squadron, No. 504, he had been moved south from Scotland to Hendon to relieve a tired and depleted squadron.

'Arty' Holmes, as he was nicknamed because of his initials, had joined the RAF volunteer reserve – the VR – when it was first formed in 1936. He was entrant number fifty-five. Fair-haired and blue-eyed, he was under five feet seven inches tall, but he had a strong, athletic frame which disguised his lack of inches. In civilian life he had earned another nickname – 'Twink', because of his bustling energy.

It was this capacity for rapid movement which surprised his colleagues in the Oxton Cricket Club, one of the strongest in the Merseyside Competition, where he made a reputation as a hitter. He once hit five sixes in an over. He was also famed for his speed and throw-in from the outfield – until Frank Dennis, the former Yorkshire swing bowler, ruled that he field in the gully, to pouch the catches that, beforehand, had kept going down off the great man's bowling.

On leaving school Holmes, after a shorthand and typing course, joined a Birkenhead newspaper as a reporter. He was following in his father's footsteps, and when his father formed his own news and reporting agency in Liverpool he joined him. Meanwhile at week-ends, when he wasn't playing cricket or rugby or tinkering with his three-wheeler sports car, he was learning to fly. Mobilized at the outbreak of war, he was eventually posted to 504 Squadron.

From September 6th 1940, when the squadron began operating from Hendon, their task was that of long-stop, backing up the forward squadrons who were intercepting the raiders nearer the coast. They were to challenge any bombers that got through. They made their first interception in the late afternoon raid of 7th September, when London's dockland was set ablaze.

After helping to break up several large bomber formations in the next few days, Holmes's squadron was released at dusk on Saturday 14th September, and that evening he visited London's West End. Londoners took little notice of the sirens during the day, work continuing in office and factory until roof-spotters sounded urgent warnings. Buses continued to run until bombs actually fell. But at night it was different. Arriving by Underground on the Northern Line, Holmes and his companions found women and children sprawled on the platforms, selecting their pitches for the night. Not all of them had been bombed out.

For the price of a three-ha'penny ticket, the troglodytes were making certain of safety. Children were doing their homework on tables fashioned from luggage, men played cards on the same surfaces, buskers and acrobats entertained.

After having a few beers – the cinemas closed at nine so there was no chance of taking in a film – Holmes and his pals set off back to Colindale. By that time women and children were sleeping, undisturbed by the thunder of the trains, and the platforms were covered with bodies to within a few feet of the edge.

Next morning, Sunday 15th September, Holmes's flight was brought to readiness at dawn. The cloud of the previous day had dispersed and it promised to be a fine late-summer's day. Yet the radar stations were reporting no activity and the squadron was stood down.

Feeling scruffy after the early call and the long wait at dispersal, Holmes took a bath. He was luxuriating in it shortly before eleven o'clock when someone banged on the door.

'Quick, Arty, there's a flap on – we're on readiness!'

There was no question of saying 'I'll be down in a minute.' He leapt out of the bath and, with no time to towel himself properly, he slipped into a blue open-necked sports shirt with no badges of rank, pulled on his blue RAF trousers, and ran out to the transport, socks in hand. Someone pulled up the tail-board after him and the truck moved off.

Pulling his socks over his wet feet was a struggle as the Humber brake bumped and swerved round the perimeter track, but he managed it before they got to dispersal, at the northern end of the grass field. As they piled out of the truck the loud-speakers were already ordering them to scramble.

Holmes ran shoeless to his locker in the dispersal hut, grabbed his flying boots and his Mae West lifejacket, and chased out to the plane, where the ground crew were waiting for him. They had already started the Merlin engine and put his para-chute harness in position in the cockpit, and they helped him on with his safety straps as he climbed in. His helmet, already connected to the oxygen supply and the radio, was hanging on the reflector sight, and he grabbed it and rammed it over his hcad, covering his bedraggled, unkempt hair. Even for Holmes it had been a breathtaking flurry of activity, and he was still wringing wet.

Ahead of him he saw the squadron leader, John Sample, already taxiing towards the far end of the field for the take-off into wind. He waved 'chocks away' and tucked in behind the other Hurricanes as they flattened the grass with their slip-stream.

Hendon was a small airfield with no runways and they would be taking off over houses. They needed a good take-off run. There were twelve Hurricanes altogether, six from 'A' Flight and six from 'B' Flight, and once airborne they would form two parallel lines, each line in three sections of two, one above the other. This was the formation they had found gave them most room to manoeuvre. Holmes was leading Green Section in 'B' Flight – the weavers, keeping a lookout astern.

The take-off itself was a shambles, each pilot ramming his throttle fully open to keep up, but as they climbed over the airfield they settled into formation. The orders were to orbit the airfield at 12,000 feet and await instructions. Soon they were climbing in tight formation through banks of cumulus cloud.

At 8,000 feet they emerged from the cloud into a clear, sunlit sky. Orbiting at 12,000, Holmes, drying out rapidly, shivered with cold.

The airfield itself, camouflaged and partly obscured by cloud, was impossible to keep in view, but Holmes picked out the silvery expanse of the Welsh Harp. Then they were ordered to climb to 17,000 feet and given a course to steer to the south-east to intercept a raid of at least thirty Dornier bombers with strong fighter escort heading north-west for London. About a hundred Dorniers had started out, but radar warning as they formed up over France had alerted the defenders and the moment they crossed the English coast at Dungeness they had to fight off successive swarms of Spitfires and Hurricanes numbering over 160 in all. Among the last to intercept, in their role of long-stop, were Sample and the pilots of 504 Squadron.

'Tally-ho!'

From the rear of the formation, flying straight into the sun,

Holmes could see very little. High above the Dorniers he expected to see the promised fighter escort of Me109s, but if things went according to plan they would be taken care of by the Spitfires, leaving the Hurricanes to deal with the Dorniers. It was still his job, for the moment, to guard his own squadron from the rear.

Ahead and slightly to the right, crossing their track diagonally, he saw what might have been a flock of seagulls, until they loomed incredibly quickly into focus and he experienced a choking sensation that told of the intensity of his excitement. He recognized all too readily the bulbous noses, like a festering blister, and the pencil-like fuselages, tapering to the delicate, toy-like twin tail. As predicted, they were Dornier 17s, a breakaway group, still forming a disciplined, symmetrical horde and heading for central London; it was the job of the Hurricane squadrons to break them up.

Holmes had come late to the Battle and he had escaped the squandering of personal resources inherent in the thrice-daily scrambles week after week that had taken such a toll of the veterans. For him, flying was fun and the prospect of combat exhilarating. For the moment, though, he looked to his leader.

John Sample, the squadron commander, was an auxiliary, one of the privileged week-end flyers, whose background and circumstances were far different from those of the impecunious VRs. But this shy, gentle, friendly man, who had enquired about Holmes's family and his journalism as well as his flying experience when he first arrived, seemed more like an accountant than a war leader. In fact he had been an estate agent. But he had already won a DFC as a flight commander in France before Dunkirk, and he inspired Holmes with confidence.

On this wing of the phalanx of bombers, the starboard wing, there were twelve Dorniers in close formation in four sections of three. Sample turned so that he appeared to be approaching at right angles, but he allowed the bombers to pass ahead of him, leading the squadron into a quarter attack, with the Hurricanes nicely placed at an oblique angle slightly astern. As the attack developed and the Dorniers, closing up for mutual protection, held their course, the Hurricanes would swing in from the starboard quarter until they were almost astern and the deflection became virtually point-blank. Just before they passed astern they would break away.

The massed Dorniers occupied a sizeable area of sky, and as the Hurricanes wheeled in, skidding and sliding as they jostled for position, the pilots in the leading sections picked their targets. One after another they said to themselves 'That one's mine'. The configuration of the Dorniers became ragged, but they put down a fierce barrage for the remaining Hurricanes to fly through. By the time Holmes, the last one to attack, had fired his first burst, the scene ahead of him was kaleidoscopic and he was uncomfortably aware of a blistering return fire.

Now to break away without exposing the Hurricane's belly to the Dornier's guns. As the Dornier disappeared from his sights to the right he did a vertical bank to the left and used bottom rudder to skid away before closing the throttle and diving steeply to make good his escape.

So far as he knew he had not been hit. He eased the Hurricane out of the dive, then climbed steeply, intent on rejoining his squadron for another attack. But as he looked round, the sky was bewilderingly empty. His colleagues, it seemed, had vanished. So had the Dorniers.

What had happened was that an unforecast headwind, gusting to ninety miles an hour, had forced the German fighters, whose range at best gave them only minutes over London, to abandon their charges and head back to France, leaving the Dorniers to cope as best they could on their own. What began as a pitched aerial battle quickly deteriorated into a series of individual interceptions. Beset either by Spitfires or Hurricanes, the Dornier crews swung round in a left-hand turn through 180 degrees, dropped their bombs at random over south London, and began what was to develop, under inspired leadership, into a brilliant fighting withdrawal.

Holmes, having lost contact, had no knowledge of this. Alone in the sky, as it seemed to him, he looked around anxiously for enemy fighters. Finally, wondering if any of the bombers had got through, he turned westwards. Far below he spotted a tightly-formed section of three, still stubbornly heading north-west for central London. This section had been on the extreme right of the formation and had become detached when their colleagues began their 180-degree turn. Much the same thing had happened to Holmes.

There was no one about to intercept these three bombers but him. These, he said to himself, are mine. He hoped there were no 109s about to interfere.

A last searching look round and he opened the throttle and dived, aiming to overtake the Dorniers on the port side, keeping for the moment out of range of their guns. A lone attack from astern, he thought, was out; it would expose him to the guns of all three. Instead he picked the wing man on the port side and angled his approach so that, as he came within range, the other two Dorniers couldn't fire at him without peppering their colleague.

He started firing at 400 yards range and was closing in steadily prior to side-slipping astern when smoke from the Dornier blackened his windscreen. He was so nonplussed that for a moment he just sat there, not knowing what to do next, but instinctively he shut the throttle. It wasn't smoke on his windscreen, it was oil, a treacly deposit that must have gushed from the Dornier's glycol tank. As the airstream dispersed it he was suddenly aware of a monstrous shape right in front of him, filling his windscreen, blotting out the sky. It was the Dornier, slowing down rapidly, and he was about to collide with its tail.

He rammed the stick forward and felt the shoulder-straps of his safety harness cutting into his collar-bone. Without them he would have gone straight through the roof. As he grazed under the Dornier's belly he thought he would hit the propellers. Then he realized with a shock that one of the propellers was stationary. He – or someone before him – had put the engine out of action, which was why the Dornier had faltered.

When he looked back, it was gliding earthwards. But the other two were still holding their course.

He would try the same trick on the other wing-man. Crossing over to the starboard side, he opened the throttle to draw level. Judging the angle as before, he crabbed in for a quarter attack.

His first burst was right on target, and a tongue of flame licked back from the Dornier.

Someone was trying to get out of the back of the plane, presumably the gunner. Holmes was aware of a white flicker of silk in front of him, but then for a moment he lost control. Correcting hurriedly, he realized that the German gunner's parachute canopy had draped itself over his starboard wing, leaving the gunner trailing helplessly below.

He had not stopped to think, before this moment, of the men in the Dorniers. His attitude was entirely impersonal, and he was concentrating on avoiding their gunfire and preventing them from getting through to central London. Now, with his own aircraft in danger, he thought only of the poor devil suspended under his wing.

He jerked the stick from side to side but nothing happened. The chap was still there. Using hard right rudder he yawed the Hurricane in a skidding movement to starboard. He saw the canopy billow slightly; then it fluttered briefly, slid along the leading edge to the wing-tip, and was gone. He had lost sight of what had happened to the Dornier.

The third Dornier – the leader – was still plodding on towards central London, apparently undeterred, speed unchecked. A flash of involuntary admiration turned as quickly to anger. The pilot must be hell-bent on some suicidal mission, like bombing St Paul's, or even Buckingham Palace. Both had been hit in the last few days.

He felt as though he was facing some resolute wing three-quarter on the rugger field, legging it for the line, with himself the last hope for the defence. He might be concussed himself in the tackle, but he had to bring his man down.

Oil was still seeping over his windscreen, and he wondered if it was coming from his own engine. Someone, in the previous attacks, must have hit him. That, with no one else about to help him, made the destruction of the Dornier all the more urgent. His engine was running roughly and the rev. counter was starting to surge. His ammunition, too, must be almost exhausted. He would have to bring this one down quickly. He thought he knew how to make sure.

Overtaking the lone Dornier, he turned to make a frontal attack, aimed at the pilot, not quite from head-on, but slightly to port, offset by twenty degrees. That would give him a chance to break away before there was any risk of collision.

The closing speed must be something like 500 miles an hour. He had only seconds left, and his thumb felt for the firing button. As the bomber came fully into focus he pressed it. He had reached lethal range when his guns sputtered to a stop.

He was hurtling straight for the Dornier. In a moment he must break away. Why didn't the German pilot give way? But he deviated not one inch from his course. There was only one way to stop him now. Hit him for six.

It was something he had never so much as dreamt of before, a split second revelation, quite unpremeditated. Minutes ago he had exerted all his strength to avoid a collision. Now, in the heat of battle, with his own machine crippled, and in a desperate bid to smash this inexorable invader before it broke through to its target, whatever that was – and he was more than ever convinced that some precision attack must be intended – he shunned the instinct which bawled at him to turn away before it was too late.

How flimsy the tail-plane looked as it filled his windscreen, as fragile as glass! The tough litttle Hurricane would splinter it like balsa-wood.

He no longer felt cold. As he aimed his port wing at the near side fin of the Dornier's twin tail, he was sweating.

He felt only the slightest jar as the wing of the Hurricane sliced through. Incredibly, he was getting away with it.

The Hurricane was turning slightly to the left, and diving a little. He applied a gentle correction. Nothing happened.

The dive steepened, and he shut the throttle. He jerked the stick violently now, forwards and sideways, but control was still lacking. His angle of dive increased almost to the vertical.

As the cloud-tops rushed to meet him he was conscious of his speed in the dive – four to five hundred miles an hour. 8,000 feet! Already he was halfway down.

He unlocked and slid back the hood. The cloud had thickened around him, blindingly white, hurting his eyes, and the screech of the dive was deafening. He undid his safety harness and tried to climb out.

The buffeting was so violent that for a moment he thought his head must be near the propeller. Yet something in the cockpit was holding him back. He had forgotten to unplug the radio lead to his helmet. He climbed back in to release it, and this time, as he struggled blindly out, eyelids clenched against the blast, the air-stream caught him with renewed savagery and draped him with arched back over the hump of the Hurricane fuselage. In doing so it snagged his seat-type parachute on some protrusion inside.

The Hurricane was diving vertically now. He could still see nothing, but he knew time was short. Kicking frantically, he thudded his boots against the control column. His boots were wrenched off by the effort, but as the Hurricane lurched into a spin he was catapulted out by centrifugal force.

Immediately behind him was the tail fin of the Hurricane, and as he was blown backwards it struck his right shoulder. He was scarcely aware of it at first, but the shoulder went dead.

The sudden cessation of noise, and a sibilant hush, told him he was out. He felt for the D-ring of his parachute, but he sought it in vain.

'Where is it? *Where is it?*'

At last his fingers closed around it. But when he tried to pull it, he could exert no pressure. His right arm, paralysed by the bruised shoulder, was useless.

He was talking to himself now, desperately, urging himself to act. He was still clutching the ripcord ring in his right hand, unable to move it, and the ground must be horribly close. What could he do?

He grabbed his right wrist with his left hand and tried to push his arm across his body. It didn't seem to work – but then there was a sudden explosion above him. For a moment he thought that with the speed of the fall his chute had collapsed. Then he found himself spinning like a top and swinging like a pendulum, all in one motion.

He reached up and grabbed the rigging lines, and that stopped the spin. He was still swinging as if on a trapeze.

Gyrating above him, in lazy slow-motion, but uncomfortably close, was the Dornier. Twisting and turning like a falling leaf, it was exuding a bright jet of flame. Its wing-tips were severed, and its tail-plane had snapped where it joined the fuselage and was falling separately. Below him, nose-down and falling vertically, was his Hurricane.

He did not know it, but his scrap with the stricken Dornier had been witnessed by hundreds of Londoners through a break in the cloud, smack over Hyde Park Corner. Knots of people were pointing excitedly upwards as Dornier, parachute and Hurricane, in reverse order, came tumbling out of the sky.

Holmes had seen nothing of the ground since the start of the scrap. Now, as he looked down, he saw that he was swinging back and forth across a vast expanse of railway lines. He estimated that they were less than 300 feet below him. Each set of parallel lines had a third line beside it. The tracks were electrified. He was drifting over the junction approaches to Victoria Station.

To the right of his lateral swing was a three-storey block. They were flats, facing Ebury Bridge Road, and their roofs were steeply raked. If he could only control his drift he might just manage to clear those flats on his next sideways swing and drop down in the road.

Within a few seconds he could see that he wouldn't quite make it. He was going to hit the roof, and he looked for some handhold or foothold. It was better than being electrocuted.

For a moment, as he touched down, the parachute supported his weight and he tip-toed on the roof in his stockinged feet like a marionette. Then the air began to spill out of his canopy.

Clawing dizzily, with nothing to grip, he started to slide and roll down the slates. Snatching in vain at the gutter, he recoiled from the vertiginous drop that stretched out below. After all he'd gone through he was now about to fall off a roof and break his neck.

A terrific jolt halted his progress. He had fallen feet first into an empty dustbin, and his toes, puppet-like again, were barely touching the ground. His parachute had wrapped itself round the top of a drainpipe and arrested his fall.

He freed himself from his harness and stepped out of the dustbin. Around him, noonday London seemed dormant, its week-day clamour strangely subdued.

He was in a garden at the back of the flats. Two girls appeared in the garden next door and he vaulted the fence to greet them. Elated at his succession of escapes, from the plane, from electrocution, and from falling off the roof, he embraced and kissed them both. 'I hope you don't mind,' he said, 'I'm so pleased to see you.' They seemed equally pleased to see him.

Inside the flats he telephoned the squadron to say where he was, then turned to see a Home Guard sergeant, middle-aged but almost twice his size, approaching with an iron bar. 'Hold it!' he called. 'I'm on your side!'

'Would you like to see your aeroplane?'

'Yes – where is it?'

'Just up the road.'

The Hurricane had come down at a cross-roads and missed all the buildings. It had plunged fifteen feet into the ground and was only just visible.

Bits of the Dornier had meanwhile landed in the forecourt of Victoria Station. Two bombs had fallen on Buckingham Palace, one on the Queen's apartments and one in the grounds; they failed to explode, but they more than justified Holmes's anger and his readiness for personal sacrifice. There were no casualties, though to what extent this was due to Holmes's heroic defence remains an imponderable.

The Dornier was the first German aircraft brought down over central London, and in breaking up it shed chunks of metal over a wide area. Meanwhile a crowd gathered where the Hurricane had gone in, and they gave Holmes a spontaneous cheer, patting him on the back and pumping his hand. Then the Home Guard sergeant, seeing that Holmes had hurt his shoulder and strained his side, walked him to Chelsea Barracks to see a doctor. It was his second excursion that day in his socks.

On the way they were joined by a civilian who proved to be a Press Association reporter. 'I'm a reporter too,' said Holmes, adding slyly, 'but I'm off duty at present. My father has a news agency in Liverpool. Could you get a message to him?'

'Sure – what do you want me to say?'

'He may hear I've been shot down, and he might think I've had it. Just tell Dad I'm OK, will you?' Remembering that it was a Sunday, he gave the reporter his home telephone number.

After he had seen the doctor at Chelsea Barracks they opened the bar in the Sergeants' Mess and it was drinks all round. 'Do you always fly dressed like that?' they wanted to know.

Someone came in with a message. 'There's a lady outside wants to see you.'

They gave him a pair of brown army plimsolls, and he walked across the parade ground to the gate. A frail looking woman of indeterminate age, perhaps still in her thirties, was waiting for him.

'Was it you that came down in that plane?'

'Yes.'

She held out a flat-fifty tin of cigarettes. 'Will you take these, as a present?'

'No, really – I couldn't possibly.'

She was neither smartly nor shabbily dressed. Just an ordinary Londoner.

'Please do. My baby was outside in his pram. They're for making your plane miss my baby.'

He couldn't tell her that at 17,000 feet, and all the way down, the last thing in his thoughts had been her baby. Nor did he like to tell her he was a non-smoker.

'Tell Dad I'm OK!' said the headlines in Monday's papers, proving that the Press Association man did his job. Holmes was interviewed on BBC Radio, received 132 letters, got a handsome leather toilet set from the Residents of Ebury Bridge Court, a metal airscrew blade from the Dornier (pockmarked with cavities from his frontal attack), and a signal informing him that 'Her Majesty the Queen has graciously commanded an audience at Buckingham Palace with Sergeant Pilot R. T. Holmes.' He was all set to go to the Palace when another bombing raid drove the Royals out of town, while he himself was temporarily grounded because of his damaged shoulder and sent on sick leave, and the squadron was transferred to

Bristol following a devastating raid on the Filton aircraft factory. So he never did get that audience.

His wartime flying career, though, remained active and colourful. He spent five months in North Russia in the autumn and winter of 1941 with the Hurricanes of No. 151 Wing RAF, was for eighteen months an instructor at the Central Flying School, and in the last year of the war flew Spitfire XIXs on photo reconnaissance over Germany. After the war he returned to news, sports and court reporting, running the agency – as he still does – when his father retired.

Post-war research into German records has led to some surprising reappraisals of the action in which Holmes was involved.[1] To begin with, the Dornier he pursued so tenaciously – it was DO172 of KG 1/76 – had come under attack shortly beforehand, one engine had appeared to catch fire, two of the crew had baled out, and the Dornier had been claimed as 'destroyed'. But since the British claims that day totalled 185 against actual German losses of not more than 60, the 'escape' of this Dornier was far from miraculous. A burst of flame and smoke from an engine might not deter a crew from pressing on to its target, nor might the fact that two of their number had baled out. Such incidents certainly occurred over Germany, the records of Bomber Command being illuminated by stories of depleted crews in damaged aircraft refusing to turn back. In any case there is incontrovertible evidence that Dornier DO172 continued on its course for central London, and that the *coup de grâce* was administered over Hyde Park Corner by Sergeant Ray Holmes.

From Lieutenant Robert Zehbe, pilot of the Dornier, through observer, mechanic and wireless operator to tail gunner, this was a determined and experienced crew. They had taken part in the initial daylight raid on London on 7th September and on other major daylight raids before that. The two who had baled

---

1. See the account by Peter Cornwell in *Battle of Britain Then and Now* (an After the Battle publication, first published 1980).

out – wireless operator and mechanic – came down in the Dulwich/Sydenham area, consistent with a heading for central London, and were taken prisoner. The observer and the gunner were probably wounded – even perhaps killed – in the earlier attacks, as they appear to have made no attempt to get out before the Dornier broke up. The pilot, although wounded – possibly by Holmes in his frontal attack – baled out and landed at Kennington. There he had the misfortune to be set upon by a group of women enraged by the carnage of the previous week. They handled him so roughly that they may well have contributed to his death the following day.

What target did this Dornier crew have in mind? What were they briefed to attack? There is no evidence that Buckingham Palace or any other prestigious or historic building was designated. Battersea was the target area, and Zehbe's seems to have been the only bomber that morning to penetrate north of the river. Why did it do so?

Pictures taken of the falling bomber, as already mentioned, show, from top to bottom, the Dornier, Holmes on his parachute, and Holmes's Hurricane. There is no trace of a second parachute, so Zehbe must have baled out beforehand. How long beforehand? Is it fanciful to suppose he had already baled out before Holmes's frontal attack, and that Holmes was firing at a pilotless, unmanned machine? If this was so, who jettisoned the bombs?

An explanation could be that when the Dornier broke up in mid-air, plane and bombs parted company. Had they not done so, the impact when they reached the ground together might have caused incalculable damage. This alone would more than justify Holmes's lethal attack. It should be remembered, though, that Zehbe's landing at Kennington was not inconsistent with a bale-out seconds before the Dornier broke up. The strong headwind, blowing him back whence he came, would have accounted for his grounding at Kennington.

All this was academic to Holmes, who recently promised that another time he would take a cameraman and a historian along with him! But he did subsequently learn something of personal interest – that his escape that day had been narrower even than he had thought. The oil that had drenched his windscreen had come not from the first Dornier's tank, nor from his own engine, but from an experimental flame-thrower mounted in the Dornier's tail, which the crew had switched on as he side-slipped astern. Fortunately for him it had failed to ignite.

There was one other piece of unfinished business – the unfulfilled audience with the Queen. When Holmes was presented to the Queen Mother at Guildhall with other Battle of Britain survivors in September 1980 he was sorely tempted to remind her of the incident, especially as she chatted informally with each one of them.[1] Would she conceivably remember that she had once invited him to the Palace? Somehow he just couldn't bring himself to ask. 'I could not help wondering,' he says, 'but, I mean, dammit – after forty years . . .'

Recently, while filming for a Battle of Britain TV programme, Holmes was taken to the flats behind Victoria Station where he landed by parachute all those years ago. 'Would you believe it!' he writes. 'We met up *quite by accident* with a man who as a boy aged eleven saw my parachute open and watched me hit the roof from a hundred yards away. He was flabbergasted when he found who he was talking to because he said the memory of the incident was so vivid it would remain with him all his life. He simply could not believe he was talking to the man on the "chute".'

1. As he relates in *Sky Spy* (Airlife, 1989).

GOERING KEEPS UP THE PRESSURE

Despite the postponement ordered by Hitler, and a noticeable decrease in activity in the invasion ports, there was no certainty that Operation Sealion would not be reactivated before winter set in, and indeed throughout the remainder of September and for much of October, and even spilling into November, Goering kept up the pressure in daylight, while the night blitz intensified. Changing his tactics, he turned to high-level sweeps by big fighter formations in which bombers might or might not be present, setting a problem of identification for Park that was eventually solved by small standing patrols whose task it was to interpret the raid and warn in good time of what was afoot. Industry – and especially the aircraft industry – was singled out for attack, and the massive fighter sweeps sometimes brought heavy Fighter Command casualties, especially amongst the Hurricane squadrons. Goering also began equipping his fighters with bomb-racks and employing them in short-range raids in the south-east, and it was on one of these raids, over Kent on 7th October, with the Spitfires hard pressed to cope, that the Hurricanes got their revenge.

'. . . *it is the opinion of many pilots that the deliberate act of ramming was entirely out of character with the RAF pilot of 1940*', wrote Francis K. Mason in *Battle Over Britain* – and this is undoubtedly right. Ray Holmes, as related in Chapter 10, had tried his luck in a crisis and got away with it. More cold-blooded was the incident involving a Hurricane pilot on 7th October.

The 'Mad Bugger':
Kenneth 'Mac' Mackenzie

KENNETH 'MAC' MACKENZIE, a twenty-four-year-old Ulster-man, circled the turgid pool of water off Hythe where the German fighter pilot had ditched. The plane, a Messerschmitt 109, had tipped forward on its nose, and Mackenzie could see the tail and fuselage sticking out of the sea like some huge cormorant searching for fish. The plane was slowly submerging and he wondered if the pilot would escape. Sure enough he glimpsed signs of movement and watched the pilot scramble clear and inflate his dinghy.

It was the end of another 109, thought Mackenzie cheerfully, and the end of another enemy fighter pilot's involvement in the war. The ditching was too near the Kent coast for any poaching attempt by the *Seanotflugcommando* – the German air-sea rescue service: one of our own lifeboats or launches, thought Mackenzie, would get there first. Because of this, he did not grudge the German pilot his escape.

He had caught up with this intruder when it had already been crippled, but he had fired his guns, and he was pretty sure he had administered the *coup de grâce*. Yet the incident left him unsatisfied. Two days earlier he had been credited with a 'damaged' and a share of a 'probable', and he supposed he might be accorded a half-share in this one. But that wasn't good enough. He wanted one of his own.

The dogfight he had recently left to chase this 109 was still going on high above him, and he could hear the controller reporting more bandits and giving fresh vectors. He still had some ammunition left, so he opened the throttle of his Hurri-cane and began climbing to rejoin his colleagues, making for the Dover-Folkestone patrol line at 23,000 feet. Meanwhile, unprotected as he was, he kept a strict watch on his tail.

For Mackenzie, the war had taken him just where he wanted to be. A sports and sports-car enthusiast right from his under-graduate days at Queens University, following an engineering apprenticeship with Harland and Wolff, he was a founder member of the North of Ireland Aero Club and had gone solo at Newtownards after only six and a half hours' instruction. Temperament, and such experience as he had, fitted him for fighters rather than bombers, and after walking out of an interview with the Auxiliary Air Force in a rage at the tomfool questions he was asked (anyway they would have trained him on bombers), he was accepted gladly by the Volunteer Reserve for training on single-engined machines. Mobilized in August 1939, he finished his training with an above-average assess-ment and finally reached an operational Hurricane squadron – No. 501 at Kenley under Harry Hogan – at the end of September 1940, just in time for the final phase of the Battle.

Good-natured and ebullient, Mackenzie shrugged off the handicap of a considerable stutter, a combination of bluntness, non-conformity and irrepressible humour making anything he had to say well worth waiting for, as his new colleagues delightedly discovered. His high spirits marked him down as something of a tearaway, and it was after his second operational flight with 501, when he got the 'damaged' and a share of the 'probable', that Hogan passed a judgement on him that was meant to be flattering. 'Congratulations, Mac,' he said, 'You're a mad bugger . . . glad to have you with us.' It was a soubriquet he was soon to justify.

For that day's operations, 7th October, things had gone badly at first, the Spitfire squadrons being hard pressed in improving weather to check a continual flow of Me109s. Around ten o'clock, however, two squadrons of Hurricanes from Kenley, Nos 501 and 605, had clashed with a flight of seven 109s, two of them out in front and five in a bunch about a mile behind. They had completed their task and were racing south-east at 25,000 feet, tilted earthwards in a shallow dive to gain acceleration, praying for a clear run home. This was the scrap from which Hogan and Mackenzie had got separated. ·

It had begun with Hogan leading 501 north and then west at 20,000 feet along the north bank of the Thames. Soon they were boxed in by a pattern of smoke-puffs from their own ack-ack. Anything flying west towards London was suspect, and the gunners were taking no chances. The other Hurricane squadron, led by the dynamic, pocket-sized Archie McKellar, flew along the south bank, avoiding the worst of the ground fire. The two squadrons held their position, two miles apart, 605 keeping slightly above and to the rear.

When the seven German pilots saw the British squadrons they realized they were being confronted head-on. Having completed their mission they were anxious to avoid further combat. Beyond the Channel lay their home airfield and sanctuary, less than twenty minutes' flying away. They had thought they were almost safe. They hadn't realized that their every move had been plotted on radar, and the intervention of the Hurricanes was a shock. They were not accustomed, either, to fighting at a numerical disadvantage, as now seemed likely.

Reacting swiftly, they made for the space between the two squadrons. But as the two 109s out in front hurtled into the gap, Hogan turned his squadron towards them. Caught in an aerial pincer movement, the two leading pilots elected to split the opposition. One pulled up and climbed to the right of Hogan, the other dived for cloud. Hogan, with Mackenzie following, had gone for the climber, with the end result, many thousands of feet below, that Mackenzie had just witnessed. ·

In their absence the other six 109s had been heavily engaged as they sought to fight their way out. In the thick of the scrap was a sergeant pilot who had fought with 501 all summer and scored more heavily than anyone: this was Ginger Lacey. Now he got another. So did a second of 501's aces, Flight Commander Gus Holden. A young pilot officer from 605 named Muirhead also got one before being shot down himself, baling out and landing in a wood. But Flying Officer N. J. M. Barry, of 501, was shot down and did not get out.

All this Mackenzie was to learn some time later. Now, back at 20,000 feet, and on his own, he heard the controller giving the position of another enemy formation. This lot were on their way in. All he had to do, if they stuck to their plotted course, was to lie in wait for them.

Presently, out to sea, he saw them – eight black specks about 2,000 feet above him, swimming into focus. Again they were 109s. There were four in a box out in front, then a vic of three, and finally a single aircraft guarding the rear. There was no doubt who was outnumbered now.

In spite of the carefully placed rearguard, that, he decided, would be his direction of attack. He turned away from them towards the sun in a wide sweep, hoping they hadn't seen him, and then turned back at them from the south. As he banked in behind them he lost the advantage of the sun, but he was still 2,000 feet below them and the chances were they hadn't seen him.

He was thoroughly enjoying himself, far more than in the earlier scrap. There had been so many Hurricanes milling about then that picking a target for himself had been difficult. Now he had eight 109s to choose from, and it looked as though they still hadn't seen him.

He kept his Hurricane in a gradual climb towards the rear vic of 109s. The chap who was doing the weaving had swung away to the left and he had a clear run.

He pulled up beautifully, just underneath the formation, less than 300 yards behind. This was the best angle of all! According to the book, you ran your sights along your target's under-belly, and one burst was enough. But as he pressed the firing button he was conscious that something had flown across his line of sight. It was the weaver. Furious, his aim at the formation spoiled, he opened up at the weaver. He could tell at once from the smoke and oil that he had hit him in the glycol tank.

The other seven Messerschmitts broke formation at once. He had been creeping up on them undetected, and but for the weaver might have picked off a couple before they got after him.

Like a good many Irishmen, Mackenzie was a man of great good temper who was nevertheless subject to occasional bouts of righteous indignation. Some things made him very angry indeed. Bloody angry. He was bloody angry now.

As the crippled 109 half-rolled and dived for the coastline, Mackenzie half-rolled after it, pushing his control column hard forward and following it closely. Down they went together, through several banks of cloud, the German pilot taking no evasive action but relying on his speed to shake off the Hurricane.

Mackenzie kept in line astern, not losing an inch, immaculately synchronized, like an aerobatic pair in a display. He fired several bursts and saw his bullets streaking into the 109. Still it kept steady in the dive. The German pilot didn't flatten out until he crossed the English coast, after which he skimmed the water at less than one hundred feet.

Now Mackenzie closed to two hundred yards and fired a long and murderous burst into the German plane. Glycol sprayed back at him from the 109's radiator and smoke poured from the engine, but somehow the pilot kept on.

He was so near the German plane he could almost have poked his guns into it, and he throttled back. If it blew up in his face with his next burst it would blast him out of the sky.

He hardly had any need now to line up his sights, but he did so yet again to make sure. The German was taking no evasive action and the 109 almost filled his windscreen. This time it would disintegrate in mid-air.

He pressed the firing button, waiting for the juddering of his eight machine-guns, holding the Hurricane down. The nose always lifted as you fired the guns. Nothing happened. He pressed again, frantically. Still nothing. He was out of ammunition.

Half-blind with vexation, he pulled away to starboard and glared across at the German. He had a sudden feeling of nakedness. Suppose this crippled pilot had enough left in his locker to hit back?

Surely he was too badly winged. The pilot must be wounded or he would have taken evasive action. He would simply be intent on crossing the Channel. And in a matter of minutes he would make it. Plane and pilot would live to fight another day. That was something he was determined to prevent. He had been happy enough, a few minutes earlier, to see a downed German escape with his life. But this man, if he survived, would be back tomorrow and the next day, and that was unacceptable. Somehow he had to force this stubborn fellow down.

The lack of aggression that the German had shown encouraged Mackenzie in a bold and near-lunatic plan. He began by pushing his throttle forward until he was level with the 109, then tucking his wing-tip in close, staring across into the cockpit. As his adversary met his eye he signalled to him to lose height and turn through 180 degrees.

The German stared back at him but made no sign. Then he looked straight ahead again, an 'eyes-front' which plainly said that he intended to take no notice, to go on heading for home. The only thing Mackenzie could do was to frighten him.

He began to 'buzz' him, skidding underneath him and diving across the top, keeping well clear of his guns, then formating on him and waving him down. Most of the time the German stared stolidly ahead.

Time was on the German's side. The French coastline was already visible. Mackenzie was getting more vulnerable with each moment, and he was running short of fuel. In a minute or so he would have to turn back. What more could he do to make the German give way?

The possibility that he might collide with the German while he was buzzing him had occurred to him, but this would be an unintentional impact that would finish them both. What about a planned collision, in which he would aim to destroy his enemy but escape fatal damage himself?

What could he knock him down with? Was there anything he could hit him with without destroying the flying ability of his own machine? What about his undercarriage? He didn't need it while he was airborne, and he could belly-land when he got back. It was an idea. He would try to knock the 109 down with his undercart.

He climbed to 500 feet and put the undercart down. Then he

tried to close again on the German. But disappointingly he wasn't overtaking him. Indeed the German pilot was pulling away. With his undercart down he had lost speed to such an extent that the crippled 109 had the Hurricane's measure. Quickly he selected undercarriage up and overhauled the German again. He must think of something better than that.

All his anger now was gone. He was left with a cold determination to complete the destruction of his enemy. There was only one thing for it. He would have to risk knocking him down with his wing.

The German would be at a disadvantage because to him the collision would be unexpected. Even if he suspected and feared what might be in Mackenzie's mind, the moment of impact would still come as a shock.

What hope had Mackenzie himself of getting away with it? He must plan the impact to give himself the best possible chance. First he must keep his propeller clear, also his tail unit. That, the tail unit, was also the German's weakest point. He must jerk his wing-tip down on the German's tail unit. The Hurricane wing was strong, and it would never snap at the wing-root. He might lose some of the wing-tip, but he had seen Hurricanes fly minus several feet of wing. The tail unit of the average fighter, though, was as flimsy and fragile as a box kite. One good blow from his wing-tip might do it.

Steadily he overhauled the 109 again and pulled up on its port side above the tail. He could see the German pilot glance nervously at him over his shoulder. The French coastline was emerging in detail now. He tightened his straps and tucked in even more closely, manoeuvring until he was directly above the German's tail.

He measured the distance with his eye. Ten feet above. It would have to be a sharp blow to do the trick, followed by a rapid recovery. The sea flashed past beneath them. They had very little height in which to pull out.

He wrenched the stick over, felt the jarring shock of the impact reverberate through the plane, and then fought for control as the Hurricane became a kicking, bucking, rearing animal bent on destroying him. The horizon tilted steeply and the sea grabbed at him. Then suddenly he was swaying drunkenly upwards, his Hurricane vibrating hideously but still flying.

Looking down he saw that the port tail-plane of the 109 had snapped just forward of the rudder, and as he looked it broke clean away and drifted down. A moment later the aircraft itself plunged into the water in a flurry of spray.

This time he did not wait to circle the wreck and assess the final plunge. Two 109s were after him. They came into the attack from above and behind, and he turned for home, flattening on to the water, weaving and jinking to and fro and up and down. He had very little fuel, and no ammunition. Three feet of his starboard wing had gone, and he had a long way to go.

The downed German pilot must have been calling for assistance. That was why he had kept peering ahead so desperately, hypnotized by the hope of aid. And Mackenzie had flown into the trap.

The two avenging pilots knew their job, and burst after burst of cannon and machine-gun fire raked the Hurricane. At first Mackenzie was able to avoid the full cone of fire by taking evasive action, but then they started coming in from opposite angles.

He kept turning towards the direction of attack whenever he could, but the damaged Hurricane was becoming more and more sluggish on the controls. Flames leapt back from the engine and the cockpit filled with smoke.

The Hurricane was now little more than a flying colander, whole areas of fabric shot away or flapping in the slip-stream, the engine coughing and spluttering and covering him with oil. But half-blinded as he was he could see the cliffs of Dover rising to meet him. It occurred to him that the German pilots wouldn't make the mistake he'd made himself. They fired two more bursts into his Hurricane and then pulled away. He could hear the last of their bullets smacking into the armour-plating behind him.

As he limped in over the coast his Merlin petered out altogether. He pulled up while he still had flying speed and looked for a likely field to force-land, easing his harness for a quick exit on landing.

Straight ahead of him he saw an anti-aircraft site, with a stretch of green beside it. He set the Hurricane down on her belly right in front of the guns and she pulled up in forty yards. But it had been a mistake to undo his harness. In the crash-landing he hit his face against the gun-sight, split his chin open, and lost four teeth. It was some time before he was able to tell a coherent story, but when he did it won him an immediate award of the DFC.

He did not know it, but the German pilot whose destruction he had so earnestly sought also survived the action. He was rescued unhurt by the *Seanotflugcommando* and lived, despite Mackenzie's efforts, to fight again.

Before the month was out Mackenzie too was back in action. But a year later, flying a Spitfire on an intruder attack over France, he was shot down and taken prisoner. Repatriated in 1944, he served in the RAF until 1967, adding an Air Force Cross to the award he received for knocking down the German fighter.[1]

Courage in the heat of battle was invaluable, and Mackenzie had this in full measure. If not exactly commonplace, it wasn't rare. It was with this cool, calculating, premeditated act of courage, at extreme personal risk, when the heat of the action was over, that Mackenzie qualified for his place among the élite of the Battle.

Efforts to discover who the pilot was have not succeeded, but the pilot of the 109 shot down earlier in the day by Hogan and Mackenzie between them and taken prisoner was repatriated after the war. His name was Lt Erich B. D. Meyer, and fragments of his aircraft were lifted from the sea-bed in the 1970s in a joint project between the Hythe Group of Channel Divers and members of the Brenzett Aeronautical Museum on Romney Marsh.[2] The results of the ensuing work of reconstruction can be seen in the Museum.

1. See his autobiography *Hurricane Combat* (Kimber, 1987).
2. See Don Everson, *The Reluctant Messerschmitt* (Portcullis Press, 1978).

THE BATTLE OF BRITAIN
MEMORIAL FLIGHT

The Spitfire and the Hurricane, the music of their Merlin engines, the feminine curves of the one and the masculine ruggedness of the other, still arouse strong emotions wherever they fly. Today the Battle of Britain Memorial Flight, based at RAF Coningsby in Lincolnshire, caters for these emotions in a nationwide programme of 150 air displays and fly-pasts a year. The Flight consists of five Spitfires, two Hurricanes and a Lancaster. The pilots, and the air crews in the Lancaster, hold regular appointments in squadron and training units, but they are backed up by a permanent staff of ground engineers, technicians and administrators who volunteer for full-time service with the Flight and willingly work the extra hours the job often entails. Three WRAF fighter controllers drive the Flight vehicles and liaise with air show organisers.

Strict display formats and limitations are followed, incorporating such safety precautions as minimum heights, minimum separation from spectators, restrictions on cloud base, visibility and wind strength, and, for the fighters, fine weather and the avoidance of cloud. Detailed requirements inevitably vary with the nature and venue of the display, but reliability comes second only to safety, and such cancellations as do occur are generally the result of adverse weather.

A Visitors' Centre, Flight Hangar and Museum were opened at Coningsby in 1986, and 21,695 people took the opportunity to visit the BBMF 'at home' in 1989. However, the Flight has not always been so firmly established as a matter of policy. Thirty years ago, fear of mechanical failure, and apprehension of the disastrous consequences that might ensue, led the Air Staff to announce the abandonment of what had become the traditional fly-past over central London: the last of these was to take place on Sunday

223

20th September 1959. Despite the care taken to ensure a successful swan-song, it was to confirm that the misgivings of the Air Staff were by no means misplaced.

12

Last of the Few

STANDING ON THE SALUTING BASE in Horse Guards Parade in front of the Battle of Britain Exhibition, the Prime Minister, Harold Macmillan, in immaculate morning dress, flanked by a similarly elegant and top-hatted Hugh Gaitskell, Leader of the Opposition, gazed upwards in pride and nostalgia at the two vintage aeroplanes, a Hurricane and a Spitfire, which were leading the annual fly-past. A glance at their watches confirmed that the RAF were on time.

The brass-hats accompanying the politicians on the dais, however, although equally resplendent, tilted their 'scrambled egg' skywards less in pride and nostalgia than in apprehension and prayer, their fingers superstitiously crossed. They were listening intently to the familiar drone of those two Rolls-Royce Merlins. Did they detect a stridency, a roughness of pitch?

They knew only too well – as Macmillan and Gaitskell did not – that for these two well-loved but ageing aircraft, mechanical failure was an ever-present risk. 'If an incident should occur,' warned the Service departments, 'the consequences could be disastrous.'

Was catastrophe imminent? In their minds' eyes the brass-hats saw one or other of the planes falter before diving murderously into the crowd.

One brass-hat whose mind was free from misgivings was forty-seven-year-old former Battle of Britain pilot Air Vice-Marshal Harold Maguire, the man in the cockpit of Spitfire XVI No. SL 574. Maguire had commanded a squadron in 12 Group, No. 229, throughout the Battle. The famous air ace who was to have flown the Spitfire that day was unwell and Maguire, who was in recent practice on the type, had taken his place. In his view, anyone would seize the chance to fly a Spitfire at any time, and this was a spectacular ceremonial occasion.

Most of Maguire's wartime flying had been on Hurricanes, and for their robustness he would always be grateful. But there was a poetry about the Spitfire, the way it responded, the lightness of the controls, which made it a joy to fly. Where the Hurricane might labour, the Spitfire seemed to be drawn effortlessly through the air as if by magic. There was no plane in the world like the Spitfire.

On this warm and sunny late-summer afternoon Maguire was thoroughly enjoying himself. He was thrilled, too, by the sight of the packed parade ground 800 feet below, and the panorama of Big Ben, Westminster Abbey and the Houses of Parliament which loomed straight ahead.

Maguire had given his Spitfire an exhaustive forty-minute test that morning at Martlesham Heath, the base where he himself was stationed and where the Battle of Britain Flight – not then formally established – was housed. Previously checked out by Rolls-Royce, the plane was declared fully serviceable in all respects by RAF ground tradesmen.

The same was true of the Hurricane. But so nervous were the Air Staff of failure that, as a safeguard, three privately-owned machines, two Spitfires and a Hurricane, had been assembled at Martlesham Heath as reserves. All five aircraft took off shortly before four o'clock that afternoon and set course in a gaggle for the rendezvous point over Hertfordshire. There they were joined by sixteen of the RAF's latest Hunter jet fighters.

When the time came to turn south for central London, Maguire's Spitfire and the first-choice Hurricane had developed no faults, and they formed up and flew together in line astern, the Hunters following, while the reserves dispersed to flying displays elsewhere.

The plan was that after the fly-past the two senior pilots would head for Biggin Hill, fifteen miles to the south-east, to show their paces and refuel. Later they would return to Martlesham Heath.

Doubts about the wisdom of routeing these obsolete aircraft

over densely populated areas had first been raised in May of that year by the Vice-Chief of the Air Staff, Air Marshal Edmund C. Hudleston. 'The time is rapidly approaching, if it is not already with us,' he wrote, 'when a decision must be taken to abandon the traditional leaders of the fly-past formation.' One day soon they would either default or crash.

In anticipation of a sentimental outcry from the public and the media, Hudleston recommended discretion in the timing of the announcement. The risk, he thought, should be accepted for this final year, the fly-past being carefully billed as 'the last formal appearance of the Hurricane and the Spitfire.' He hoped this would disarm criticism.

The Public Relations men at the Air Ministry feared that if something went seriously wrong after such an announcement and lives were lost, the RAF would get a very bad Press. But in August the decision was confirmed and the announcement made.

Early on that Sunday afternoon the parade assembled at Wellington Barracks and marched to Westminster Abbey for the Thanksgiving Service at 3.15. By 4.30 the various elements, civil and military, had marched back past the Cenotaph and formed up in Horse Guards Parade for the salute to be taken.

Right on cue the Hurricane and the Spitfire approached from the north, their much-vaunted speed of twenty years earlier now seeming oddly sedate. This was especially disconcerting for the pilots of the Hunter jets who were hanging on somewhat precariously behind.

To the brass-hats on the ground the planes seemed to loiter interminably as they passed down Whitehall, prolonging the agony. Big Ben was indicating 4.35 as they receded.

For thousands of spectators it was a poignant moment, the last occasion – so they had been told – that they would see these two legendary aeroplanes fly over the city they had defended so desperately. For many, vision was blurred by emotion.

Crossing the Thames, and leaving the Elephant and Castle under his port wing, Maguire overflew Camberwell and Peckham and continued steadily on his south-easterly course. In less than five minutes he would be in the well-remembered circuit of Biggin Hill. He was still in buoyant mood, and as he surveyed the TV masts sprouting from Crystal Palace to his right a mischievous thought occurred to him. Those who had stayed at home to watch TV and thus missed the fly-past would be momentarily reminded of it by the 'wobble' they would get on their screens.

In the next second Maguire's moment of smug satisfaction turned to shock and dismay as, without warning, and quite unaccountably, his engine spluttered and stopped.

What could have happened? It was worse than any nightmare. The engine had been purring away so contentedly he couldn't believe it. But he switched at once to his emergency radio frequency.

'Mayday! Mayday! Mayday! I have engine trouble and may have to crash-land!'

Although frantically busy trying to locate the source of the trouble, he noted subliminally that he was still flying over the vast and apparently boundless built-up area of south-east London, a closely-woven pattern of tiled and sloping roofs which threatened disaster for any attempted forced landing. He had never seen so many chimney pots in his life.

He pulled the nose up while he still had the speed to do so, giving himself more height and more time to think. He suspected a blockage in the fuel supply. What could he do about it?

In this mark of Spitfire there were two fuel tanks, one above and feeding into the other, giving a total endurance of ninety minutes. He had been airborne for forty-five minutes, which would have exhausted the capacity of the lower tank. Somehow the gravity feed from the top tank must have failed.

If he had extended his air test at Martlesham for another five minutes he would almost certainly have discovered the fault and got down safely, giving time for the fault to be traced. It was too late now.

The feed system was automatic, or should have been. There were no fuel cocks for the pilot to check, no emergency methods of operation. He began pumping the primer of the carburettor to try to get the flow going and restart the engine, but he was losing height, and he soon realized that if he persisted with this he would still be pumping when he crashed into the roof-tops.

Fortunately the plane was lightly loaded, with no guns or ammunition, and this was a comfort. He settled her down at gliding speed, between 110 and 115 knots, and looked around urgently for a place to land.

He could see Biggin Hill in the distance, but he knew there was no hope of reaching it. Then, ahead and to the right, he glimpsed what looked like playing fields, with an open grassed area in the foreground, ideal for his purpose. It was some kind of park, and the approach was partly screened by trees, which presented a hazard. But it was his only chance.

He planned to land diagonally across the grassed area with the wheels up – there was no room for a wheels-down landing. He was descending nicely, slowing down gently in the glide, and he could feel from the controls that he had got speed and rate of descent just about right. He selected flaps down, which acted as air brakes, and concentrated on the point he had chosen for the bellyflop, avoiding the trees.

He was down to 300 feet when the open grassed area suddenly filled with a kaleidoscopic throng of tiny specks which his horrified glance multiplied into hundreds. The field was swarming with children.

He had committed himself to the approach, and without power there was little he could do about it. There seemed no choice but to carry on, hoping the multitude would part and let him through. But in the same instant he realized this was unthinkable. His muted approach meant that few would see him or hear him. They would be taken unawares, bringing unimaginable carnage.

It was exactly the kind of catastrophe the Air Staff had feared.

There seemed no alternative, yet he knew he had to come up with one. He had read many times of pilots sacrificing their lives to avoid hitting towns when they might have baled out. But at this height he did not even have the option of using his parachute.

The only escape for those children was to aim his Spitfire deliberately into the trees. It was just possible he might survive the consequent crash. His mind was almost made up when, beyond another clump of trees on the far side of the park, he saw a cricket pitch.

Moments earlier a group of white-clad figures, statuesque as flies in aspic from the air, had been absorbed in their game. But so late in the season the match was scheduled to finish early, because of the light. At 4.40 it had been time for the captain of the batting side to declare. In those agonizing moments when Maguire had faced what seemed an insoluble dilemma, the players had gone in to tea.

It was not a large cricket field, and there were houses and trees on the approach, a boundary fence, and more houses beyond. But if he could reach it, he might just get in.

Directly on the approach line was an avenue of poplars which he doubted if he would clear. By manipulating the throttle and pumping the primer he sought to coerce one final burst out of the engine, but nothing resulted. Turning left to avoid the poplars, he side-slipped perilously back into line. Skimming a few feet over the roof of a house, and bisecting a gap between two others, he narrowly avoided an oak tree before dropping down towards the edge of the field.

Assistant groundsman Raymond Beavis, nineteen, was on his way out to tend the wicket between innings. He was pulling a roller and carrying a brush. He heard a sudden sibilance and saw a plane coming straight at him from over the sight screen. He abandoned the roller and ran.

On the nearby Shortlands golf course, a foursome on the second tee heard the plane and looked up to see it banking on one wing-tip over the roofs of some houses. It looked certain to crash.

Scraping the ground at a hundred miles an hour in a belly-landing that raised a blinding trail of dust and smoke, the Spitfire careered on into the field and across the cricket pitch, shearing the stumps at one end. It finally came to rest on the far boundary just short of the fence, beyond which a surprised suburban family hastily abandoned their alfresco tea.

Groundsman Beavis, thinking the plane was on fire, ran across to rescue the pilot. 'I'm all right,' Maguire told him, 'but

I've hurt my back.' Beavis helped him out of the cockpit and supported him across the field to the pavilion. 'I'm very sorry,' apologized Maguire, 'if I've upset your game.'

As a final throwback to the experience of RAF pilots shot down or crash-landing in the Battle of Britain, Maguire was asked the traditional question, 'Would you like a cup of tea?'

The golfers on the second tee at Shortlands stood amazed. 'How the pilot managed to miss the houses and flatten out in time baffles me,' said one of them. 'It was a miraculous piece of flying.'

Meanwhile the splintered stumps were replaced, the wicket was brushed and rolled, and after firemen and police had mounted a guard on the Spitfire to deter souvenir hunters, the game was resumed. Although the result now seemed less important, the players agreed that the declaration had been brilliantly timed.

When the fuel system was examined no fault could be found, Rolls-Royce concluding that whatever had blocked the feed must have cleared itself in the crash. Flights over built-up areas by Hurricanes and Spitfires were duly banned, though the notion that the two old war-horses might disappear from public aerial display for ever proved to be highly unpopular all round. Yet unless the brass-hats relented – and events had fully justified their fears – such fly-pasts were over. That was the position when a special presentation of some splinters of wood, reminiscent of the presentation of the legendary 'Ashes', was made afterwards in the following terms:

These stumps were presented by Oxo Limited to Headquarters No. 11 Group RAF.

They were broken during the forced landing of Spitfire SL 574 piloted by Air Vice-Marshal H. J. Maguire, CB, DSO, OBE, on the Oxo Sports Ground at Bromley.

The aircraft was taking part in the Battle of Britain fly-past on 20th September 1959.

And this was the last flight of a Spitfire by the RAF.

Happily, second thoughts, as philosophers and poets have said, were best, and it was not long before a Battle of Britain

Memorial Flight was formally established, with rebuilt and refurbished machines, and the ignominious end of the 1959 fly-past could be forgotten.

For Maguire, the impact seems to have cured the symptoms of an earlier back injury which had inconvenienced him over the years. 'You won't have any more trouble with your discs,' said the RAF specialist. 'They're locked in with your vertebrae now.' Today, at seventy-seven, he confirms that the specialist was right.

The Spitfire flown by Air Marshal Sir Harold Maguire, as he became – SL 574 – was originally built as a Mark XVI at Castle Bromwich in 1945 and entered service after the end of World War II. Following its engine failure and forced landing in 1959 it stood as a gate guardian at Bentley Priory for fifteen years, except when it was refurbished for the Battle of Britain film, and over the years it suffered inevitable deterioration. Eventually, starting in 1986, it was restored by volunteer enthusiasts of the RAF Halton Aircraft Renovation Society, a task which took them two years.

Meanwhile the Eagle Squadron Association, representing the group of volunteer American airmen who flew with the RAF before the United States entered the war, wanted to acquire a Spitfire, and they offered in exchange a P51D Mustang, the fighter which, fitted with a Packard-built Merlin engine, escorted their long-range bombers so successfully in the latter stages of the war. On 20th April 1989, Maguire had the pleasure of presenting Spitfire SL 574 to the Americans and of accepting a Mustang in return. Today this Spitfire is on display in the Aerospace Hall of Fame at San Diego, while the Mustang is in the RAF Museum at Hendon.

The official establishment of the Battle of Britain Memorial Flight, however, ensures that the esteem and affection in which the Spitfire and the Hurricane are held is continually renewed, and that neither of these historic aircraft is totally relegated to the role of museum piece.

INDEX

*(For Service personnel, ranks shown
are normally those current at the time.)*